ADOLESCENT SUBCULTURES AND DELINQUENCY

ADOLESCENT SUBCULTURES AND DELINQUENCY

Herman Schwendinger
and
Julia Siegel Schwendinger

PRAEGER

New York
Westport, Connecticut
London

Library of Congress Cataloging-in-Publication Data

Schwendinger, Herman.
Adolescent subcultures and delinquency.

Bibliography: p.
Includes indexes.
1. Juvenile delinquency. 2. Juvenile delinquents–Psychology. 3. Subculture.
I. Siegel Schwendinger, Julia R. II. Title.
HV9069.S44 1985 364.3'6 84-26329
ISBN 0-275-90161-0 (alk. paper)
ISBN 0-275-91656-1 (pbk.: alk. paper)

Library of Congress Catalog Card Number: 84-26329

ISBN: 0-275-90161-0
0-275-91656-1 (pbk.)

First published in 1985

Praeger Publishers, One Madison Avenue, New York, NY 10010
A division of Greenwood Press, Inc.

Printed in the United States of America

The paper used in this book complies with the Permanent Paper Standard issued by the National Information Standards Organization (Z39.48-1984).

10 9 8 7 6 5 4 3

For Leni and Joe,
who played ball in the alley behind the field office
and managed to grow up and develop their own talents
while their parents gathered data
and developed a theory of delinquency.

Contents

PART IV. PHASIC DEVELOPMENTS AND DELINQUENT MODALITIES

Acknowledgments

While making field observations of delinquent and nondelinquent groups, we found enormous gaps in the traditional explanations of juvenile misconduct. Development of an adequate explanation required years of work and demanded the study of economic, political, and historical information as well as observation of youth actively involved in delinquent behavior. While we conducted our research, we were helped by wonderful people from many walks of life. First we want to express appreciation to the library and computer facility staffs at the University of California, at Los Angeles and Berkeley. We are deeply grateful for the wholehearted assistance of the staff of the Soujourner Truth Library and the Computer Center at the State University of New York, College at New Paltz. The research edition would not have been completed without the support of the Computer Center director, Jon Lewitt.

We are especially indebted to a unique group of bright people who paved the way among some of our primary sources—adolescent streetcorner groups. Among these special people were Cowboy, Marty, Roger, Nick, Matt. Without their trust, help, and advice, our contact with and understanding of Greasers, Eses, Little People, Bad Dudes, Heists, Connections, Punks, Flunkies, and Cons would have been difficult to establish. Our thanks to Dan Whelan, who guarded our lives.

There were numerous people with conventional credentials who supported our later research. We are grateful to Armand Attia, Harriet Bellinson, Nick Curcione, John Davis, Betty Friedman, Ann Goolsby, Fred Hoffman, John Irwin, Ronnie London, Don Long, Nancy Mangin, Naomi Robison, Stan Taylor, and others.

We will be eternally grateful to two faculty members at UCLA: the late Richard T. Morris, a magnificent teacher; and John Horton, who stood by us especially when times were rough. More recently, our work has been encouraged by the editors of *Crime and Social Justice*, Tony Platt and Paul Takagi.

Finally, we would like to express our appreciation to Herbert Blumer, Malcolm Klein, Dragan Milovanovic, John Quicker, Don Spielberger, Joseph Weis, and Alan Wilson for critical responses to parts of the manuscript and gracious help in expressing some of our ideas.

The National Institute of Health (MHO 7077) supported our research.

Introduction

There is a theoretical crisis in criminology. It began when self-report questionnaire studies uncovered an unexpected amount of middle-class delinquency. These studies, as Empey (1982:118) later observed, "hit like a bombshell." They indicated that delinquency cuts across class lines to a greater degree than police statistics suggest. The self-report studies therefore contradicted theories explaining delinquency on the basis of lower-class conditions. They also lent credence to Tittle and Villemez's (1977) extraordinary claim that social-class relationships have nothing to do with criminal behavior.

The debate over the self-report studies has reached an intensity unprecedented in theoretical criminology. (For some examples, see Braithwaite, 1981; Clelland and Carter, 1980; Elliot and Huizinga, 1983; Hirschi, Hindelang, and Weis, 1979, 1982; Kleck, 1982; Schwendinger and Schwendinger, 1982, 1983a; Stark, 1979; Tittle, Villemez and Smith, 1978.) In this debate, we have argued that most of the responsibility for the current crisis lies with the opportunity-structure, social-disorganization, and differential-association theories (Cloward and Ohlin, 1960; Cohen, 1955; Kornhauser, 1978; Sutherland, 1947). In addition to a dependence on official statistics for their credibility, these theories have never dealt adequately with either social-class or delinquent relationships.

Social-control theories share the responsibility for the crisis and also fail to explain delinquency adequately. These theories depend on the fiction that Hobbesian tendencies are "set free" by poor socialization, by alienation from school as a result of scholastic failure, and by other factors that prevent the integration of delinquents into conventional society (Hirschi, 1969; Wiatrowski et al., 1981). Contradicting these assumptions, our own research discovered whole categories of delinquent youth who had been subject to none of these conditions. Our participant observation of middle-class delinquents—called "socialites," for instance—emphasized their socialization and subscription to the dominant (materialistic) norms of our society (Schwendinger, 1963). The socialites' high social status among peers demonstrated their integration rather than alienation and lack of control. Chambliss' (1973) widely published ethnographic study, *Saints and Roughnecks,* provided further evidence. The delinquent middle-class Saints included members who were "wheels" in the high-school student organizations. They were not, by any stretch of the imagination, "school outcasts," and, because they did well in school, their delinquency could not have been caused by weakened social controls resulting from scholastic failure. Consequently, social control theory cannot explain the middle-class delinquents found in either of our studies.

Adolescent Subcultures and Delinquency offers a solution to the current crisis in delinquency theory that comes to terms with the social-class anomalies found in self-report delinquency studies and with social-control anomalies reported by ethnographers. Furthermore, our solution relies on genuinely new causal "locus candidates" for analyzing peer-group delinquency. In our work, locus candidates are basic social units for explaining social relationships at particular levels of reality (Edel, 1959:172). The basic interpersonal units employed in our explanation are *adolescent* subcultures. However, let us emphasize that the choice of these units does not place our theory in the conventional subculture school of thought. The subcultures we examine are fundamentally different from those specified by other criminologists. Opportunity-structure and differential-association theorists depend for their basic units on lower-class *delinquent* subcultures or on simple dichotomies comparing group members' attitudes toward illicit behavior. But locus candidates based on delinquent subcultures do not even pretend to explain middle-class delinquency; and Sutherland's differential-association theory provides no feasible guidelines for distinguishing delinquent middle-class peer groups from the delinquent streetcorner groups in urban ghettos. Research into differential association has, in fact, hardly gone beyond using peer groups to prove that individuals in delinquent groups are influenced by their friends.

Because our theory proposes certain adolescent subcultures as locus candidates, this work explains these subcultures and shows empirical evidence of their utility for delinquency research. The explanation was initially developed while we observed peer groups in working-class and middle-class communities over a four-year period (Schwendinger, 1963). Theory formation was further supported by a four-year research project in which we collected data on several targeted areas of interest, including linguistic behavior, network relations, and delinquent conduct. Throughout the 1960s, we concentrated on procedures for measuring these peer relationships. The late 1960s and early 1970s witnessed the development of the macroscopic aspects of the theory (Schwendinger and Schwendinger, 1976a). In 1983 we returned to Southern California and found that the major adolescent subcultures mapped almost 20 years earlier had survived with only minor alterations. Consequently, our perspective on delinquency emerged from a careful long-term appraisal of theoretical ideas, methodological strategies, and research data about adolescent relationships.

In our theory, we propose that certain *stratified networks* of adolescent groups mediate the relationships between macroscopic social processes (including socioeconomic conditions) and the modal patterns of delinquency occurring among peer groups. These delinquent patterns involve life-cycle changes and learned outlooks in adolescent groups on all class levels. The members of these groups are frequently classified by such adolescent names as "Greasers," "Homeboys," and "Hodads"—or "Socialites," "Preppies," and "Elites." Even though the Greasers, who adopt subproletarian styles of life, and the Socialites, who adhere to bourgeois styles, violate the law more often than other youth, these types are not essentially produced by stressful conditions or the lack of commitment to conventional goals. Instead, both types represent subcultures that have emerged historically with the rise of capitalism, and their styles of life present themselves as conspicuous consumption or other status accompaniments to commodity circulation relations.

Organization of the Book

This work is divided internally into various parts. Part I, entitled "Political Economy and Adolescent Subcultures," associates the historic rise of capitalism with certain varieties of youth and their formations. This part describes the flow of labor from rural to urban areas and the appearance of such types as the Wilde Dells, Wilde Rogues, and Blackguards, who were sixteenth- and seventeenth-century counterparts to contemporary "streetcorner" youth. Today, especially within the third-world "cordons of misery" (squatter settlements) and in metropolitan slums and ghettos, international historical processes continue to generate a distinctive stratum of adolescent types that adopt subproletarian styles of life. On the other hand, there are delinquent groups with bourgeois styles of life that have also existed for centuries. Together with the streetcorner groups, these "socialites" comprise the perceptual "end anchors" of the *stratified informal peer networks* that are most visible in (but not restricted to) communities with a heterogeneous social-class composition.

Although this work deals with the impact of economic and political relationships on adolescent subcultures, it also describes the linguistic behavior and network relationships that characterize these subcultures. Therefore, in Part II, entitled "Social-Type Metaphors and Adolescent Subcultures," we provide concrete examples of stratified peer networks at particular localities and periods of time. We analyze the networks, giving special attention to their parameters and socioeconomic variations. Various hypotheses about the networks in communities with different economic, ethnic, and racial characteristics are proposed. Employing examples from participant observation and interviews, readers are systematically acquainted with the adolescent metaphors used for classifying members of these networks. In addition, we explain our analytic categories for describing the networks. In another section of Part II, we introduce the larger context of the "local peer society," which includes peer formations *outside* the stratified networks mentioned earlier. With this addition, we establish the basis for comparing widely varying types of peer groups and their delinquent or nondelinquent modes of behavior.

In our exploration in Parts I and II of *multiple levels of reality,* we employ a special analytic strategy for explaining adolescent (and delinquent) relationships. This method "progressively concretizes" the causal analysis by moving the reader from predominantly macroscopic and international relationships to the microsociological structures established among local groups of adolescents. (See Theotonio Dos Santos, 1970, for the concept of "progressive concretion" as he applies it to the study of class consciousness.) Our analytic method assumes that causal determinants exist on social psychological and psychological levels of reality that are not distinguished by macroscopic theory. Although political economy should be central to any scientific theory of delinquency, adolescent and delinquent relationships cannot be understood from political economy alone. Consequently, we also examine how ethical standpoints, local conditions, and subcultural developments affect delinquency.

In Part III, "Ideology and Ethical Behavior," we shift the analysis to the second half of the causal equation, namely, the direct relationships between delinquency and adolescent subcultures. However, once again, we begin with the macroscopic background for our analysis. Therefore, in the opening chapters, we describe the structural conditions underlying the ethics that support antisocial conduct. This part also includes chapters on the concept of moral rhetoric (Edel and Edel, 1959) which we use to challenge conventional theories about delinquent rationalizations. We then deal with specific types of ethical discourse that directly influence the developmental phases of delinquent groups.

In Part IV, "Phasic Developments and Delinquent Modalities," we discuss our ethnographic observations of socialite and streetcorner groups. We deal with the relationship between delinquency and the developmental phases through which stratified networks of groups often evolve. We provide material that further clarifies the subcultural contexts within which delinquent activities develop. These contexts include, among others, the status relations that stimulate intergroup violence, the high-school fraternities and their injurious pledging and hazing practices, the effect of car clubs on vehicle violations, and the impact of marijuana consumption on group solidarity. Part IV concludes with an analysis of *adolescent* illegal markets.

Parts I to IV comprise the paperback edition of *Adolescent Subcultures and Delinquency.* These parts are sufficient for understanding our theory of delinquency. The hardback edition, however, incorporates an additional part, entitled "Quantitative Methods and Research Findings." In this part, we deal with the methodological procedures and empirical data that make credible the theoretical propositions in this work. (The procedures are applied to a study of several thousand adolescents.) We begin with procedures for collecting the linguistic data that establish adolescent subcultural identities. We also describe a sociometric algorithm for distinguishing informal groups and intergroup networks. After identifying subcultural types and informal networks, the parameters of delinquency among these subcultures are measured with a "self-and-other" report questionnaire. Our procedures then provide individual-level and group-level data that go beyond the conventional data base on delinquent relationships. After describing these procedures, we employ the data for testing theoretical ideas, including those resolving the current crisis in delinquency theory. As a supplement, these procedures are useful beyond merely testing empirical generalizations. They can serve as "instruments of discovery" to help researchers generate further understanding of adolescent and delinquent behavior. Thus, in the final chapters of the hardback edition, *Adolescent Subcultures and Delinquency* introduces new methodological procedures for extending the theoretical ideas mentioned in the paperback edition. It now remains for the reader to judge whether our ideas represent a fruitful alternative to conventional practice in criminology today.

I

POLITICAL ECONOMY AND ADOLESCENT SUBCULTURES

1

Developing Capitalism and Official Delinquents

Every political economy generates its own material causes and legal categories of crime. Young lawbreakers certainly existed before the sixteenth century, but the monumental changes initiated by the capitalist mode of production created their own causes and definitions of youthful behavior. With regard to the material causes, the historical facts are incontrovertible: capitalism ripped apart the ancient regime and introduced criminality among youth in all stations of life.

Subproletarian Formations

This chapter begins our account of the class variations in delinquency. It broadly sketches the macroscopic changes that created delinquent subproletarian formations in many parts of the world. Certain English developments are used to illustrate these changes, because they registered the rapid increase in crime accompanying the annihilation of precapitalist economies. As mercantile capitalism destroyed the older modes of production, thousands of "masterless" children found themselves without employment. Reaching adulthood, which, at the time, fell anywhere between the ages of 14 and 17, these youngsters took to the roads, singly or in bands. They roamed the countryside by day, slept in barns or damp fields at night, and stole, pillaged, and begged from the population at large.

Throughout the fifteenth and sixteenth centuries, some of these youth, dubbed "Wilde Rogues" and "Wilde Dells," could still be seen in the countryside. Others, however, traveled to urban centers and became acquainted with pickpockets, gamblers, and confidence men; they joined the ranks of the city prostitutes or apprenticed themselves to the thieving beggars. Still others, on leaving their rural communities, quickly found work as casual laborers and were swallowed up in the poorer communities of the larger towns.

Meanwhile, a carnival of crime erupted from the recomposition of precapitalist relationships. New criminal populations became stabilized and began to reproduce themselves generationally. The children of "harlots," "hedge priests," and "sturdy beggars" were being taught "evil tatches" instead of the skills of the ploughman, spinner, and artisan. In Alsatia, a thieves' quarter centered in the very heart of London, and in the poorer districts on the edge of the city, one found the prostitutes called "Walking Morts," the "Doxies" accompanying city Rogues, and the "Bawdy Baskets" who stole linen while hawking lace, needles, and pins. These women instructed their sons, the Kynchen Coes, and daughters, the Kynchen Morts, silently to "creep in at windows and cellar doors" and diligently to pursue a life of crime (Aydellote, 1913; Harmon, 1930; Jusserand, 1931).

The descendants of prostitutes or thieves, the apprentices to the city Rogues, and the young rural vagrants were not the only youth considered lawbreakers. Immediately surrounding the thieves' quarters, there lived a population of working men and women and their numerous offspring. The children passed the time with one another, laughing, playing, and brawling in the streets. There, boisterous youth took their own places among the precapitalist repertoire of troublesome social types.

Their rowdy behavior was not tolerated for long. As early capitalism evolved, influential citizens condemned the "idle" and "mischievous" lives led by the children of the poor. Firmin (1681), a seventeenth-century philanthropist, claimed to have observed these children "in whole companies at play" in the outer parts of the city. He denounced their continual wrangling, cheating, swearing, and fighting. He alleged that they were a menace to equestrian traffic: they were fond of throwing stones at passing coaches, and they even caused the deaths of horsemen by maliciously whipping the horses and causing the hapless riders to be cast to the ground!

To alleviate this problem, Firmin urged the creation of a workhouse for destitute youth in every parish. Around 1698, the governors of the London Workhouse established their institution partly with this very purpose in mind. They also proclaimed that the institution would control "Vagrant orphans, known by the name of the Black Guard whose parents being dead, were reduced to the greatest Extremities; and being destitute of Relations, Friends, and all the Necessaries of Life, were become the Pest and Shame of the City, by Pilfering and begging about the Streets by Day and lying therein almost naked in all the Seasons of the Year by night" (Maitland, 1739). The name "Black Guard" was derived from the phrase "black art" (which signified the art of burglary) and the word "guard" (which indicated that these young thieves operated in peer groups). The Black Guard also contained youth who were not orphans. By choice or necessity, the children of the poor left home early; and some of these waifs joined the gangs that roamed the streets of London.

In a 1753 letter to the *London Chronicle,* Saunders Welch (1753) complained that poor families in manufacturing towns often allowed seven-year-old children to leave home without instructing them in the habits of industry. He stoutly maintained that the workhouse would actually prevent these youngsters from becoming "a dreadful nuisance to society." This institution, however, seems to have had no effect: long after workhouses had been established, thousands of youth were still to be found clothed in rags, sleeping half naked in city streets, or living in cheap, filthy lodgings.

Early Theories and Causal Conditions

Even before the industrial revolution, such institutions as asylums, prisons, workhouses, and half-way houses had become familiar social landmarks. Also, at the onset of this revolution, categories central to modern views of young criminality, such as "juvenile delinquent" and "delinquency," were added to the rhetoric of social control by bourgeois reformers.

Yet, whenever the causes of delinquency were in question, writers still emphasized personal destitution and parental supervision. The facts certainly spoke for themselves: in 1790, for instance, a boy was caught in the act of theft while his companions escaped. The young culprit did not live with his family, but, a constable reported, he slept "in a cellar in St. Giles, where fourteen or fifteen boys of different ages assemble, and pay two pence a night for their lodgings." Upon examination, the constable found that "the cellar where [the boys] all lay was filthy beyond description" ("Home Investigation of a Juvenile Delinquent by a Constable upon Order of a Magistrate," 1790, in Sanders, 1970:91). The boy's thieving could, therefore, be accountable to his destitute condition and the simple lack of parental care.

Criminality among the young was also attributed to other relationships. Even prison conditions were considered a causal factor. For instance, reformers in 1776 said that older criminals corrupted the morals of juvenile delinquents in prison by telling them innumerable tales of criminal adventures, stratagems, and escapes. Exposure to hardened criminals in prison caused these delinquents to engage in ever greater crimes (Smith, 1776).

Thus, as the industrial revolution leaped forward, delinquency was being ascribed to a variety of causes. In 1816, the first official survey of delinquency, a London Commission observed that thousands of boys and girls (many of them in gangs) were committing crimes within the city. After conducting the survey, the commissioners took pains to enumerate the multiple causes of delinquency. They stated that youth had become delinquent because of the lack of education, improper parental supervision, the want of employment, the association with thieves and prostitutes, the severity of the criminal code, the defective state of the police, and the inadequate system of prison discipline ("Report of the Committee for Investigating the Causes of the Alarming Increase of Juvenile Delinquency in the Metropolis," 1816, in Sanders, 1970:102–6).

But the commissioners' findings did not indict more general conditions introduced by the rise of capitalism, even though such conditions had been mentioned centuries earlier by state officials. Back in the sixteenth century, for instance, the Sheriff of London, Thomas More, suggested that crime was increasing sharply because of impoverishment and the disintegration of parish life. In 1516, he wrote that these conditions were due, in turn, to the private appropriation of communal lands, the burgeoning unemployment among household retainers, and the growing avarice among clergymen, nobles, and gentlemen. His famous work *Utopia* attributed these factors to the increasing organization of society around cash payments rather than traditional obligations. In fact, More was fully persuaded that social justice and individual happiness could never be attained for the greater part of humanity unless private property was abolished. He may have been wrong in some aspects, but history would show that he was pointing in the right direction. The property relations he condemned eventually created a social order that transcended any plutocratic society that even he could have imagined. More would have been astounded at the seventeenth-century speculation in trading ventures. The merchant adventurers alone numbered 7,200 members. Tens of

thousands of slaves were being shipped to the Caribbean Islands to produce cash crops. Over 100,000 slaves were abducted from Africa by a single trading company, and the proportion of wealth enjoyed by the joint-stock companies had increased a thousandfold (George, 1971:396).

Such events changed the structural foundations of English society. By the turn of the sixteenth century, the main forms of feudal servitude had been weakened by the consolidation of a class of independent peasants and artisans. But in the sixteenth and seventeenth centuries, even these types of petty property relations were being transformed by the fusion of the domestic market with the world market, the rise of the great landowners, merchant-capitalists, and joint-stock companies, and by the imperial plunder of overseas civilizations. These developments created new social-class relationships: A bourgeois class rapidly expanded in town and countryside; simultaneously, parts of the propertyless and hitherto property-owning classes were changed into a class of able-bodied paupers and wage-earning proletarians.

The State Consolidates These Causal Conditions

Thomas More connected the increase in sixteenth-century crime with the impoverishment accompanying the changes in the class composition of English society; but he did not realize that the state would play an essential role in the endless reproduction of these relations. For example, at first the monarchy provided sporadic opposition to capitalist trends. Later, however, the government imposed economic policies that overwhelmed the customary rights of feudal aristocrats, petty guildsmen, and sturdy yeomen. Struggles against these state policies occurred on all class levels, in all parts of English society. For instance, because of the imposition of oppressive fines, high rents, and the forcible enclosures of communal lands, farmers rebelled violently against wealthy landowners throughout the sixteenth century. However, these rebellions were brutally suppressed by the government. The largest rebellion—led by Robert Ket in the seventeenth century—was crushed by an army of 6,000 men. Ket and other leaders were decapitated, and their heads, mounted on long poles, were set before the gates of Norwich. With the support of the state, the disastrous effects of the commercialization of English rural life continued unabated (Tawney, 1912).

The great landowners and mercantile capitalists relied on the state to support their unchecked control over the means of production. Equally important, however, was the government's role in securing every conceivable species of labor power for their expanding enterprises. Depending upon the economic circumstances, the state enabled members of this social class to obtain and employ wage labor, bonded labor, convict labor, and slave labor for the accumulation of profit. By the end of the seventeenth century, officials had utilized sword, musket, and the hangman's gibbet to enable the ever-increasing appropriation of labor power by the bourgeoisie.

These political conditions placed countless individuals between the jaws of a vise, fashioned largely, on the one hand, from the annihilation of preexisting modes of production and, on the other, from a repressive, restricted, and unstable market for labor. People from many walks of life—small landholders, artisans, monks, friars, military retainers, other servants, and wage laborers—were being cast off by the dissolution of the older modes of production. They became a surplus labor force. Even when they did sell their labor power, they were barely able, or unable, to support themselves and their families.

Children were also hurled into the vortex of these developments. In an anonymous tract, "A Supplication of the Poore Commons," 1546 (Pinchbeck and Hewitt, 1969), parents of such children, painfully wrote:

> Many thousands of us which here before lived honestly upon our sore labor and travail, bringing up our children in the exercise of honest labor, are now constrained some to beg, some to borrow, and some to rob and steal. And that which is most like to grow to inconvenience, we are constrained to suffer our children to spend the flower of their youth in idleness, bring them up to bear beggars' packs, or else, if they be sturdy, to stuff prisons and garnish gallow trees.

Child Labor and Redundant Youth

Throughout the seventeenth and eighteenth centuries, the surplus labor force and its population of economically marginal families became a permanent feature of English society. However, the expansion of industrial capital, especially in the nineteenth century, also forced industrial proletarians into the surplus labor force and criminal activities. To describe these changes, we shall turn to the New World, where the social foundations of working-class delinquency eventually caught up with the changes in England.

The great geographical shifts in population did not end the delinquency problem. Marginal families in England were pushed and pulled in all directions. Some families uprooted themselves completely from England and settled in the American colonies. Delinquency subsequently emerged in the wake of the nascent capitalist conditions established in the New World. Consequently it is not surprising to find the lamentations of the sixteenth-century commoners being echoed by early nineteenth-century North Americans. In 1821, a Boston Commission noted that children were to be found everywhere "begging in the streets, or haunting our wharves, market places, sometimes under pretence of employment, at others for the purpose of watching [for] occasions to pilfer small articles, and thus beginning a system of petty stealing; which terminates often in the gaol; often in the penitentiary; and not seldom, at the gallows" ("Report of the Committee on the Subject of Pauperism and a House of Industry in the Town of Boston," 1821, in Bremner, 1970:753).

Citizens in Philadelphia and Baltimore were also worried about delinquency among the poor. Suggestions reminiscent of the English workhouse for the control of these youth were made throughout the following decades. For example, in 1840, the inhabitants of Baltimore were confronted by a proposal for "a manual labor school" that would only care for "the class of boys [which forms] a distinct portion of the population of all large communities" (Latrobe, 1840). In particular, this class of boys included the half-fed, half-clothed, idle, and delinquent children of the indigent.

In the second half of the nineteenth century, the surplus labor force had also become associated with other European immigrants, who sallied out from slum communities at the crack of dawn "to do the petty work of the City, rag-picking, bone gathering, selling chips, peddling, by the thousands, radishes, strawberries, and fruit through every street." A New York journalist stated in 1853 that these immigrants hung about "the German boarding houses in Greenwich Street, losing their money, their children getting out of control, until they at last seek a refuge in Ward's Island, or settled down in the Eleventh Ward, to add to the great mass of foreign poverty and misery there gathered" (*New York Daily Times,* 1853).

On the other hand, the economic status of adolescents was not necessarily determined by their parents. Regardless of whether or not their parents were jobless, propertyless children were an easily exploitable labor force, sought out for cheap employment. From the beginning of the nineteenth century, the expansion of the North American economy had incorporated large numbers of children who, along with their parents, had previously been employed in agriculture. Paradoxically, however, underemployment among adolescents (as well as adults) was eventually encouraged by the growth of industry itself. To compete successfully, industrialists invested in machine technology; hence, the same number of commodities could be produced with increasingly fewer hands. Wherever the expansion of capital was unrestricted, living labor was replaced by machines, and capital accumulation incessantly generated a redundant population of workers.

These redundant young workers joined the ranks of the unemployed seeking further employment. However, the reemployment of young technologically displaced workers was largely contingent upon the expansion of capitalist production and the subsequent expansion of job markets. But the expansion of production was beset by contradictions, leading to periodic overproduction of commodities, including capital, the means for producing commodities. As a result, job markets fluctuated enormously, with periods of growth and depression.

Stable employment for youth was also offset by other long-term industrial trends. Although the rate of capitalist expansion surged sharply upwards after each economic crisis and gradually increased, on the average, throughout the nineteenth century, it was generally never high enough to absorb all the young workers into the labor market. As a result, the process of capital accumulation—which above all involved the production and overproduction of the means of production—continuously replenished the population of redundant youth. Cut off from the supportive natural economy, where agriculture and industry were closely related, the companies of ragged thieves appearing in the streets of London and Baltimore demonstrated the continued lack of support for unemployed adolescents.

Articulation Relations That Prevent Delinquency

The sketch of political and economic conditions just presented is based on a classical model of capitalist development. In this model, as indicated, the expansion of industrial capital further transforms the economy after the mercantile period; and it continues to annihilate precapitalist modes of production. The double movement—the *expansion* of the capitalist mode of production and the *annihilation* of older modes—is important for explanations of working-class crime and delinquency, because it establishes its own conditions for the further development of the surplus labor force.

However, the classical model is not the only explanation of subproletarian crime and delinquency offered by a study of political economy. The growth of industry may not lead to criminalization of many working-class members, because industrialization alone is not sufficient. The effects of industrial growth depend on how the capitalist mode of production is articulated with other economic relationships. Since the concept of *articulation* is important and new to delinquency theory, we shall illustrate it with research based on South African and South American political and economic developments. The South American examples will serve a number of other purposes. Research based on articulation theory introduces political and economic factors that influence delinquency in third-world countries, and it will clarify the changes that occurred in nations such as the United States and England centuries ago.

Also, our use of articulation theory will further highlight the differences between our theory and other delinquency theories. It sets the stage for this contrast in Chapter 2. For example, some theories attribute high rates of delinquency to advanced capitalism and its lack of social control resulting from the segregation of youth in late-twentieth-century high schools. These theories also emphasize declining participation of youth in modern labor markets (Christie, 1978; Greenberg, 1977). Yet, even though we completely agree that modern schools and labor-market conditions are important, depending upon the level of analysis, we have already contradicted these alternative theories in certain fundamental ways. We have suggested that delinquency is due to complex macroscopic processes that have varied significantly at different stages of capitalism and in different parts of the world. The reader has learned that delinquency expanded when England and the United States were as yet *undeveloped* capitalist nations because of major historical changes in class relationships and worldwide economic conditions. The social alarm over delinquency also developed centuries *before* the public high-school and modern labor-market conditions existed. Let us now turn to modern underdeveloped nations, because the causes of delinquency continue to be altered by worldwide economic developments. These political and economic changes will further underscore the limitations of theories that rely primarily on the lack of social control in public high schools or in modern labor-market conditions.

As indicated, the study of changes in third-world countries suggests that the effects of capitalism both on precapitalist formations and on delinquency are more complicated than the classical model (based on the traditional economic history of England) would suggest. That model assumes the systematic destruction of all productive precapitalist units such as the tribal group, family farm, cottage industry, and guild system. In actuality, however, capital appears in some cases to have conserved these units or at most to have encouraged a spotty and gradual rate of decay. So long as these units survive, they restrict the recomposition of class relationships and reabsorb part of the labor force thrown off by capital. Youths make up part of this labor force, and, when unemployed, they return to the family farm, artisan's shop, and cottage industry, where they are reintegrated into traditional social relationships that prevent delinquent behavior.

Thus, while delinquency exploded with the rise of capitalism, some societies, even though they were affected by capitalist developments, did not experience this explosion. These societies were relatively exempt from youthful crime, because they conserved precapitalist units of production in local economies where agriculture and industry were closely related. Since such units continue to absorb surplus labor forces (especially in Africa, Asia, India, and South America), they explain why delinquency among poorer youth is minimal in certain countries, despite the domination of capitalism.

A concrete example is offered by Hartjen (1982), involving agrarian communities in India where delinquency is much less frequent than in advanced industrial societies. Pointing to the large-scale demand for child labor in farming, cottage industries, and other small-scale enterprises, he emphasizes that this labor integrates young people into a network of role relationships that involve a variety of obligations regarding kin, subcaste, and community. This integration into viable communal relationships exerts traditional controls that support lawful behavior and impede the alienation of youth and the development of their own subculture (Hartjen, 1982:466–467).

Yet behind this integration there is a set of socioeconomic relationships based on the "articulation" of capitalist and precapitalist modes of production. Wolpe (1980) describes such articulated relationships between "the reproduction of the capitalist economy on the one hand and the reproduction of productive units organized around precapitalist relations and forces of production on the other." It is important to note that such relationships, in some cases, are due to resistance by precapitalist formations, which limits the expansion of capital politically and preserves traditional relationships with their ideology of community and kin. Marx (1962:328) comments on this precapitalist resistance in India:

> The obstacles presented by the internal solidarity and organization of pre-capitalistic, national modes of production to the corrosive influence of commerce are strikingly illustrated in the intercourse of the English with India and China. . . . English commerce exerted a revolutionary influence on these [village] communities and tore them apart only insofar as the low prices of its goods served to destroy the spinning and weaving industries, which were an ancient integrating element of [a] unity of industrial and agricultural production. And even so this work of dissolution proceeds very gradually.

On the other hand, aside from precapitalist resistance, capitalist enterprises, at times, purposefully avoid devouring precapitalist units of production simply because these units absorb the costs for reproducing the labor force that capital might otherwise be forced to expend on wages or taxes. In this regard, Meillassoux (1980) observes that self-sustaining agricultural communities are preserved because they are able to fulfill the social security functions that capital prefers not to assume in underdeveloped countries:

> Once people undertake wage earning activities in order to pay taxes and gain some cash, if the capitalist system does not provide for old age pensions, sick leave and unemployment compensation, they have to rely on another comprehensive socio-economic organization to fulfill these vital needs. Consequently, preservation of the relations with the village and the familial community is an absolute requirement for the wage earners, and so is the maintenance of the traditional mode of production as the only one capable of ensuring survival (Meillassoux, 1980:198).

A report from the Mine Native Wages Commission in South Africa illustrates why capital might maintain the system that enables families to adopt security functions. The report states,

> It is clearly to the advantage of the mines that native laborers

> should be encouraged to return to their homes after the completion of the ordinary period of service. The maintenance of the system under which the mines are able to obtain unskilled labor at a rate less than ordinarily paid in industry depends on this, for otherwise the subsidiary means of subsistence would disappear and the laborer would tend to become a permanent resident upon the Witwatersrand, with increased requirements. . . . (Meillassoux, 1980:198).

Finally, the reproduction of capital at the expense of other modes of production is also limited by the instabilities inherent in capitalism itself. The expansion of capitalist enterprises among the indigenous population is frequently constrained not only by the lack of sustained markets for capital goods in economies with low levels of development, but by periodic fluctuations in the markets for these goods. When markets expand, petty entrepreneurs recruit workers into small factories that are expanded as far as the economy allows. However, when the markets drastically contract, the boom inevitably ends. Factories are bankrupted, and petty entrepreneurs revert to the traditional modes of survival based on subsistence farming, shopkeeping, and artisanry. Wherever these productive units remain viable and support traditional communal life, delinquency is lower.

Other types of articulated relationships can be mentioned, but they would merely provide further evidence of the lower incidence of crime and delinquency in certain regions of the globe despite the capitalist mode of production. Articulated relationships also show that the dominance of capitalism alone is not sufficient to encourage delinquency among the poor. To create delinquency, the movement of capital must also establish the complete separation of the producers from the ownership of the means of production on a large scale and, at the same time, must minimize the possibility for their reabsorption into an alternative mode of production.

Articulation Relations That Heighten Delinquency

On the other hand, articulation relations that encourage crime and delinquency among economically marginal populations can also be found throughout the third world. Petras (1976) describes nations on the periphery of the world capitalist economic system where the reabsorption of excess workers is minimized. In this world system, imperial metropolitan nations at the core exploit the nations at the periphery. This exploitation establishes an economic structure in which one segment of the labor force is incorporated into industries financed by international capital. As capital inserts advanced technology selectively into the periphery, it generates a new stratum of industrial workers. At the same time, a larger layer of the population leaves home to find work. Capitalist forces and relations of production undermine the traditional craftspeople and subsistence farmers, driving them into urban slums as underemployed laborers.

The flow of capital regulates this process. Capital inflows from metropolitan countries introduce technologies requiring relatively fewer workers. At the same time, cash and commodity outflows diminish the remaining local capital. Devoid of local capital, jobs cannot be provided for workers ejected from the precapitalist and early capitalist units of production. Eventually, population movements follow the flow of capital, moving, as Petras (1976:26–27) says, "From areas of surplus appropriation to areas of surplus disposal: from hinterland to capital city, from periphery to core."

In the peripheral nation, this capital flow expands the infrastructure which, in turn, stimulates the growth of an enormous variety of tertiary occupations and subproletarian pursuits. For example, the country's residual surplus funds are channeled into the multiplication of bureaucratic, commercial, and service occupations that maintain the economic power and life style of imperial patrons. Petras (1976:27–28) observes, "Civil servants, small and large businessmen, bankers, peddlers, prostitutes, personal servants, message boys, cab drivers, hotel workers, restaurant and barkeepers, military officials, pimps, and procurers gained part or all of their livelihood through their relationship with the imperialist class and their apparatus." Some of these people provide recreational facilities for wealthy patrons, others police the local population to protect the articulated relationships benefiting comprador classes and imperial agents. Still others congregate around nightclubs, casinos, hotels, and resorts that become hotbeds of crime and corruption. They soon become replicas of prerevolutionary Havana, which was known then as the "Bordello of the Caribbean" (del Olmo, 1979).

In this process, the ethos of a substantial number of individuals is radically altered. The commercial and service sectors increasingly define individual life styles. Consumption is heavily skewed in the direction of individual services, luxury goods, commercial enterprises, specialty shops, and personal indulgences. Illegal enterprises and political corruption sustain ruling families. Even persons at the lowest levels of society adopt the notion that hustling for themselves or for foreigners beats working in a factory.

Using articulation theory, the analyses of other Latin American authors like Obregon (1980) also provide important keys to the causes of crime among the poor in peripheral countries. Obregon observes that capitalist expansion has produced heterogeneous and *segmented* Latin American economies composed of precapitalist units, transnational corporations, highly competitive industries, and latifundia estates. This type of segmentation can occur with the abrupt insertion of advanced capitalist forces and relations of production into developing economies where the advancing economy combines with but does not completely eliminate the old. Thus, small farms often remain, but the insertion of technology into agriculture gravely depresses the living standards of small farmers, who cannot compete with these economic developments.

Further, Obregon observes, while living standards improve for some urban inhabitants, others find archaic forms of production and petty hustling increasingly necessary for survival. Survival methods based on handicrafts, petty trading, and illegal services are adopted by economically marginal people, because the sectors based directly on the capitalist mode of production provide little support. In addition, the traditional subsistence economy is so severely depressed, it cannot feed relatives unable to find work elsewhere. Many cannot find work because the monopolies utilize a technology that requires a relatively small labor force, and therefore marginal workers find themselves completely superfluous. The competitive industries are the traditional haven for migrant laborers, but those industries no longer require migrants even in the reserve army of labor. There are already many more people in the surplus labor pool than are necessary to keep wages low and productivity high among the employed in competitive industries. Therefore, certain members of the proletariat and petit bourgeoisie are forced to take refuge on the fringes of economic life. Their solutions to economic survival rarely lead anywhere, because they generate extremely diminished incomes from "popular markets" formed by the indigenous population itself.

Delinquency, as indicated, is encouraged by these structural changes. Cordoba, an industrial city of over one-half million people in central Argentina, illustrates this phenomenon. DeFleur (1971), in an ecological study, reports that in this city, squalid slums are scattered along the steep banks, on fields in danger of being flooded, and in empty lots near noisy industries. Slum inhabitants live in huts of cardboard, tin, old bricks, and discarded boards like the "Hoovervilles" of the depression period. Appropriately, these enclaves are called *villas miserias,* cordons of misery, because of the emiserating poverty suffered by their inhabitants. DeFleur (1971:299) notes, "The slum dwellers of Cordoba, from which the bulk of the delinquent population is drawn, are internal migrants. That is, they are rural people who are being displaced from the land as Argentina undergoes a period of industrial growth and social change." Finally, DeFleur's study found that most officially reported delinquents lived in or near the *villas miserias*. There were some official delinquents in middle-class and upper-class communities, but these were primarily low-waged service employees such as servants.

In Cordoba, the incidence of official delinquency is undoubtedly influenced by the demoralization of family life and the inadequate social and economic supports provided for rural migrants. Both the demoralization and the inadequate support are caused by the combined and uneven development of capital and not merely "industrial growth and social change," as DeFleur suggests.

Consequently, the destructive effects of capitalist development on family life are curbed only when peasants and urban workers are able to struggle against the life-destroying encroachments by capital on their communities. But, where class struggles cannot resist these encroachments because of fascist death squads and military juntas, for instance, it is more difficult for men and women to pass into one mode of production and back again when the labor market constricts. When capitalism finally absorbs the hinterlands, living standards among the traditional small producers in the agrarian sector simply decay. These producers must either perish or join the great migration to the cities. In the urban centers, the exploitative ethos of capitalism floods the popular consciousness, and, inevitably, some of the children bred by the *villas miserias* become predators themselves.

NOTE

1. Christie and Greenberg both observed the tendency of crime to peak at lower ages in contemporary societies. This observation is a striking contribution to the field. Our disagreements with them rest solely on the conventional mechanisms they use to explain this long-term trend.

2

Class, Communities of the Poor, and Informal Sectors

In this chapter we deepen our analysis of articulation relations by examing South American urban communities composed of rural migrants. In their new urban settings the migrants have problems making ends meet. The necessities of life in urban communities are usually purchased, whereas in their village communities the migrants might have been able to acquire some food, clothing, and housing through their own labor or through the cooperative efforts of joint family groups and neighbors. Because such acquisitions are not purchased, they will be called "noncommodity" values. The migrants find that the acquisition of such values is more restricted in urban communities where, to a greater degree, people must have money to survive.

Consequently, in the urban communities, the rural migrants attempt to revive or create cooperative relationships that lessen their dependence on money earnings. These relationships are evident in "household economies" composed of family members who prepare meals, make clothing, repair furniture, and so on. They are further expressed in networks of mutual aid and reciprocity established between neighbors, friends, and family groups formed to reduce the cost of foodstuffs, housing, clothing, fuel, electricity, and other necessities of life. Although they may be influenced by traditional values, these economic activities emerge in urban settings because they help people survive and improve their living standards. We shall see that insofar as they support *cooperative* forms of communal life, these activities make delinquency less probable even in the face of economic insecurity.

Because the probability of delinquency may increase when socioeconomic processes divide working-class communities internally, we will also examine how families become stratified within poor communities. Such divisions are due, once again, to the great importance of commodity relationships in everyday life. Since poor as well as other communities in most societies are dominated by commodity relations, an ethic of individualism emerges among families. Such an ethic reinforces the effects of occupational instability on family life and child-raising practices. It also makes the styles of life adopted by families more susceptible to the effects of inequality in money and resources due to labor market conditions. Thus, we concretize the causes of delinquency by showing how class relations are recomposed among South American rural migrants as their communities become stratified internally. For example, once migrants have settled in urban communities, two contrasting trends become evident: one trend leads to the development of stable petit bourgeois and working-class family patterns; another leads to highly insecure and unstable family relationships. Let us begin the discussion of these relationships with a study of a Venezuelan squatter settlement.

Class Recomposition and Styles of Life

Squatter settlements in Venezuela and other South American countries are expressions of "hyperurbanization," wherein urban populations become much larger than existing rates of economic growth can bear (Bairoch, 1975). Some of the causes of hyperurbanization involve the international flow of capital, as mentioned in the previous chapter. The inflow of capital from metropolitan countries encourages some industrial expansion within peripheral countries; but, because of the massive outflow of profits, growth is constricted, and industrial labor markets do not expand sufficiently. In addition, the industries created by the inflow of capital are capital intensive and only support a relatively small labor force. In addition to many established urban poor people, rural migrants who are pushed or pulled into urban centers are unable to find jobs in the industrial sector, and they turn to the tertiary, public, and informal sectors to survive. This informal sector includes illegal enterprise as well as archaic methods for making a living.[1] The rural migrants therefore also support themselves through bartering and engaging in cottage handicrafts or other archaic forms of production and exchange. They survive by providing personal services and carrying on petty illegal activities, even though these alternatives rarely provide adequate sources of income. Consequently, once they are in the cities, the migrants minimize the gap between income and cost of living by converging in squatter settlements.

Peattie (1971), an anthropologist, describes a settlement that is similar to the one studied by DeFleur in Cordoba, Argentina. Unlike DeFleur, however, Peattie actually lived in the Venezuelan *barrio des pobres* ("community of the poor") from 1962 to 1964. The barrio is in a city whose population tripled in a single decade, and, although it is not one of the "company towns" built by large corporations, the barrio is adjacent to the Iron Mines Company of Venezuela, a subsidiary of Bethlehem Steel.

The regular sources of income among the adults in the barrio, at that time, epitomize hyperurbanization on the community level. For instance, Peattie reports that only one person had a fairly well-paying professional job, and he was an accountant in a construction plant. Eighteen people had jobs either with Iron Mines or with a recently established mining subsidiary of U.S. Steel; 19 were in a variety of other jobs, from school teacher to cab driver; 11 were petty proprietors, most of whose business activity took place in the "popular market" in the barrio itself (there were six small businesses selling liquor, groceries, soft drinks, and so on). Twelve women worked as domestic servants or washerwomen in nearby company towns. The poorest household was composed of two old women, one of whom was helped occasionally by a married daughter, and the other, having no kin, begged for a living (Peattie, 1971:291–292). Since there was no system of public welfare and since unemployment among men 19 years of age and older ranged between 30 and 40%, almost all the people in the barrio were at least partly dependent on the 81 persons who possessed more-or-less regular yet mostly poor sources of earned income. At the time of Peattie's census, the barrio had 490 inhabitants, living in 80 household groups. This means that a household averaged 6 or more people. More than half were juveniles, and the persons possessing regular sources of income were not necessarily distributed evenly among the households.

Peattie's observations showed that class relationships were being recomposed because of differences in economic support for family life. This recomposition was expressed by distinct trends in both socialization of children and styles of life. One trend was identified with those having a consolidated economic base in labor markets, or popular markets, or both; the other emerged among those who had not consolidated such a base. The first trend included working-class and petit bourgeois parents who were able to save, invest, and plan for the future. Parents in this group controlled their children, taught them to be obedient and clean, and made them attend school regularly. If they worked for the big companies, their obligations to the children were supported by fringe benefits as well as higher incomes. In addition to housing and medical care, the companies provided schools for the children, free school busing, and school books and supplies. Since educational entry requirements were becoming more important in favorable job markets, the economically stable families were securing the futures of their children.

The second trend, on the other hand, was seen among those who had not consolidated a stable economic base. Peattie (1971:298) reports that these people were adjusting their values and aspirations to highly restricted possibilities in life. Concretely, this adjustment was considered a response to "the institutional structures which provide the poor with crowded housing, which weaken the father's role, and which inform the children of the poor that they should not expect too much or try too hard." Since these people were not able to consolidate a secure economic base quickly, they were going to be at a much greater disadvantage than they would have been in prior decades, when the industrial expansion absorbed many people regardless of educational background.

Peattie was impressed by the degree to which the men in the second group were preoccupied with *machismo*. She recognized that *machismo* is traditional in Latin America, but the men who "acted macho" in the barrio reminded her of Harlem. It is implied that this conduct was a compensation for economic instability among the males rather than a result of modes of child raising. She states:

> The proletarian situation, in my *barrio* as in Harlem tends to produce a number of matrifocal and female-headed family groups. For people in this situation, there is almost nothing to hold a family together. . . . Both men and women can earn money, and although jobs for women are very scarce, jobs for

> unskilled men are not to be counted on, either; thus, neither spouse is a secure economic base for the other.

She reports that 20% of the households in the barrio were headed by women. These households were becoming what she calls "small matrilineal lineages" (1971:294–295) and were in an extremely vulnerable economic position. Sexual divisions and individualism increased the instability of family relations. According to Peattie (1971:294):

> [T]he worlds of men and women are separate, the women [oriented] to the house, to children and their female kin, the men to "the street" and the bars. Both men and women are active and individualistic in sex, quick to form new sexual alliances. It thus happens that in such families if there is a man in the household he is there at the margins, and he may easily slip off altogether. In this situation it seems to me remarkable that so many couples stayed together.

However, whether they were headed by or composed of men or women, the households and friendship groups appeared to provide some degree of economic security. Both patriarchal and matrifocal families, as well as friendship groups and multifamily groups, employed various mechanisms to support living standards and to ameliorate the destructive effects of unstable sources of income. Whether kin or friends, these groups adopted cooperative projects, reciprocal exchange, mutual aid, and redistributive arrangements for allocating food, clothing, and other necessities (purchased from the earnings of a few persons) among all members of the group, regardless of their earning. These supportive systems were qualitatively different from exchanges based on the circulation of equivalent values at market prices; yet they encouraged relationships that bind different families together and make social life in the *barrios de los pobres* more cohesive.

Marginalization and Disorganization of Communal Life

Peattie observed economically stable and unstable families in the Venezuelan settlement. Her study implies that family relations were strained but not necessarily destroyed by unemployment, because mutual aid and reciprocity compensated somewhat for economic insecurity. Her observations also imply that when economic insecurity increases and supportive communal relationships decrease, families fall apart and crime and delinquency increase rapidly.

Evidence for such a trend toward delinquency is provided by Perlman (1976) who studied the *favelas* (another name for squatter settlements) of Rio de Janeiro. Although they were poor, the residents of these settlements worked cooperatively together to build their own shacks, schools, churches, streets, and electric power lines and sewage and water networks in the *favela*. They paid no rents or mortgages. Perlman describes the social cohesion and mutual aid among the settlement inhabitants, but she also points to the disastrous effects of government policies that forcibly uprooted the residents of one settlement and burned their houses to the ground to make way for high-rise apartments for wealthy families. The residents were relocated in housing projects, where they no longer lived close to relatives and old friendship circles or to recreational gathering places such as beaches and sports fields, which had been accessible previously. Because they were forced to travel much further to their workplaces, employed fathers began to stay away overnight from their wives and children, and some began to take up with other women.

The residents of the projects also faced a situation where all "the advantages of modern living" had a price. Because individual families were scattered throughout the new housing districts on the basis of income level rather than social and familial ties, the supportive family networks of the *favela* failed to survive the relocation. High unemployment further exacerbated the situation, and families began to default on rent or mortgage payments. The desire to maintain their living quarters declined in the atmosphere of distrust and dissatisfaction with community conditions. As the community deteriorated, the crime rate soared. Perlman (1976:218) reports, "People who live in the projects repeatedly say there is more violence there than in the *favela*, more street fights, more maltreatment of children, and less concern for others. They say they are afraid to go out into the streets at night, and meanwhile the government procrastinates in installing street lights."

To explain the crime and economic condition of the *favelados*, Perlman rejects social disorganization theory and suitably turns to South American political economists. (We noted some of their ideas in Chapter 1, when we discussed the huge proportion of people in the subproletariat, created by capitalism in dependent nations.)

Perlman (1976) uses the idea of economic marginalization to explain why people are in the *favelas*. She cites Jose Nun's observation that "the unemployed can represent a reserve labor army for the competitive sector and a marginal mass for the monopolistic sector" (p. 257). Furthermore, she mentions Obregon's view that the marginals are largely composed of the "marginalized bourgeoisie"—e.g., self-employed craftsmen, small businessmen, shop owners, and managers in the competitive sector—and "marginal proletariat"—migrants from agriculture, workers in low echelon jobs: domestic servants and messenger boys (p. 255).

Perlman (1976:191–231) excoriates the social scientists who attribute the marginal status of the *favelados* to social disorganization and the breakdown in social controls or to a culture of poverty and a lack of commitment to values that integrate society. She describes the scholarly stereotypes of the urban poor and contrasts them with the actual characteristics of the *favelados*. She observes that the largely rural immigrant residents generally value hard work. They share the aspirations of the bourgeoisie, the perseverance of pioneers, and the values of patriots. Although they conform politically, when they do take radical steps to benefit themselves they are forcibly repressed. After summarizing her findings, Perlman insists that the adverse conditions experienced by the rural migrants are determined by structural relationships backed by political coercion and manipulation, rather than the personal or cultural characteristics of the residents. She (1976:258) concludes:

> . . . the defining characteristic of the marginalized sector is its role in the accumulation process characteristic of dependent nations. It is from this condition that other expressions of marginality arise, be they ecological manifestations in the emergence of squatter settlements, psychological characteristics of the "marginal" personality, [or] sociocultural characteristics of "marginal" behavior.

Reactive Effects of Illicit Activity on Communal Life

Among the relocated inhabitants of the housing project, crime and disorganization of communal institutions seemed to emerge together. But is crime always accompanied by disorganization? Lin's (1958) study of Chinese delinquent peer formations in Taiwan provides a negative answer. Traditional Chinese delinquents engaged in violence or economic crime for their families or themselves. These youths had little or no education, and they resided in the old sections of cities and small towns because they were mostly from poor "lower-middle" or "lower-class" families. These delinquents, Lin (1958:247) observed, were not alienated from communal institutions. They followed customs rooted in local traditions, and their group structures were "intimately interwoven with that of the community." Lin even noted that the criminal status of delinquent leaders provided them with a voice in communal affairs through connections with temples and elders. These young criminals maintained a strong grip on the economic affairs of the area by using their subordinates as agents, particularly in prostitution, gambling, trading with stolen goods, black-marketing, and narcotics peddling.

Obviously, the emergence of illicit activities can provide greater security for some families and support traditional institutions. Illicit activities can also interact with these institutions and affect the quality of life or even child-raising practices. An example of the effect of the illegal market on family life can be found in *La Vida,* Lewis' (1966) study of a Puerto Rican barrio in San Juan. To appreciate the social significance of the study, the similarity between Puerto Rico and other third-world countries should be noted. For example, industrial development is limited, and the service sector is enlarged. And, after more than half a century of colonial rule by the United States, Puerto Rico has a 40% unemployment rate, and 60% of the population survives on food stamps. The average income is only $1,212, and welfare payments are taken without gratitude because they are insufficient for family needs. The government is much more interested in the welfare of wealthy corporations than the welfare of the poor. Government concern for poor people is symbolized in Lewis' work by the mayor's wife, who distributed gaudy red paper to slum residents so that they could decorate the exteriors of their ramshackle, rat-infested homes to please the American tourists flying overhead on their way to a "happy holiday" in "sunny Puerto Rico."

Under these conditions, the informal labor sector expands enormously, at a considerable social cost. Although, as indicated, this sector may shore up standards of living, it can impact on family relations significantly. One type of impact is shown by the anthropologist, Berry Burgum (1967), who notes that the biographical information in *La Vida* inescapably connects Lewis' so-called culture of poverty with the effects of capitalism. The lives of "los pobres" are caught up in a familiar web. The only source of income for the barrio's illiterate males is working on the docks when the ships come in; and large numbers of barrio women support themselves by prostitution, servicing the endless crowds of naval and merchant sailors on leave.

Because of these conditions, families seem, at times, to be held together by nothing more than a mother's love for her legitimate or illegitimate children; and, finally, the ties between mothers and daughters become the only stable core of these relations. When sons get into trouble they fend for themselves, while the husbands and lovers are frequently unreliable, financially or otherwise, and hovering on the fringes of family life (Burgum, 1967:332). On the other hand, despite the centrality of the mother–daughter relationship, family stability is almost nil. There is no hint whatsoever of the "mother domination" that is often attributed to these kinds of families by sociologists and criminologists. Burgum (1967:333) correctly notes,

> Such a society could hardly be called a matriarchy. Women could scarcely be called a regulating influence. Whereas in primitive societies sexual freedom promotes an organized society, here it induces the opposite [consisting] of social and moral deterioration. Every stabilizing factor seems to dissolve. One example of matriarchy [in *La Vida*], the superior influence of some strong-minded woman, was meaningless as a social pattern since this matriarch never had any authority over the males, so that there could not be any training of the children for responsible mature sexual attitudes. We are left with no other binding social influence beyond the temporary genetic attachment of mother for child.

In addition, the so-called "culture of poverty" among the prostitutes is deeply affected by the interaction between the restricted job markets for men and the women's informal labor market activity. Burgum (1967:331–332) observes,

> The men who earned little and had no expectation of more were in sharp contrast to the women whose income was scarcely limited since American sailors were notoriously loose with money. Sex thus became more than a source of income; natural instinct stimulated in this way became an obsession, and if not as engufing a one as that of the American in the nineteenth century to become a Commodore Vanderbilt, it was soley because this generic love of children restrained it. But the consequence in personal relations was that sex permeated all interpersonal contacts. Mothers intoxicated their children with

> sexual fantasies and stimulated, particularly in their daughters, physically and otherwise and by the coarsest vocabularies, an interest in sex which was a parody of the normalcy practiced in most primitive societies.

Clearly, then, child raising expressed the commodification of social life. Even talk about sexual relationships between a mother and daughter was influenced by the market in sex. Also, to attract the North Americans, women commanded a higher price when well dressed. To increase their earnings, prostitutes bought expensive clothes, and the contrast between how the women looked and how they lived when with their children was glaring.

Informal Sector and Social Disorganization

For almost a century, social disorganization theory has attributed prostitution and other forms of crime and delinquency to the destruction of the traditional family, uncontrolled individual behavior, and disorganized personality characteristics. (The theory further implies that delinquency is produced by temporary imperfections in industrial society due to rapid urbanization and social change.) But crime and delinquency among the poor has been sustained by the *recomposition* of such structural relationships as social classes and not merely by the temporary destruction of specific institutions such as the family or the family farm. Moreover, the most worrisome forms of delinquency reported by criminologists in the past were concentrated within the surplus labor force and its population of economically marginal families. Surplus laborers have been a permanent stratum in capitalist societies. Consequently, the disorganization and demoralization that reinforce criminal behavior in poor communities are due to profound structural conditions that are ignored by vague references to personal deficiencies, labor market conditions, urbanization, or social change in social disorganization theories.

Furthermore, studies indicate that crime and social disorganization are independent phenomena and are not necessarily linked with one another. An ethnographic study by Whyte (1943) describes a poor North American urban community that is partly integrated—not disorganized—by criminal organizations. Lin's study of delinquents in Taiwan, mentioned previously, also reveals stable accomodations between leaders of major communal institutions and criminal organizations. Crime and delinquency do not, necessarily, therefore, come from disorganized communities or mean the inevitable destruction of communal institutions. On the other hand, the kinds of communal relationships that really impede crime may suffer most when criminals strongly affect community life. Whether they are traditional or not, such communal relationships enhance the power of peer people to control their own lives.[2] After the residents of the *favela* in Perlman's study had been relocated, crime expanded as social relationships organized around mutual aid, reciprocity, and cooperative communal enterprises disintegrated. The previous existence of these social relationships suggests that the residents had had greater freedom to organize their social and physical environment in their own interests. In the *favela,* many residents had been able to cope with adversity by redistributing the necessities of life on the basis of need. They had also had enough control over physical resources to conduct cooperative projects aimed at improving housing, streets, water supply networks, and so on. Despite their lack of legal title to land use, they had even had some control over the utilization of urban space. However, they lost all control in the relocation housing project where urban planners and housing authorities completely determined the location and construction of the housing as well as the disposition of all other physical resources. The relocation meant, therefore, that families lost both individual and collective power to determine their lives in the face of adversity. It is this kind of power that is destroyed when externally imposed disorganization paves the way for crime and delinquency.

Even though social disorganization theory is more than a century old, scholars upholding this view rarely ever conduct field studies aimed at first-hand examination of the causal interactions between disorganization and crime. Such an investigation might indicate that there is a greater variation in the temporal sequencing of disorganization and crime than social disorganization theory suggests. For instance, the obsession with sexual relations and the conspicuous styles adopted by the prostitutes in San Juan could not have been produced by the disorganization of traditional family relationships, because each of the pertinent elements—the prostitution and the invidious ethic of conspicuous consumption—were equally dependent upon the international economic developments that were destroying the traditional family. The forces unleashed by such developments were demolishing patriarchal family relationships and encouraging women to engage in prostitution as a source of family income. Among the marginal families these two sets of relationships—the female-headed family and prostitution—were therefore correlated only because of their relationship to similar causes. Furthermore, the woman's involvement in prostitution was itself a causal factor: through its feedback on the relationships between the mother and children it reinforced the changes in the family and stimulated an obsession with sexual relations in child raising. The informal sector can sometimes be as influential as other economic sectors in recomposing traditional relationships.

To the social-disorganization theorist, the entrance of capital is seen as a force for modernization whose wake produces disorganization and *then* crime and delinquency. But the fundamental causes of these illegal relationships lie in a different direction. We have seen that capital creates new forms of organization and cooperation that become endemic, whether they are in conflict with the law or not. Within the San Juan barrio, these new forms of organization include the market for prostitution as well as other economic relationships supporting the naval base and the transnational corporations binding Puerto Rico to the United States. Capital recomposes class relationships and produces a population of marginals within working-class and petit bourgeois families. The disorganization and informal economic structures that characterize these particular populations are products of this recomposition, although they eventually reinforce each other and further intensify the harmful effects of international economic developments.

NOTES

1. The phrase "informal sector" is used by world system theorists, but it has sharp limitations. It appears to be a residual category that usually refers to a variety of activities on the fringes (or outside) of the capitalist mode of production. When referring to illegal sources of income, other scholars prefer the phrase "irregular economy" or "subterranean economy," because these sources are distinguished from those open to the public and regulated by law.
2. It should not be assumed that mutual aid and reciprocity is only stimulated by traditional relationships. Mutual aid projects can be organized by political parties and nontraditional family support, including communal child-care arrangements, is also important in this context.

3

Streetcorner and Intellectual Prototypes

Thus far we have concentrated on communities of the poor in peripheral and semiperipheral nations. We will shortly describe conditions supporting delinquency in North American ghettos. Some of these conditions, such as restricted labor markets and internal divisions in a community, are familiar because they were equally evident in studies of communities in the less economically developed countries. On the other hand, there are some conditions in less developed contries that are not as evident. For instance, squatters' settlements hardly exist any more in the United States, and poor people almost never occupy land or houses without paying rent, especially in urban areas. Propertyless residents cannot modify other urban resources to improve their lives without purchasing these modifications or influencing government policies. Furthermore, although the massive production of use values remains in household economies, everyday life in the United States is overwhelmed by the mass media and commodity markets.

There are other social conditions that are especially important for understanding delinquency in the United States. Welfare systems and especially child support programs are usually more extensive in the United States. These systems remove economic barriers to high-school attendance and thereby reinforce universal compulsory education laws that concentrate adolescents in schools. The importance of that concentration, however, is not that it segregates adolescents from adults and thereby undermines adult controls (Christie, 1978; Greenberg, 1977). This concentration is important because it provides fertile soil for the development of a larger variety of adolescent social types, peer networks, and status groups within high-school districts. An adolescent's "community," therefore, is expanded beyond fairly limited residential areas. Furthermore, these types, networks, and status groups are incorporated into a number of adolescent subcultures and not into a single "youth culture," as many scholars believe. The subcultures cannot be readily classified on the basis of social-class terms because they include bourgeois adolescents that adopt subproletarian styles of life and working-class adolescents with bourgeois lifestyles. Since delinquency is often associated with both of these styles of life, even the phrases "working-class delinquency" and "middle-class delinquency" become inappropriate. To arrive at the impact of high-school conditions on such adolescent developments, we will now turn to the United States, starting with the discussion of comparisons between North American ghettos and the South American settlements.

North American Ghettos, Sources of Income, and Social Types

The previous sections have noted that Puerto Rico has a very high unemployment rate, and most of the population requires some form of welfare such as food stamps to survive. Thousands of people have responded to these conditions by migrating to the United States mainland, where the standard of living is generally higher and opportunities for social mobility are greater. Nevertheless, in 1970, the vast majority of mainland Puerto Rican school-age children were born in the North American "barrios de los pobres." Most resided in New York City ghettos, where almost three in ten Puerto Rican families were headed by women. In the rest of the city population, only the proportion of black female-headed families exceeded this number. Obviously, there are many similarities between poor families in Puerto Rico and metropolitan United States.

Again, labor markets regulated by the interplay between economic sectors encouraged certain family characteristics. The 1970 census found only 72% of the mainland Puerto Rican males over the age of 16 employed in legitimate labor markets. The majority of these men worked in the least desirable and lowest-skilled occupations. In addition to the large number of female-headed households, there were very few double-income families. A mere 28% of Puerto Rican women were gainfully employed, and families on welfare just barely survived on their monthly payments. As many as one-third of all these families lived at or below the poverty level, and this proportion was increasing (U.S. Department of Labor Statistics, 1975).

Also, because of these labor market conditions, numerous mainland Puerto Ricans hustled for money in the informal sector. Like their counterparts in San Juan, some found occasional unregistered jobs with small businessmen, including self-employed Puerto Ricans, who normally ran one-man operations with a high risk of failure. Others turned to burglary, gambling, extortion, prostitution, trafficking in drugs, and other crimes to fill the income gap.

Analysing such modes of survival, Harrison (1975), a political economist, notes that ghetto residents in the United States rely on the "welfare economy," the secondary labor market, and the "illegal economy" to make ends meet. (The "illegal economy" includes some of the activities identified previously with the "informal sector.") Utilizing Harrison's categories, in 1978, Moore, in an important study entitled *Homeboys,* observed that Chicanos in Los Angeles barrios adopted all three of these economic means of survival. Their income, according to Moore (1978:30–33), is derived from a "tripartite economy." The "tripartite economy" is also implicated in Sharff's (1981) anthropological study of a marginal family's coping styles and the economic roles adopted by Puerto Rican youth. How might the tripartite economy be implemented? Sharff describes a female-headed family in which an articulate daughter regularly accompanies her mother to fight for family needs at the City's welfare bureau. Another daughter is doing well in school, and the mother sponsors her continued education so that she will be able to support the family in the regular labor market after achieving a technical or professional job. The sons also fill roles in relation to family support. One son with an accommodating disposition is encouraged to obtain regular employment at a factory or service job; but another son, who is an aggressive streetcorner boy oriented around life in the street, plays his economic role in the informal sector. He hustles for money and deals in drugs to supplement family income. Thus, within the same family, each youth engages in different sectors of the economy to maintain standards of living.

Class, Community, and Social Types

Poor North American families generally enjoy a higher living standard than their counterparts in third-world countries. Despite this difference, there are still cleavages within the ghetto communities that are similar to those found by Peattie's study in Venezuela. For example, Hannerz (1969:39–58) studied a Washington, D.C., black ghetto neighborhood and found socioeconomic distinctions between "mainstream" and "streetcorner" families and between "swingers" and "streetcorner men." The mainstreamers are composed of stable working-class as well as petit bourgeois families who are relatively better off than the streetcorner families. There was hardly any unemployment among the mainstreamers. They owned their own homes (here rather than in the suburbs, because of racial segregation), accumulated relatively expensive furniture, and were highly concerned with the style and comfort of their surroundings. Streetcorner families were confronted by different conditions: A great number of these families fell below the poverty line, and many were composed of the "female-headed" families that comprised between one-third and one-half of all the families living in the neighborhood. The streetcorner families also had "looser internal relationships," and husbands and wives spent most of their leisure time apart. Further divisions in the ghetto included a younger "social set" composed of "swingers" who were largely composed of young men and women from the mainstream families. These young adults led a fast social life and frequented commercial cabarets or periodic dances held at an old "middle-class" Negro fraternity lodge. Although they tried to act like high-society socialites, many swingers were members of the working class and had a high rate of job changes because of periodic unemployment. But they were better off than the streetcorner men, who were even more likely to be unemployed, for even longer periods, or, in the case of some, permanently. The streetcorner men usually spent their days together at a single hangout, talking, drinking, shooting craps, playing cards, or just hanging around. Hardly any had graduated from high school, and some were relatively recent migrants from the rural South.

We can see a parallel between North American ghettos and South American barrio family patterns. Hannerz' account of the mainstream and streetcorner families recalls Peattie's description of the Venezuelan barrio, where some families were consolidating a relatively secure economic base in labor and popular markets while others were afflicted with persistent underemployment. Whether or not adolescent peer formations are related to these class developments cannot, however, be determined from Hannerz's study. Adolescent groups are only mentioned by Hannerz in relation to the development of sexual attitudes. On the other hand, we can extrapolate such youthful formations from another study by Ellis and Newman (1971), who report social distinctions among black adolescents that seem to parallel Hannerz' swingers and streetcorner men. Ellis and Newman interviewed ghetto youth in Chicago and found a variety of adolescent social types in the ghetto, including the Ivy Leaguer and the Gowster, who were seen as opposite types. An Ivy Leaguer belonged to a social club such as a fraternity, and he dressed quite fashionably even "by middle-class standards." He wore button-down collars and Brooks Brothers-style clothing to effect an "Ivy-league look." Reportedly, he emulated "middle-class behavior," was considered a good boy by his teachers, finished high school, and was well liked by authorities and family. However, the "raggedy Gowster" (who was considered "a rebel against middle-class society" and usually did not finish school) was called the most "distinct role" in the ghetto. The Gowster preferred baggy pants, long-tip-collar shirts, loose Italian-knit sweaters with cuffs turned under, and brand-name "Stacy Adams" pointed shoes. He sported a hat worn "ace-deuce," that is, low to one side, sometimes worn over a "dew rag" or kerchief in order to protect the "conk," a processed pompadour hair style. He also had a unique manner of walking, belonged to a "gang," and perceived himself as a warrior. "Don't mess with that cat, he's a Gowster," people would say.

Redundant Youth and Marginal Relations in School

The emergence of the Gowster can be explained by structural and institutional factors but not by the mere lack of youth employment. The effects of youth labor markets affect Gowsters and nonGowsters alike, since adolescents, in general, have no independent economic status in advanced industrial societies. This lack of independent status in the United States is rooted historically in advanced capitalist developments. Taken together, the replacement of living labor by machines and the technical and scientific revolution limit the expansion both of the unskilled labor force and of the labor force as a whole. Because they are generally employed in unskilled jobs, children and adolescents have been particularly affected by these developments (Bremner, 1970:753). Therefore, since the 1930s, youth have been gradually but not completely eliminated from the economy—first in basic industries, and last in agriculture. They have been excluded because job markets are influenced by economic developments as a result of the changing composition of capital and its decreasing need for unskilled labor.

These same economic developments have also encouraged the universal system of secondary education, which only fills part of the gap created by the decline of child labor.[1] Today, youth, whether in school or out, are usually dependent upon parental support until the end of adolescence. (Some are even dependent through young adulthood.) Most adolescents cannot maintain themselves in gainful employment, and, because their educational activities do not produce immediate profits, their parents, rather than capital, have been forced to continue to bear the primary costs of their subsistence. As a result, millions of young people become subject to an extraordinary variety of social problems that accompany the status of dependent able-bodied persons in our society.

Certain relationships within the school and the family also determine modern adolescent developments. Socialization efforts by the school and the family interact with each other and become extremely significant because of youth's prolonged dependent status. This socialization uniquely recreates a process of marginalization *within* the school itself, as we shall see. The factors underlying this marginalization process include socialization practices within the family and school that reproduce labor power. To grasp these practices abstractly, it should be recalled that capitalism matures with the generalization of commodity relations. This generalization refers to the transformation of all the factors of production into commodities. In capitalism, therefore, workers, whose value-creating power is a factor of production, become commodity owners. They own their own creative power—that is, their labor power. In exchange for wages, workers sell to employers the right to dispose of their labor power in production. This labor power has been nurtured by the family and by the school.

To clarify this point further, let us note that certain requirements must be met daily to *reproduce* the commodity of labor power. This power is not a lasting power: workers "use up" their powers on the job. To renew their energies for each succeeding work day, they require, among other things, food, shelter, and clothing. Labor power, therefore, requires the appropriation and consumption of the necessities of life for its own reproduction. Finally, certain long-term relations are necessary for the reproduction of labor power. Where do youth learn to become effective workers? Labor power is a quality formed by the energetic acquisition of certain abilities—that is, by the acquisition of knowledge, skills, experience, and discipline. Some of these abilities can be acquired on the job, but, before or after employment has begun, many basic skills, work attitudes, and so forth can be partly learned within socialization agencies such as the family, school, and church.

Most socialization agencies concentrate on youth who will generally become proletarians and who, therefore, require certain types of services for the production of their labor power. (The organization of such services will be called "reproduction relations," because they instill the work habits, technical knowledge, and so on, that reproduce labor power intergenerationally.) These services are largely provided by parents and teachers, whose efforts, as indicated, are exerted within families and schools. With regard to the reproduction of labor power, both socialization agencies seem to operate separately, while in fact they are quite interdependent.

Various kinds of interdependent relations characterize these agencies: obviously, a child's success in school is partly dependent upon his family relations. Empirical studies further indicate that the family, compared with the school, is a stronger determinant of the child's eventual "success" as a labor force participant. But *determination* of individual success cannot be equated with *domination* of the general standards that regulate successful striving. The family is forced to regulate its own reproduction (socialization) relationships according to the meritocratic and technical standards exerted by the school (Papagiannis et al., 1983; Wilcox and Moriarity, 1976; Wittig, 1976). With regard to the long-term reproduction of labor power, therefore, the school is the dominating agency.

The reproduction relations in the school are, in turn, largely dominated by industrial relations. Economists suggest that educational standards "correspond" somewhat to the hierarchical organization of the labor force (Bowles and Gintis, 1973:65–96). The standards used to reward and punish a student's behavior within the school are, therefore, synchronized with the standards used by managers to control workers.

The reproduction relations within the family are also dominated by industry, but this form of domination is partly mediated by the school. As mentioned previously, the school, despite appearances, essentially organizes its reproduction relations around industrially related standards. By dominating production relations within the family, the school as well as industry imposes these standards on parents and children.

These dominating relations are expressed in the same general laws of investment and profit maximization that culminate in the uneven development of various groups and nations (Bluestone, 1972). Operatively, this means that investments in the development of the labor force are allocated unevenly. These investments concentrate on those groups of persons who are considered to have a greater potentiality for meeting the merit-oriented criteria prevailing in educational institutions. Conversely, the investment of private or public resources—which are calculable in terms of money, equipment, facilities, faculties, and even in the teacher's time, attention, and expectations—will be minimal for the development of those groups of persons who do not appear to meet these merit-oriented criteria.

Consequently, the allocation of educational resources frequently (but not always) favors those youth who have already been the recipients of superior resources. They receive more because of the economic and cultural advantages that are passed on to the members of certain ethnic, racial, or occupational strata, or because of the compensatory time and energy expended on them by self-sacrificing parents. During the elementary-school period, a mutually reinforcing relationship is set up between the activities of youth who show the productive signs of superior familial investments and the patterns by which resources are selectively allocated within educational institutions. Throughout the child's formative period, educational capital continuously builds on the most favored students.

Simultaneously, the competitive position of the least favored students deteriorates, and a process analogous to marginalization within the economy occurs in the context of the school and the family. This process has inadvertent consequences that are expressed in anarchic behavior patterns by youngsters who never were strongly motivated to achieve or who have lost this motivation because of persistent failure.[2] Consequently, they do not make any disciplined effort to achieve, nor do they actually acquire the cognitive and the non-cognitive traits that generally favor sustained labor force participation in the future. Although their chances for future employment are somewhat independent of their status in socialization agencies, these children manifest early in life some of the adaptive characteristics that sometimes evolve among owners of the least valuable forms of labor power. On one hand, these children are distinguished from most subproletarians because they galvanize their lives to a greater degree around personal consumption values and informal relations rather than labor-market activities and family relations. Yet they are forerunners of the adult "streetcorner" crowds. Although their adulthood is also influenced by conditions that are independent of adolescent life, we will use the phrase "streetcorner youth" to classify these adolescents. Streetcorner youth can also be justifiably called proto-marginals rather than marginals, because their status is not actually determined directly by economic institutions. The members of this population are *not* usually counted among "the employed" or "the unemployed." Instead, they are regarded as students, and during most of their adolescent years workaday life is very far from their minds.

Streetcorner and Intellectual Prototypes

Within communities throughout the United States, adolescents speak about these streetcorner youth, and such names as Greaser, Ese Vato, Dude, Honcho, Hodad, and Homeboy appear whenever they are mentioned in conversations. These metaphors refer to *individual* streetcorner youth; nevertheless, they also signify their *social regularities* in personal behavior. They point to the forms of conduct, carriage, attitudes, gestures, grooming, argot, clothing, and delinquent acts exhibited by members of the same peer formations. Although different names may be used in different localities, these regularities are often the same. Of course, their life styles, just like adult life styles, change over time.

We shall discuss these names and their referents more fully in later chapters. Unless otherwise indicated, the term "streetcorner" (or "marginal") simply refers to "prototypic" rather than developed adult streetcorner or marginal relationships. For now it should again be emphasized that the marginalization processes under discussion are not directly determined by labor market relations. The effects of this marginalization will therefore be reflected in family and school relationships, but they are not classified by any official economic category.

To avoid any misunderstanding, it is taken for granted that certain types of family conflicts or "breakdowns" definitely enhance the possibilities of marginalization. On the other hand, these possibilities are also mediated by parental resources. Wealthy families can employ such "absorption mechanisms" as psychiatric counseling, boarding school, and the tutorial trip abroad to cushion the effects of family disturbance on the child. If these mechanisms are unsuccessful, then their wealth further provides children who are becoming marginalized with a second chance later in life. Some of these children, in fact, never have to concern themselves with labor market activity: they can be sustained by inherited property.

By contrast, petit bourgeois and working-class families are exposed to greater hardships and difficulties. Absorption mechanisms are relatively unavailable, and family problems directly influence the parents' and child's active contribution to the production of the child's labor power. They interact with the already disadvantaged competitive relations engendered by the school.

Consequently, one can assume that a child's productivity in school is also influenced by individual capacities and by family factors such as the cultural background and values of parents, which are partly independent of socioeconomic status relationships. Nevertheless, traditional socioeconomic factors, such as the parents' income, education, and property, also affect the likelihood of marginalization. Because of the long-term effects of the uneven development of capital, a greater proportion of marginal youth can be expected among lower-status families. Alternatively, marginalization can certainly be expected among *higher*-status families (or among "middle-class" families), but to a lesser degree.

Since we have been concerned with educational factors, let us now turn our attention briefly to youth who, from the standpoint of the school, represent the most highly developed forms of labor power. (Our attention to this social type is brief because this work is concerned with delinquent youth.) These are the high academic achievers, who strikingly epitomize the division of labor among mental and manual workers in capitalist societies. They are usually very articulate, and some have broad political, cultural, and scientific interests. Others, noted for their narrow academic and technical interests, symbolize the degree to which young personalities have been influenced by the extreme labor force segmentation among mental workers. Their personal interests are "overspecialized" and organized largely by experiences based on the appropriation and dispensation of technical knowledge.

The term "intellectual" (or "proto-intellectual") will be used to characterize these youth. With regard to adults, the word "intellectual" classifies the aggregate of persons who devote their occupational activities to the formulation of ideas, to the creation of artistic representations of ideas, or to the application of ideas, such as the application of scientific-technical knowledge to human affairs. The development of modern intellectuals can be traced back to the early capitalist period. But this development has been accelerated enormously by the expansion of monopoly capitalism and the modern state (Schwendinger and Schwendinger, 1974:143–87, 360–61). Today the category of intellectuals includes writers, city planners, university teachers, and scientists. The term "proto-intellectual," on the other hand, refers to youth who manifest the personal interests and characteristics that have been generated among adults by the developments mentioned above. Historically, educational institutions have played a very important part in regulating the formation of this particular population. The schools have selected intellectuals from virtually every stratum in the population. Certain families have, however, contributed candidates disproportionately. Bourgeois families, including small farmers as well as independent professionals, have supplied the greatest proportions. In recent years, the established families of such "mental workers" as teachers, technicians, and scientists have also been contributing relatively higher numbers of proto-intellectuals.

Because of bourgeois educational policies and the intergenerational effects of uneven investment, young women, youth of both sexes who belong to racially oppressed groups, and children of unskilled workers become candidates to a lesser degree. It has been chiefly the white families of higher socioeconomic status that have established a mutually dependent relation with the school. The children of families that *have* more *get* more, because the public educational system converts human beings into commodities and builds upon *that* human material which already has considerable investment value.

In communities across the United States one finds that the names for these types of youth also appear in peer conversations. Included among these names are Intellectual, Brain, Pencil-Neck, Egg-Head, Book-Worm, and Walking Encyclopedia. We shall discuss these names and their referents in later chapters. For now, it should be noted that by contrast with many marginals, these youths are paragons of virtue. In fact, they are foremost members of the least delinquent population in a local society of youth.

NOTES

1. Adolescents, therefore, have not been excluded from the labor market simply because of child-labor laws, the decline of the "family economy," or the emergence of a *highly specialized* division of labor. See Dollard (1941) and Coleman (1962) for explanations based on such factors. Also, the secondary school was first developed for technical "labor in general"—that is, to provide education commonly required for work performed by skilled blue-collar workers and clerical workers, who move readily from one kind of job to another in the mature phases of capitalist development. It was not developed because of the increasing specialization of the division of labor, as Coleman (1962) believes.
2. In this context, the research by Polk (1972, 1973) is also important, because he provides insights into school and delinquency and shows that negative high-school experiences affect delinquency and later criminal behavior.

4

The Prototypic Socialites

Previous chapters discussed historical conditions underlying the development of streetcorner youth and intellectuals. We can now describe some of the conditions underlying a third type—the socialites. Early capitalism gave rise to the bourgeoisie and the predecessors of today's youthful socialites. These young "gallants" (who were the children of the high bourgeoisie) will be discussed in this chapter. But, first, a word about the composition of their social class. Because the bourgeoisie emerged largely from the expansion of commerce, especially in agrarian commodities, its membership was certainly not limited to city burghers, independent craftsmen, merchants, and guildmasters. Certain members of the nobility and other large landholders born in the countryside were likewise members of this new class (Wallerstein, 1974:240–44).

Noting the degree to which economic changes in sixteenth-century England were based on a revolution in agrarian relations, the eminent historian, Tawney (1947), called the beneficiaries of this revolution "the gentry." Thus, the gentry were usually landholders, though some were also distinguished by the aristocratic titles of the lesser nobility. Often, they held no title at all; they were simply prosperous "clodhoppers."

The Young Gallants

At the very beginning of the sixteenth century, this new social class began to exhibit a highly conspicuous pattern of personal consumption. To wit, in 1516, when Thomas More (1964:27) condemned the growth of avarice, he also pointed out that "alongside of . . . wretched need and poverty you find ill-timed luxury. Not only the servants of noblemen but the craftsmen and almost the clod-hoppers themselves, in fact, all classes alike, are given to such ostentatious sumptuousness of dress . . ." Ostentatious dress was also mentioned at the universities. The officials at Cambridge complained that the attire of the student offspring of the gentry and the aristocracy had become "disordered" and "excessive," "tending to the decay of learning, & other dissolute behavior" (Cooper, 1863:613, 616).

Because of their opposition to traditional, austere consumption standards, the younger gentry were particularly vulnerable to social criticism. However, they were not alone. Traditional restraint was also being swept aside by their socially active families. The seasonal tides of squires, gentlemen, ladies, and lesser nobility, in particular, rapidly transformed London into a notable center of conspicuous consumption. The standards of the younger gentry were modeled after the older, more rakish members of their class. As their fortunes rose, these older members adopted the leisurely patterns of the aristocracy. Some speculated furiously in the expanding money market and indulged compulsively in luxuries that threatened them with personal ruin. For others, however, life in the city became a pleasant, lasting social occasion. They beguiled themselves on warm summer days "with music and cup in barges upon the water." Hours were spent riding in coaches about the city streets. Libraries were turned into gambling saloons, and the royal parks were used for dueling, commercial bowling, and quaffing wine leisurely under the trees (Fisher, 1948).

An expanding network of luxury trades and civil associations supported the life style of the London gentry. Hackney cabs appeared on the streets, and the exclusive club sprang into being as gentlemen from similar parts of the country gathered together in their favorite taverns. The institution of the commercial theatre and new trends in architecture were sustained by their demand for commercial entertainment and housing. These emerging styles of life represented aspects of "the first complete bourgeois revolution" in social, cultural, economic, and political affairs (Hobsbawm, 1954:63).

This style of life and its ostentatious use of dress, jewels, and perfumes were captured sarcastically in Ben Johnson's writings. He advised propertied men first to discard their responsibilities in the country if they wanted to become accomplished gentlemen; and then, before traveling to London to live among the gallants, to exchange "four or five acres of [their] best land into two or three trunks of apparel."

The reader will recall that this same bourgeois revolution produced the idle and mischievous companies of poor London youth who were castigated by Thomas Firmin. However, while the scions of the landed gentry were less identified with gainful employment and obedient conduct, Firmin advanced no schemes for imprisoning them in a workhouse or for punishing their wrongdoings decisively. In fact, their misbehavior was rarely censored by officials, even though they were, if anything, more malicious than the youngsters in the outer parts of the city.

Hibbert (1963:45), for instance, describes the drunken escapades of the Bold Bucks, a group of young gallants who committed rape frequently and with impunity. "An expectation of inviolability," Hibbert notes, "was indeed, shared by many, if not most young men of [their] class." Another gang of young gentlemen also committed crimes without fear of punishment. In a letter to a friend, Jonathan Swift (1901) complained in 1711 that the streets were not safe, and that he was terribly afraid of being beaten by "a race of rakes" called the Mohocks. In another letter, he wrote: "Lord Winchelsea told me today at Court that two of the Mohocks caught a maid of old Lady Winchelsea's at the door of their house in the park, where she was with a candle and had just lighted out somebody. They cut all her face, and beat her without provocation." An additional report, this time by Lady Wentworth, indicated that the Mohocks "put an old woman in a hogshead and rolled her down the hill." They mutilated other persons, cutting off their noses, hands, and so forth, also without provocation (Swift, 1901:419–32). Allegedly, the Mohocks never took money from anyone; they were simply maliciously violent, yet always remained "young gentlemen." One member of the gang was a baronet's son, another the youngest son of the Bishop of Salisbury. The Bishop's son was an ill-reputed young man about town, but he entered the profession of law eventually. He was appointed a judge in 1741 and knighted four years later (Swift, 1901:419–20). Though earlier his own violent acts had been committed with impunity, for all we know this knighted judge may have imprisoned or executed indigent youth for similar crimes.

The Apprentices

Bourgeois double standards were applied to a wide range of personal conduct, including sartorial preferences, sexual activities, and recreation. While the younger gentry were free to dress and live as they pleased, the style of life among the nascent petit bourgeoisie, the ordinary apprentices, was regulated by stringent and detailed prescriptions. The guildsmen and the authorities, of course, had always indicted and severely punished apprentices for being riotous and truculent, and for stealing from their masters. From the sixteenth century onwards, however, apprentices were condemned for keeping mistresses, for frequenting taverns and playhouses, and for displaying "great excesses in clothes, Linen, periwigs, gold and silver watches, etc." (Besant, 1904:324–26). Of course, the sexual behavior of apprentices was not unusual by contrast with the rest of society. Regarding the fifteenth and sixteenth centuries, Brinton (1959:250–55) writes, "as far as I know, [it] is the only period in the history of the West when the male wore very tight lower garments ('hose') with a conspicuous codpiece, which was often ornamented." Women also demonstrated a rough-and-ready equality in certain sexual matters. Their low-cut decolletage, provocatively flaunting the breasts, and the wild, hot pursuit of earthly pleasures by both sexes were among the factors that provoked the clergy to cry out against the changing standards of sexual morality.

The attempts to control apprentices reflected the standards restricting personal consumption within single occupational groups. Legal statutes were particularly applied to everyday attire, because dress was associated with the wearer's servitude. The appropriate attire for apprentices traditionally included a flat round cap, coarse side coats, cloth stockings, and other such severe apparel (Besant, 1904:329). As early as the sixteenth century, city ordinances specifically forbade extravagant dress being displayed by apprentices on the streets of London. In 1582, the Common Council proclaimed that from hence-forth all apprentices must

> wear no Hat [other] than a Woolen Cap, without any Silk in or about the same . . . enriched with any manner of Gold, Silver, or Silk . . . wear no Pumps, Slippers nor Shoes, but of English leather, without being pinked, edged or stitched, nor [garnished] Girdles nor Garters . . . wear no Sword, dagger, or other Weapon, but a Knife; nor a Ring, Jewel of Gold, nor Silver, nor Silk in any Part of the Apparel (quoted in Besant, 1904:325).

Punishments were meted out to no avail. Although punishment included public whipping and the addition of six months of service to the time specified by the indenture, these ordinances did not eliminate errant behavior; it persisted for centuries, and eighteenth-century writers, like Sir William Maitland, continued to complain that apprentices as well as lawyers' clerks "are under no Manner of Government; before their times are half out, they set up [like] Gentlemen, they dress, they drink, they game, they frequent the Playhouses and intrigue with the Women. . . ." Even at the very end of early capitalism, therefore, noted citizens demanded more effective laws to curb the so-called "destructive practices of our Modern Apprentice" (Besant, 1904:325).

The ordinance of 1586 was among other legal codes controlling apprentices. These codes required the master to provide the apprentice with the minimum requirements in food, clothing, and shelter. In exchange, the master appropriated the full product of the apprentice's labor. In certain respects, the codes protected the apprentice, but they also buttressed the unequal terms of the master–apprentice exchange. Apprentices, under these conditions, could not legally adopt modes of consumption exceeding the necessities provided by the master; they did, however, acquire money for greater consumption by embezzling from their masters or covertly selling their services to others. Consequently, further ordinances had to be enacted to insulate them from the temptations, the personal discontent, and the unlawful conduct that were being stimulated by the ostentatious and materialistic styles of life manifested by youth in the wealthier classes. Regardless of the proliferation of legislation, the pull of conspicuous consumption was overwhelming, and it continued.

Beneath the surface of these ordinances lay the effects unleashed by money capital's increasing domination of everyday life. One effect was that exploited and exploiters alike were being influenced by the changing expectations that accompanied the competitive struggle for material advantage. In those sectors of mercantile and industrial production that were being vigorously propelled by capitalist developments, this struggle provided further fuel for rising expectations and status usurpation. Also, the economic changes that consolidated the means of agrarian production within the hands of capitalist farmers and the means of industrial production as the property of merchant capitalists and merchant guildsmen intensified the lines of stratification in English society. The lines cut in diverse directions. The chasm separating the great landowners from the landless proletarians was obviously widened but, in addition, class divisions were sharpened between the guildmasters, on one hand, and the journeymen and apprentices, on the other. Status differentiation among poor and wealthy guilds deepened, and the status accompaniments of growing economic inequality intensified feelings of deprivation on all class levels.

Bourgeois Versus Petit Bourgeois Youth

Although the apprentices were being generally subjected to harsher conditions by the ordinances, their desires were stimulated by these status concerns. Apprentices, particularly from the wealthier guilds (Pinchbeck and Hewitt, 1969:232), eagerly adopted the ostentatious styles set by the foremost fraction of the rising bourgeoisie, the landed gentry. Their conspicuous consumption was, however, grounded materially within the limits of the guild system. Because apprentices expected to join the ranks of the masters eventually, they generally aspired only to becoming members of the petit bourgeoisie. Some, however, aspired to acquiring the greater powers of appropriation bestowed on the wealthier guildsmen. The development of trade and domestic industry placed these guildsmen among the nouveaux riches of early capitalist society. The apprentices, however, were not yet masters and were subject to legal and economic forms of class exploitation and domination.

These legal and economic controls hardly applied to the younger gentry. Their mode of consumption opposed traditionally austere consumption standards, but they were not whipped in public for their transgressions. Young gentry were constrained to live within their means, but their disposable income was certainly not limited to that resulting from self-earned property. Though their social lives were determined by commodity relations, they were the beneficiaries of other people's labor.

Wherever possible, the gentry organized status relations in their own interests. To be conspicuous, their consumption certainly had to be enviable, and it cultivated the sins of avarice, gluttony, and pride. Moreover, the malicious violence inflicted, particularly on social inferiors, by young rakish gentlemen such as the Mohocks was the quintessence of their class arrogance and brutality. In every class society, the morals of rising classes have been organized centrally around exploitative relationships. The gentry's morals were molded by their own struggle for the control of agrarian commodity production and exchange. Although first expressed by transitional rhetorical categories such as avarice and pride, the struggle for control was quickly and completely rationalized by expedient bourgeois doctrines defining all persons of lesser status essentially as natural social inferiors (Tawney, 1947). For example, the "industrious poor" were denigrated by these doctrines, but the unemployed laborers and displaced farmers were considered the epitomy of inferiority. According to these new doctrines, these marginals got what they deserved, even if their "just due" was akin to life in Hobbes' state of nature—namely, poor, nasty, brutish, and short.

By contrast, the younger gentry who did not work at all were accorded status by other classes, because their parents owned the land that was used by tenants, laborers, and slaves to produce their revenue. But they were also set apart by the fine houses, clothing, food, and the personal services that were at their disposal through, once again, their parents' vast economic power. This power was not to be denied. In fact, poorer aristocrats grudgingly intermarried with bourgeois families to acquire land deeds, stock certificates, and ready cash. The status of a lesser noble could moreover be purchased directly. Thus, the scions of the landed gentry acquired social honor that was symbolized by the aristocratic title, the genealogist's chart, and the emblazoned family shield.

Although noted for their own ostentatious fads, the settled members of the aristocracy were generally contemptuous of the gentry's garish tastes, apish manners, and crass materialism. Some gentry, in turn, were sensitive to this hypocritical scorn, but their sense of humiliation was more than offset by the comforts of the money they possessed. It was further tempered by the obvious comparisons with the squalid realities they had imposed on others while acquiring and maintaining their own wealth. The gentry had learned the lessons of contemporary life accurately, even if Hobbes did not. They were not at all freed from the state of nature by a willing obedience to a common sovereign power. Their freedom was predicated squarely on the expansion of their own powers. In early capitalism, only the selfish use of power made their lives rich, pleasant, merciful, and long.

Styles of Life and the New Industrialists

The young gallants and apprentices, and the material conditions that sustained their existence, eventually metamorphosed into today's socialites. But the historical background of the modern socialites was not limited to the early *bourgeoisie*—the thriving merchants, wealthy guildsmen, and landed gentry. An important contributing group were the industrialists, and we need to know more about how their history and cultural characteristics molded a certain type of youth. Although English industrialists also indulged in the delights of conspicuous consumption, the self-made men among them were at a momentary disadvantage. They possessed limited resources with which to launch themselves into the riptide of competition. Immediate profits supplied these self-made men with their revenues for personal consumption; but the profits also had to be divided into capital, wages, etc. to ensure production on an ascending scale. Since expenditures for luxuries sharply diminished their capital, these "men on the move" viewed conspicuous consumption with ambivalence.

By the eighteenth and nineteenth centuries, Protestant doctrines provided distinct moral standards for resolving this ambivalence. However, the competitive market had little regard for personal anxieties or moral principle. If the self-made man was interested in the pursuit of money, then he had to favor progressive accumulation. Until his fortunes rose, he was compelled to invest his profits and to abstain from a luxurious life. It should be noted, however, that various "theories of abstention" view the self-made man differently. Some, for example, insist that his abstemious behavior was dictated by bourgeois piety. Rather than a mundane practicality and a greedy desire for personal gain, his religiosity, frugality, and asceticism created anxieties that drove him to accumulate incessantly. Because of these bourgeois virtues, it is said, the self-made man scorned the immediate joys of life. Anxiously sustained by the dictates of his calling, yet with little more in his hands than the sweat of his brow, the ascetic Protestant tightened his belt, bit the bullet, and accumulated an immense hoard of wealth.[1] However, the "theories of abstention" mystify the process of capitalist accumulation. The self-made man accumulated capital, but the essential mechanism involved was *exploitation,* not self-denial. If any population was truly forced to abstain from the joys of life, it was the population of slaves, indentured servants, convict laborers, and wage earners that had been created by capitalist developments.

The infamous Manchester textile manufacturers went through several phases before they expended their revenues on luxury goods. In the beginning, they encouraged the lowly cottagers to pay a high premium for allowing their children to work as apprentices; but the children, who were starved and driven to exhaustion on the job, learned no trade; they merely tended machines. At the same time, since their average profits were low, these manufacturers had to be parsimonious and live like misers (Marx, 1959:594). The life styles of succeeding generations of manufacturers adjusted to developing circumstances. From 1779 onwards, the fortunes of the Manchester textile manufacturers soared. Concomitantly—as John Aiken observed in 1795—their "expense and luxury . . . made great progress, and [were] supported by a trade extended throughout every part of Europe" (Marx, 1959:594–95). When revenue and capital were no longer severely restricted, these manufacturers abandoned plain living. Adopting the air of the capitalist who had been born wealthy, they conspicuously indulged themselves in luxuries. According to Marx (1959:594),

> [t]he progress of capitalist production not only creates a world of delights; it lays open, in speculation and the credit system a thousand sources of sudden enrichment. When a certain stage of development has been reached, a conventional degree of prodigality, which is also an exhibition of wealth, and consequently a source of credit, becomes a business necessity. Luxury enters into capital's expenses of representation.

In the world of business, conspicuous consumption is as essential as money in the bank. Everyone knows that clothes make the man and diamonds are a girl's best friend. The reasons are simple: conspicuous consumption reinforces patterns of status, deference, and domination. The generalization of commodity production, however, adds new dimensions to this consumption, which mitigate against thrift and self-denial. In this context, conspicuous consumption is important, because capitalism makes individual worth equivalent to economic worth in social as well as economic relations (Veblen, 1953). Whenever capital throws up a new stratum of wealthy bourgeoisie, the crass material foundations for bourgeois status relations are reaffirmed.

For example, in the last decades of the nineteenth century, the *nouveaux riches,* born aloft by the expansion of monopoly capital, entered the American upper class in an orgy of conspicuous consumption. Families of finance capitalists led a luxurious and leisurely life. Establishing a social world of salons, circles, and intercity communities such as Newport and Saratoga Springs, these families became known as "high society." In the 1890s, high society's leisure activities contrasted with its ruthless and exploitative business practices. The former were distinguished by rounds of genteel parties, attendance at the opera and theater, and participation in the arts. Sports on land and sea, including tennis, polo, sailing, fox-hunting, and gambling, were varied by the seasons or combined with the trip abroad. Like their English predecessors, the members of this society developed mannered and ritualized modes of flirtation, eating, drinking, speaking, and fashionable dress. They also developed snobbish exclusion standards to maintain the status distinctions between themselves and the new newly rich of each succeeding generation.

The Children of the Rich and Very Rich

Before the Civil War, upper-class status in the United States had been based on social and economic interrelations within relatively isolated, regional business and family networks. After the war, however, these institutional networks expanded. Certain institutions outside the family, such as the exclusive Eastern boarding school and the fashionable Eastern university, then became significant for the children of the very rich.

With regard to this development, Baltzell (1958) states, "In an age which marked the centralization of economic power under the control of finance capitalism, the gentleman bankers and lawyers of Wall Street, Walnut Street, State Street, and LaSalle Street sent their sons to Groton, St. Paul's, or St. Mark's." After receiving their secondary education at these boarding schools, the youth attended private universities such as Harvard, Yale, and Princeton, "where they joined exclusive clubs such as *Porcellian, Fence,* or *Ivy.*" Marrying in the same circles, living in similar suburbs, commuting to the same places of business, and attending comparable clubs, these young men carried on and reproduced anew the contemporary patterns of upper-class life.

Baltzell also mentions Exeter, an Eastern boarding school that caters for both upper-middle-class and upper-class families. Booth Tarkington, for example, attended Exeter, although, according to one biographer, his father was "a lawyer of modest means."[2] In varying degrees, Tarkington's friends at Exeter seemed to have leavened their educational priorities with rowdyism, carousing, stylish clothing, and old-fashioned whoring. His school friends, who shared the same "regular old fraud" of a landlady, "raised more hell than any other six students in Town," and the fashionable Eastern sartorial tastes acquired at school brought him ridicule when he returned during vacations to his midwestern home. During his senior-high-school year, he remarked to a friend that some of his classmates "are handsome, some of them witty . . . but what a hot-bed of foulness and muck! Portsmouth houses [of prostitution] are full of them every night—Boston ones, every holiday" (Woodress, 1955:47–48).

Because he was born into a "proper Philadelphian" (upper-class) family and attended Groton, George Biddle's autobiography is also instructive. It provides insight into upper-class attitudes toward education and high society:

> My mother grew up in a large family. . . . her upbringing was chaotic. There was no regular schooling, no disciplined routine. Uncle Moncure had unusual gifts, but he suffered from weak eyes. Grandfather persuaded him to throw up his studies and gave him horses to keep him out of mischief. *Before he was twenty* he was a gentleman jockey in the hardest drinking crowd in America [our emphasis] (Biddle, 1939:43).

By contrast, Biddle graduated from Groton and Harvard:

> I had four happy years at Haverford School when it was decided, upon due consultation, that my education could be improved—intellectually, morally, physically, socially—by the benefits of a New England boarding-school at Groton, Massachusetts where my elder brother had already preceded me. Here I stayed for five years and another six at Harvard and the Harvard Law School (Biddle, 1939:32).

His experiences at Groton do not reflect a climate of strong commitment to academic studies. Although he describes the atmosphere at the high school as "socially conservative rather than actually hostile to scholarship," his accounts suggest a conservatism largely lacking in enthusiasm for the advancement of knowledge (Biddle, 1939:43).

"To succeed at Groton, as later at Harvard," Biddle (1939:45) remarks, "three paths lay open; athletics, social success and administrative ability." With regard to athletics, he (1939:44) complains "we had to play football and baseball, no matter how thoroughly we disliked them and how indifferently we played, unless the doctor actually forbade it." Social success was accepted without qualification. It involved circles, rituals, clubs, and parties. At Groton, it even demanded a strict conformity to modified English "fag and hazing traditions." According to Biddle (1939:46), these traditions simply imbued a "mutuality of respect for the rights of the younger as well as the older." In actuality the traditions fostered sentiments that augmented personal manners and poise with a sense of power, confidence, and social superiority.[3]

Social success was also important at Harvard.

> At Harvard, then, the New England boarding-school boy went in for clubs—social success. If that were not one's line, one

> opted for major athletics—although even in the field of major athletics there were social overtones. . . . From a social point of view one never went in for scholarship. One carried one's honors lightly, with just a note of depreciation. High honors did not actually leave one in bad odor, so much as under a cloud of suspicion" (Biddle, 1939:82).

Administrative ability was the third path to success. The importance of this ability was largely taken for granted because many Groton students were certain to become financial and business leaders. The frank recognition of its importance at Groton was directed at maintaining the power of upper-class families on an hereditary basis.

Biddle was aware of the enormous resources made available for the development of the upper-class child. He (1939:66) stated,

> Ninety-five percent of these [Groton] boys came from what they considered the aristocracy of America. Their fathers belonged to the Somerset, the Knickerbocker, the Philadelphia or the Baltimore Clubs. Among them was a goodly slice of the wealth of the nation, little Morgans, Whitneys, Webbs, McCormicks, Crockers, Stillmans. On the whole the equipment and the teaching were more admirable [at Groton] than at any other school in America.

But Biddle (1939:66) complained that these educational resources were being wasted:

> Generally speaking, this aristocracy, this wealth, this admirable educational training was destined to flow into one channel—Wall Street or its equivalent. There were, of course, exceptions. Of the fifty-six of my two Groton forms the names of seven have even been listed in *Who's Who in America*. The greatest number, however, could in terms of manhood, be listed as absolute failures: parasites on the community, cheats, drunkards, lechers, panhandlers, suicides.

Undoubtedly, some of these "absolute failures" had adopted parasitic and deteriorating styles of life in adolescence that survived into adult life. For those able to sponge from their own families or prudently live on incomes from their own property, the consequences of this adolescent–adult life style are less serious. On the other hand, the consequences for others may be unmitigated disaster: despite family monetary support, ruling classes in capitalist societies have produced their own share of downwardly mobile persons, whose decline is accelerated by gambling debts or other effects of their irresponsible behavior.

The downward movement of the older rich is matched by the upward movement of the newly rich, who conspicuously reproduce upper-class styles of life. The production of millionaires has not ceased: immense fortunes are still garnered by exploitation, by denying workers the fruits of their labor. One can now find wealthy communities in Dallas, Denver, Phoenix, and Los Angeles as well as in Philadelphia, Baltimore, or Boston, with their yearly "coming out" debutante affairs, exclusive circles, and preferences for particular private schools. Here we also find metropolitan newspapers whose "women and society" sections carry the latest reports on the charity balls, fashion shows, nights at the opera, and prominent socialites.

These newly rich families still send their children to "upper-middle-class" and "upper-class" colleges. In a 1982 article, "Crime and deviance on a college campus: The privilege of class," Hills mentions such a school, but, disguising its name, he calls it "Preppy University." Hills notes that Preppy University is a small private liberal-arts college in the Northeast, which is featured prominently in a recent best-seller, *The Official Preppy Handbook*. Hills (1983:257) writes,

> Its affluent students are mostly white and upper middle class students, neatly attired in the de rigueur uniform of jeans, alligator shirts, and L.L. Bean footwear. Yet the parents of the attractive young people who attend this socially popular coed college are probably unaware . . . of the large number of serious criminal acts that involve Preppy students: "rape dates," property damage, burglary, larceny, auto insurance fraud, illicit drug use, drug trafficking, cheating the telephone company, and many other forms of behavior that violate other people's dignity, privacy and possessions.

The few injurious acts that are discovered by administrators are treated as "pranks," lapses of judgment, or expressions of "bad taste" and are usually ignored or covered up by the authorities.

Although restricted by more limited revenues, similar relationships are generated among other fractions of the bourgeoisie, including the lower levels of the managerial stratum, the independent professionals, the commissioned salespersons, and the smaller businessmen and women. Members of these fractions may derive their revenues for personal consumption from capital return. Others may acquire money for consumer spending from self-earned property relations and the sale of professional services. In fact, even though they have no property of their own, some of these persons may pay for their style of life by managing another person's property.

The less affluent bourgeois parents may also send their children to private schools, for instance, a military academy, where children are prepared for the military or for other bureaucratic institutions. On the other hand, these parents may prefer a private "progressive school," where the children are socialized for the independent professions or the independent labor market. Generally, however, the children are sent to immense public high schools and are thereby provided with a variety of educational programs that also fixate student developments at uneven levels.

Within these public institutions, the children of the less affluent bourgeoisie become living contradictions. Because of their bourgeois backgrounds, they generate highly invidious and consumption-oriented styles of life imitating those of the rich and very rich. They are, furthermore, particularly sensitive to the unremitting "sales efforts" as well as other pressures aimed at increasing aggregate demand among consumers. However, in advanced capitalist society, the metropolitan public school is increasingly unable to accommodate the social needs of petit bourgeois youth. As a result, their styles of life and sensitivities create special "tension management" problems with regard to school activities. Relatively mediocre scholarship, absenteeism, and an almost exclusive attention to extracurricular activities are some of the choices made in resolving these problems.

Caught in the flux of economic change, these youth who come from bourgeois families may not remain in the social class of their birth, but while in school they form various status groups. Although the instabilities of self-earned property, the separation from professional parents, and the attractions of extremely unstable occupations may eventually send them in other directions, for the short period of their adolescence these youth constitute their own prototypic forms of bourgeois life. Whenever they are concentrated, they sustain complex status formations characterized throughout adolescence by loosely knit, interlocking crowds and cliques. During high school, moreover, fraternity and sorority clubs frequently emerge within the crowd formations.

Although these social networks emulate status relations that have been generated by the bourgeoisie, their membership is not restricted to bourgeois youth alone. Like the apprentices of bygone years who turned the products of their labor over to their masters, there are youth who conspicuously emulate bourgeois styles of life regardless of their ascribed class position. Some adolescents from working-class families fix their eyes on these styles of life and join formations of socialites in their own community.

More than emulation lies behind a working-class youth's adoption of conspicuously bourgeois styles of life. Under capitalist production a "free wage laborer" has autonomy in personal consumption when compared to the feudal mode of production. Also, the commodification of social life expands enormously under capitalism, and this expansion affects the styles of life adopted by working-class youth. Finally, the status accompaniments to the capitalist mode of production generate attitudes toward personal consumption which create a sense of deprivation among people in all classes.

Consequently, over the recent decades, in communities with skilled-worker as well as bourgeois families, one finds a variety of faddish names for these socialites appearing in peer conversations. Such names include Socialites, Elites, Shiddities, Colleges, Ivy Leaguers, Swingers, and Preppies. We shall discuss these names and their referents in later chapters. For now it should be noted that by contrast with the streetcorner youth, that is, the Greasers, Hodads, Homeboys, or Ese Vatos, these socialite prototypes are less likely to be involved in the most serious violent and economic forms of delinquency. However, we shall also see later that with regard to vehicle violations, vandalism, drinking, gambling, petty theft, truancy, sexual promiscuity, and other garden varieties of delinquent behavior, the socialites are frequently equivalent to streetcorner youth, or not far behind.

NOTES

1. For a discussion of these views, see Marx (1959:591–98). Our caricature of these views, however, is patterned after a work not mentioned by Marx because it appeared in this century. That work is Max Weber's (1958) *Protestant Ethic and the Spirit of Capitalism.*
2. Tarkington may implicate benevolent admission practices as well the "sponsored mobility" generally applied to students in upper-class institutions. For sponsored mobility, see Turner (1966).
3. See, for instance, the comments about "the upper class mind" and the reference to Fitzgerald's *The Rich Boy* in Baltzell (1958:333).

II

SOCIAL TYPE METAPHORS AND ADOLESCENT SUBCULTURES

5

Introduction

The long-term historical processes underlying socialite and streetcorner youth have been discussed, but these processes are insufficient for understanding the particular ways in which these youth present themselves. Technical–industrial developments and local conditions further concretize adolescent social types at a given historical moment. The mass production of relatively inexpensive automobiles in the postwar years, for instance, generated thousands of car clubs among streetcorner youth as well as among socialites. Greaser car clubs were especially noticeable where working-class families were highly dependent on private transportation.

To understand these youth, other factors should also be taken into consideration. Socialite and streetcorner groups are embedded in "peer societies" that are usually composed of thousands of youth from similar high-school districts. Peer society members therefore include not only socialite, streetcorner, and intellectual youth but also additional types such as athletes, surfers, and hot-rodders. Though socialite and streetcorner youth develop independent networks, these other social types influence their styles of life and network developments.

Consequently, the forms taken by socialite and streetcorner youth are not just simple reflexes of macro-relationships. These youth emerge in already established communities, and their networks are affected by local conditions. Obviously, the theoretical unraveling of their subcultures requires a *multilevel causal analysis* aimed at the progressive concretion of socialite and streetcorner relationships. Because such an analysis represents a departure from conventional criminology, we devote Part II to concepts and observations enabling us to understand the structures of *peer societies* before we consider delinquency. This part of our exposition on adolescent subcultures will be dominated by concepts dealing with linguistic behavior, small groups, and extended network relationships. We have already emphasized the historical processes behind the emergence of certain types of adolescents and their subcultures in Part I; Part III shows how these adolescent subcultures mediate between macroscopic processes and delinquency. But in Part II we establish the intervening link in this causal chain by shifting the focus to the peer societies and subcultures themselves.

Of necessity, different time frames and levels of analysis will also be used to establish the causal link between the macroscopic process, subcultures, and delinquency. But, even though recent years and other parts of the United States are mentioned, our exposition will converge on adolescent life in specific southern California communities between 1959 and 1967. This fortuitous time period coincided with the peer formations at their apogee in southern California. Postwar prosperity was lingering on, industrial growth was increasing, and the conservatism of the 1950s was just leveling off. The formations at this time and in this place were crystallizations of the long-term peer patterns that had extended from the previous historical period and have continued on into the present. The "resurgence" in the late 1970s of the same socialite and streetcorner patterns that had been markedly evident during our research serves to remind us of the degree to which these patterns are grounded in the fundamental characteristics of our society. To appreciate the continuities between the earlier period and the 1980s, we would like to point to 1970 media revivals of music and film subjects popular in the 1950s and 1960s. Box office hits such as *Animal House* and *Grease*, which accentuated the rowdy and carefree life among fraternity clubs and street-corner crowds, are examples.

At first glance, it may seem that the styles dominating young people's lives in the 1950s and early 1960s *disappeared*, only to be revived after a period of social upheaval in the late 1960s and early 1970s. Media corporations have added to this impression by resurrecting old movies from their film mortuaries. In these movies, cool cats like Elvis Presley strum guitars and sing about hound dogs and blue suede shoes; and performers like Pat Boone contrast their blue blazers and crisply creased pants with Elvis' leather jackets and ducktailed hair. A music revival even took place in the early 1970s, when some academics believed that the counterculture had revolutionized culture tastes and swept the past aside. At that time, the music industry granted Elvis Presley, Chuck Berry, and Rick Nelson a new lease on life. Furthermore, extremely popular contemporary music groups epitomizing these types started their careers in the 1970s. Sha-Na-Na, which occupied one of the prime TV time slots in 1981, is an example. The corpses of the overdosed and older Flower Children of Haight Ashbury in San Francisco were still warm when Sha-Na-Na began its climb to stardom in the wake of a 1950s music renaissance. As if making our point, while addressing their listeners, Sha-Na-Na's show in 1981 still opened with the chorus: "Hi There! All You Greasers!" Neither the revival of the clothing styles nor the recording of the "golden oldies" validates the claim that such fundamental types as the Greaser and Socialite actually disappeared. While their preferences in celebrities and music changed, the enduring existence of the social types themselves underlies not one but repeated revivals of preexisting fashions.

In 1971, Chicago's WIND radio station adopted a golden oldies 1950s revival format and increased its listenership from 596,000 to 800,000. In the summer of 1972, Boston's WBZ held a "Greaser weekend," replete with songs from the 1950s and 1960s and with patter by aging rock deejays from that period. The revival at that time included fashions that had been popular in the 1950s and 1960s, including the black-on-black and charcoal-black-and-pink color combinations. By 1972, outstanding movie directors had cranked out films about adolescent life such as the *Last Picture Show*, which featured Socialites and Outcast peers from a small Texas town. A later film, George Lucas' *American Graffiti* portrayed the full panoply of adolescent social types in Los Angeles, where young people—boys in ducktails and girls in ponytails—cruised up and down flashy Sunset Strip and the parking lots of drive-in restaurants. In the early 1980s film, *Nice Dreams*, Cheech and Chong snorted coke and smoked grass with all sorts of zany social types, but they call themselves "Eses" (or "Essays") from "Vatoland," and Vatoland still referred to the East Los Angeles Barrios. (Ese—derived from Ese Vato—is the classic name for Mexican–American streetcorner youth in southern California.) Finally, the violent conflicts between the socialite and streetcorner youth (described in the coming chapters) were featured in Coppola's 1983 film, *Outsiders*, based on S. E. Hinton's popular story about the rivalries between Santa Fe working-class Greasers and middle-class Socs (pronounced "soshes"), the "high-society" kids.

Regardless of media "revivals" of preexisting styles, each decade witnesses a continuity in adolescent styles of life. Even though the social upheavals of the late 1960s had some effect on adolescent populations, this effect varied greatly from community to community.[1] Furthermore, in many communities socialite and streetcorner youth were hardly altered by these changes. In 1967, for instance, these social types were key organizing forces in southern California peer societies. Several studies made in the 1970s and 1980s demonstrate this fundamental continuity of basic types in other places. Poveda's (1970) study of a predominantly working-class high school in the San Francisco East Bay Area registers the appearance of the socialite youth called High Society or Upper-Class Kids, streetcorner groups called In-Crowd and Party Goers, and highly conforming youth called Lames and Super-Duds. Weis' (1973) study of an upper-middle-class California community shows similar findings. He observed the use of such terms as Socialite or Elite and Greasers or Hard Crowd. Larkin's (1979) study of a New Jersey suburban high school also found the Socialites and Greasers, the very same types we had first observed 20 years earlier and over 3,000 miles away in southern California. Owen, a journalist, passed himself off as a 1980 senior-high-school student in a predominantly working-class New York State community. His book, *High School* (1981), records his interaction with exemplars of an utterly conventional peer society typical of the early 1960s. Finally, in 1983, we returned to a southern California city and found the socialite networks still concentrated among relatively affluent youth. (The terms Preps and Preppies, however, had replaced Socs and Socialites.) Consumption patterns among two groups styling themselves after popular music trends, the Punkers (i.e., Punk Rockers) and Heavy Metalers, had made inroads among older white streetcorner youth. These patterns, however, were not reported among the Afro-American or Mexican–American streetcorner youth, who were called Homeboys or Ese Vatos. (These minority youth were generally poorer and had much less discretionary buying power than the white streetcorner youth.) We also observed a great variety of dress and grooming styles displayed at teen clubs ("new wave," "mod," "flash dance," "punker," 1920s and 1950s styles) as well as styles originally introduced by the Flower Children of the late 1960s.

Adolescent Hippies should be given a brief mention, even though this social type represented a short-term or limited addition to the high-school social scene. We witnessed the development of the Hippies in the late 1960s and early 1970s, but to us they did not seem to change fundamentally the extended structures created by the socialite and streetcorner youth in California. And, from our impression of Hippie developments in the San Francisco Bay Area, also toward the end of the 1960s and early 1970s, these types were much more highly concentrated among middle-class families to begin with. In addition, we felt that the Hippies had a relatively small effect in most American communities. Where their presence was observed, their numbers were not large. At the beginning of the 1970s, Poveda (1970) found the Hippies to be a very small minority. At the end of the decade, Larkin (1978) noted that the Hippies and Freak Radicals had appeared earlier but that their numbers had substantially declined. Owen (1981) makes no observations of Hippie types. And in 1983, in one southern California community, we found that distinctive networks of adolescent Hippies were no longer evident.

The decline of the Hippies can be seen in the context of utopian middle-class movements, which rapidly lost their influence among adolescents during the early 1970s. The diminution of these developments was concurrent with the national swing to the right and the reinforcement of conservatism, individualism, and political apathy. These developments were also undermined by recurrent economic crises marking the end of the longest economic boom period in American history. Hippie styles of life are still evident (especially among middle-class individuals), but the social upheavals of the late 1960s and early 1970s rose and declined among high-school students within a fairly short span of time.

The expansion of drugs, in our opinion, also did not obliterate the socialite or streetcorner youth, nor was drug usage introduced by the Hippies. (Drug use was firmly established among streetcorner youth decades before the Hippie developments occurred.) Furthermore, our observations indicated that expanded drug use was concentrated among preexisting varieties of youth. (See also studies by Blumer et al., 1967; Friedman, 1969; Poveda, 1970; and Weis, 1969 and 1973.) The so-called "drug cultures" emerging among adolescents around the turn of the 1970s were largely (but not totally) absorbed by the more enduring subcultural variations in behavior that will be described in our work.

Research on adolescent styles of life is always dated by time-bound observations. However, in the coming chapters we transcend this sense of data time by using concrete observations to support *theoretical generalizations* about more enduring relationships. The peer cultures of the late 1950s and early 1960s represented a high point of postwar adolescent development, and they provide coordinates that help us chart the complex microsociological processes still affecting adolescent life today.

NOTE

1. They also vary from one country to another. Examples can be found in a number of excellent studies emphasizing working-class youth published in the 1970s by British authors (Brake, 1974; Clarke and Jefferson, 1976; Mungham, 1976; Parker, 1976; Pearson, 1976; Reynolds, 1976; Taylor and Wall, 1976).

6

Social Type Names and Schemes of Gradation

Throughout the year, and especially during the hot summer months, adolescent crowds gather in parks, beaches, corner hangouts, and at countless other places. Each crowd hums with endless gossip about Socialites, Preppies, Elites, Athletes, Greasers, Homeboys, Hodads, Brains, Hot-Rodders, Surfers, Insiders, In-Crowders, In-Betweens, or Regular Guys and Girls. Some of these names signify personal attributes that have been valued over the years. Others symbolize ephemeral styles of life that change with the season. Still others distinguish peers who are acceptable companions yet not quite one-of-the-boys. Certain names, such as Clod, Wierdo, Square, Lame, and Spaz (or Spastic), simply refer to youngsters defined as worthless human beings.

This outpouring of names fluctuates over time and space. Around the turn of the 1950s, metaphors such as Hot Rodder, Car Clubber, and Cycle (pronounced "Sickle") Rider appeared in the western and southern United States. By the end of that decade, words like Ese, Socialite, and Surfer had saturated the air along the coast of southern California; then some of these terms invaded beaches on Long Island in New York. In the late 1960s, the phrase Flower Children became fashionable in San Francisco, but it rapidly disappeared. In its wake there remained such names as Freak, Hippie, and Long Hair.

Geographical locations may spawn the same or differing names for similar types. In 1983 interviews, the word Preppy was found in the Mid-Hudson Valley (New York State) and Santa

Monica (California) to classify the same type of youth. We found that the word Socialite or its abbreviated expression, Soc, was commonly used in the 1960s by adolescents throughout the western part of Los Angeles, the San Fernando Valley, and as far south as Long Beach, California. On the other hand, we found other metaphors pointing to similar types on New York's Long Island. While white socialites were called Colleges (short for Collegiates) in Long Island, black socialites were termed Shiddities or Sedates in Berkeley and Los Angeles. While certain metaphors may pop up in two or more places 3,000 miles apart, some names may be virtually unknown in one part of the same city even though they are used repeatedly in another. In sum, authors over the last few decades have reported the use of various and sundry names—Socialites, White Shoes, High Society, Ivy Leaguer, Party-Goer, Upper Class, In-Crowd—for adolescent socialites in cities across the nation. (See, among others, Blumer, et al., 1967; Gitchoff, 1969; Friedman, 1969; Kinney, 1983; Larkin, 1979; Riggle, 1965; Poveda, 1970; Schwartz and Merten, 1967; and Weis, 1969, 1973.)

What characterizes the youth signified by these names? A strong interest in dress and grooming is one of the most stable features of a socialite style of life. On the other hand, while the interest remains high, sartorial fashions tend to fluctuate enormously over the years. When our study began at the end of 1958, Soc boys and girls in western Los Angeles were identified with "ivy leagues," "continental dress," white tennis shoes, and cashmere sweaters. The boys' favorite hair styles were cut fairly close, even "crew cut" and straight, while girls styled their hair in "bubbles" and "guiches." Socs certainly no longer groom themselves in the same fashion. Crew cuts and guiches may, at times, be seen on adults, but Socs now regard them as passe—remnants of a very dim and "funky" past.

Moreover, in 1958, socialite fashions contrasted sharply with the stylistic characteristics among streetcorner youth whose peers called them Greasers, Eses, Rowdies, Jo-Bads, Dudes, or Hoods. Regardless of their local names, these youth usually had their own similar life styles. During the early years of our research, Anglo Greasers and Chicano Eses sported "blue denims" or "khakis." The boys often wore "Sir Guy shirts" and meticulously groomed their long hair, combing it straight back at the sides.[1] In front they allowed their pompadours to flop forward in "jelly roll" style, and in the back it was shaped like a "ducktail" or "duck's ass." The girls also had hirsute preferences—namely, high-combed "ratted" hair—and in contrast to the Socs they outfitted themselves in longer or shorter skin-tight skirts, tight sweaters over pointy brassieres, and long hanging earrings.

Yet despite these differences socialite and streetcorner youth shared many values. Both were preoccupied with commercialized leisure-time activities, and often they had ambivalent, indifferent, or even antagonistic attitudes toward academic achievement. And, importantly, both were "insiders," looking down upon the Clods and Weirdos, who were "out of it."

On the other hand, intellectuals, who were called Intellectuals, Brains, Pencil Necks, Bookworms, or Egg Heads, were partly distinguished by their perseverance and interest in academic pursuits. These youth often associated with peers who spent a greater amount of their time after school doing homework, helping in household activities, or participating in adult-directed youth organizations. In the very early years of our research, the Intellectuals and Brains dressed quite conventionally, with no distinctive characteristics. By the end of the 1960s, however, many of them had joined other types in adopting Hippie styles of dress and grooming. Still later, toward the end of the 1970s, these styles were curbed by the harsh realities of economic recession, and then the intellectual youth trimmed their beards, long hair, and dress to meet traditional expectations. Their flamboyant styles faded somewhat, leaving a modified yet conventional image of intellectual youth for the 1980s.

The networks formed by adolescent types also change in time and space. Socialite and streetcorner networks emerge first in elementary school, where small cliques of boys and girls seem to spend every spare moment grooming their hair or displaying clothing that sets them apart from the others.[2] At first these faddish cliques represent a small minority, but they increase gradually up to the final year of elementary school. During that final year, preteens feverishly begin to anticipate adolescence, and their teachers frequently become disturbed by the insolent spirit permeating the classrooms. These Big Shots and Smarty Pants, as the sixth-graders are sometimes called by younger children, are often seen strutting around in a flamboyant display of arrogant and superior airs. Their preoccupation, at this age, with peer norms, status, and conflicts also becomes painfully evident to parents and other adults.

A profound cleavage marks the patterns of conduct among young people in the years of transition from childhood to adolescence. Most preteens remain relatively unchanged, retaining the personal interests orienting them toward home or school activities or toward organized peer relations in secular and religious institutions. However, especially in urban areas where there are large concentrations of youth, the preteen world witnesses the consolidation of independent peer formations. Characteristically, the members of these formations are excessively competitive and insensitive to low-status peers. These breakaway preteens are also frequently identified by a narrowness of social vision and an extremely self-centered preoccupation.

For a moment, let us observe these unfolding relationships through the eyes of some elementary-school girls. In one case, Lorraine, a fifth-grade girl, reported that the upper-grade girls' bathroom in her school had become a focal gathering point for combing and singing activities by the older girls. Once inside, they hung around as long as possible, combing their hair and simultaneously presenting loud renditions of the "top 40" (popular) tunes. In order to prevent the resulting crowding and noise, a student "safety monitor" was assigned to supervise the area. However, the fifth-grader noted, the monitor herself often joined in with the singing crowd. Lorraine complained: "Some of the high fifth-graders comb their hair in the bathroom. The high sixth-graders, who are safeties, let the girls comb their hair and sing songs and things like that . . . and chase the lower graders that don't like it out of the bathroom. They tell us "We're Safeties. Now get out!" And they push us around in the bathroom. The rest of the people get out while they stay and comb their hair."

Lorraine added, "Most of the guys in school are all football and baseball types; but there is a gang of boys who tease the younger kids. These boys call each other nicknames like "Whitey" and they are in the sixth grade. They dress mostly like the other boys. They always pick on someone chubby and say nasty things. They even scared a little two-year old on the way home—pretended to hit him and he cried. A lot of these boys and girls like to push people around."

In Lorraine's replies we find no use of highly abstract terms to classify peer behavior. Instead, she makes reference to the *football and baseball types*, the rowdy *gang of boys* who tease younger kids, and the *crowd of sixth-grade girls* who incessantly comb their hair and sing popular songs in the bathroom. By contrast, as they grow older, the previously mentioned metaphors—Squares, Athletes, Greasers, and Socialites—will be substituted by young people to signify the youth singled out by Lorraine. The metaphors can rapidly spring to the junior-high adolescent's mind, because there is wide observation and commentary on the metaphorical referents—

the hair, clothing, and behavior styles. In junior high school, some youth, becoming aware of these social regularities, are able to locate and label the social types of their provincial society with the aid of colorful language.

During early adolescence, in junior high school, the most frequently observed group relationships are the cliques and crowds. These groups rarely have distinctive names, insignia, or officers; moreover, they vary in size and structure. As one adolescent pointed out, "Sometimes there is only a big crowd and sort of like little buffer states of close friends around it. Or sometimes there is more than one crowd." The small crowds tend to be composed of youth representing compatible social types; and, in junior-high-school graduating classes, the "main crowd" may be more accurately referred to as a complex of the smaller crowds.

On the other hand, the social type composition of a crowd frequently includes a sprinkling of incompatible adolescent types. Even the Squares will occasionally refer to their membership in the "main crowd," especially when there is a reason for everyone to feel a common bond. The Squares' participation is encouraged by the sense of unity that springs up when they enter the graduating classes. On this occasion, for a short while, something happens. A senior classmate observed: "Everybody feels like they are all part of the same crowd because they are all graduating. It doesn't matter if you are a Greaser or a Soc or anything."

However, invidious relationships and their schemes of status gradation, which rank certain types as superior and others as inferior, begin at some point, unscheduled and unannounced. As boys and girls grow older, progressing from elementary school to junior and senior high school, the schemes of gradation become more distinct, and the number of markedly status-oriented circles swells in proportion to the number of outsiders. The fact that the gradations are there is certified by the comments the groups make about each other. To find out about these schemes, let's listen to what the types, at various ages, say about each other and themselves.

The View from Outside

An elementary-school child observed, "Sometimes [groups] make fun of other kids by calling them Punks . . . because they don't do their things or because they are fat. They are teasing the smaller and the chubbier ones. They say, 'If you walked on a swaying bridge it would break down.'" In saying this, the child is reflecting on her own experience. She complains about the scapegoating that sets these particular types of groups apart from others.

The complaints by "outsiders" may turn on the duplicity of the "in-group" members. Further observations from elementary-school children indicate that the manipulation of out-group members may be sly rather than taunting, hypocritical as well as instrumental. Attracted and yet repelled by a popular circle of peers, Angie pointed out, "Sometimes they treat . . . sometimes they get a little funny with you. Then, like when they want to find something out, then they're real friendly with you. Then, they just go and leave you alone. Then, in their own bunch, they act real friendly. They have their own secrets and everything."

Sometimes bigotry enters the invidious social equation, and this evil prompted Sarah's complaint. She noted, "They make fun of the kids who are outside . . . and, well . . . sometimes this happens to me . . . they started making fun of me because I was a Jew."

Another out-grouper, Amy, anxiously reported, "Sometimes they act like real big shots, like throwing you out in the street or something. They are real mean and they call you names and make you so unpopular that you feel like a dunce."

Indignant, Betty snapped out, "They'll always walk around together holding hands or something like that. They'll have a long line and they'll always get into trouble because they go *right through* the game areas [pushing other children out of the way] and they act real smart."

Streetcorner Views

By junior high school, however, the chasm between circles of peers widens further as group boundaries are more intensively supported by invidious economic distinctions. We can see these standards reflected in an interview with a junior-high-school streetcorner girl who used the socialites as her reference group and who was deeply affected by her inability to buy a fashionable graduation dress. She was aware of her family's low economic status, which she tried to cover up by defensive reactions. She minimized the importance of buying a stylish gown that would equal those worn by the socialites. "You know," she added, "the Socs care more about graduation than I do. They are always saying, 'Oh, I'm going to get such and such a dress at Saks Fifth Avenue.' Why, there are girls who go up to the teacher and say, 'I know more French than *you* do. I'm going to Switzerland this summer.' They are such *snobs*."

The boys who belong to streetcorner groups, like Greasers, may also be aware of the Socs if the latter exist in their community. Some of their observations provide another perspective. Joel joined a streetcorner formation toward the end of junior high school. Afterward he admitted: "I heard that these Socialites were saying these girls here were pretty cheap and all that—and that Charlotte and her friends were Bads. So I didn't go with Charlotte for a long time. Now that I know her real good I think that she is real nice, and her friends are considerate. It's mostly hearsay. Like I heard a bunch of stuff about her last year and it wasn't really true. The Socs are always trying to bring people down."

When networks of streetcorner youth emerge in communities dominated by socialites, they react sharply to the others. Comparing themselves to socialites, the streetcorner boys express their indignation. Ned hotly exclaimed, "Socs dress funny and look funny!" Maxie complained, "It has always got to be better with the Socs. If I had tennis shoes and a Soc had tennis shoes—just alike—the other guy would come up to me and say: 'You've got new tennis shoes just like me, but mine are better!' They've got this always on their minds."

These responses to the Socs are partly grounded in the streetcorner youth's own standards of conduct. Dress standards are stressed by a streetcorner girl, Patty, who said, "None of us girls wants to be Socey—going around wearing Frenchy heels." A streetcorner boy, on the other hand, emphasized masculinity. Bob commented, "Those Bermuda shorts and continental clothes are kind of feminine to me. The Soc boys wear pants that are like Capris for the girls." "If you see them in a big crowd they go around singing and acting like fools. The [Soc] boys act like girls," said Leo.

Such responses are backed up by a litany of the streetcorner boy's virtues and a chorale of the socialite's vices. The socialites are said to be insincere and subservient upstarts. One Greaser complained: "Socs are always bragging." Another declared: "They think they are better than the next guy. There are some Bad Socs but they still are flunkies." Dutch sarcastically disputed the point that Socs even exist: "There is no thing as a 'Soc,'" he said. "There are only 'social climbers.' One trying to climb on top of the other."

But the status standards that dominate capitalist societies weigh heavily in favor of the socialites; and these standards frequently force streetcorner youth into defensive postures. These youth consider the hegemonic standards to be hypocritical; they counter their rivals' reputation for being "clean-cut American youth," loudly asserting that Socs are just as immoral as Greasers; and, therefore, it stands to reason, they cannot be superior. With great indignation, John, a Greaser, declared: "They say we are wild and we get drunk. They drink as much as we do!" Randy pointed out: "The Soc sticks his nose in everybody's business. He's no different than us. He'll run somebody down with a 'stick car' [a sports car with a stick shift] and we'll stick somebody with a knife." Nodding in agreement, his friend, Mike, added: "The Soc boys have gotten into more Soc broads than any girl we layed on this beach. The Socs think that they're better than us in the way they treat the girls but they're worse! At least we take care of business privately. The Socs fool with their girls in a group."

Some of these angry comments were recorded with a crowd of streetcorner youth in a community where Greasers and Socs were status rivals. However, opinions vary from one rival to another, and some Greasers are aware that the Socs have diametrically opposite opinions. Diego remarked, "If a Soc came around an Ese group he would be considered dirt. The same if an Ese came around a Soc group." The socialites have their own standards, which counter the Greaser's slanderous remarks with equal contempt.

Socialites Have Their Say

Members of a socialite high-school crowd also had their inimitable things to say about the street corner youth in their community, youth to whom they referred as Eses and Jo-Bads. Their remarks emphasized the Ese's deficiencies—especially in dress, grooming, manners, and morality. One Soc remarked, "The Eses [boys] have a big jelly-roll hair cut and try to make a big impression. Why, they don't even comb their own hair." When asked to describe an Ese, Michael, a Soc boy, exclaimed, "The Eses—they drink! And they drink only for the sake of drinking. They love to drink. The Eses will say, "Where's the liquid refreshment?" before they ask for anything else when they come into the house. We Socs don't care about it that way. We say, "Where's the booze?" and enjoy ourselves without making pigs of ourselves. But it's like addiction with the Ese." In this comment an Ese is reputed to be snobbish because he uses such contrived words as "liquid refreshment" when requesting an alcoholic drink. The Socs, by implication, do not have to resort to such transparent status devices. (On the other hand, they unconsciously manipulate vernacular expressions and use words such as "booze" to signify that they are not snobs.)

Substituting the term Jo-Bad for Ese or Greaser, another Soc, Tommy, concluded, "There are some groups that are very social; the Socs. That's us. Some are the Athletes that don't do anything but athletics. Then there are the guys who are the Brains that only talk about their work and don't go out for anything social. And then, there are the guys who don't care about life or anything at all. They don't think about the future. They are the Jo-Bads."

Because of their status conflicts, Socs see Eses in harsh negative terms: pigs and addicts. "Eses are disgusting," Franklin flatly announced.

Other groups exist, and Socs are aware of the differences. Compared with Soc views about Eses, their comments and attitudes about the Intellectual circles in senior high school are benign. Intellectual circles are less concerned with "making it" in the local "social scene"; to some degree, they dance to a different drummer's beat, and, therefore, there is less cause for such defensive socialite rationales.

Intellectual Versions

The intellectual circles include some of the most articulate members of a peer society, and when intellectuals become aware of other social types, they have a lot to say. First, as one might expect, they recognize obvious differences in styles of dress and grooming. "You can tell the Socs by the fact that they have tight, white Levis on. The Eses have jelly-roll haircuts," said Alicia, girl intellectual.

Other intellectuals' opinions reiterate the commonly observed streetcorner youth's preoccupation with status, power, and violence. Consequently, these views do not have to be repeated here. Frequently, however, Intellectuals perceive similarities as well as differences between the Greasers and Socs. Chris noted, "The Bad Kids are very much like the Socs. They are popular in their way and worry more about their prestige than about their achievements. They have a strong group awareness. If you are not a member of a club you are nobody. If you are not a Nazi, you are a nobody."

The Intellectuals' standpoint toward Socs is framed by an awareness of their economic aims and backing. Sidney explained,

"The Socs are known by external trappings. They are trappings of wealth and style." Josh thoughtfully reflected, "It seems to me that the Socs are the epitome of today's society and goals. They want status. To be rich. They want to marry well."

Intellectuals recognize that individual personality traits and peer contacts as well as family status and family contacts are important to the Socs. Albie noted: "You get into a [high-school] Soc fraternity by making an external impression by means of your personality traits, or force of character, or you can inherit a position by being a younger son of an old fraternity alumnus who has made good or who is an important man. You can also get into this club by coercion—by taking out one of these girls and making her have a good impression of you or a bad impression of herself. Or you can have one of the boys take you out and get into the group that way."

Intellectuals are not always purely objective but show their feelings in their comments. Some are struck with envy by the Soc's status. With a tinge of jealousy, Charlie said, "A Soc can be identified almost 90% of the time by just looking at the person. He has a certain air of confidence of position. Because they can have an air of superiority—not of intelligence or of personality—but just superiority of position."

In fact, most intellectuals point out that the socs' status is not based on personal ability or any other legitimate grounds. This opinion is reflected in remarks that downgrade the Socs by depreciating their styles and ways of acting. For instance, Lenore, an intellectual, reasoned, "Say two girls came to the school. Like my friend and I did when we moved from the eastside. I wasn't looking for this [Soc girl's group] . . . but all my friend could say was, "I finally made it! I finally got to a rich school." What happened was that she sought out this [socialite] group. If [being accepted by the group] meant that everyone was wearing skirts above their belly buttons—she would wear skirts like that. If everybody had their hair in a flip, she would take out her braids."

In many communities the socialites monopolize school politics, and their power is recognized by intellectuals as well as others. One intellectual boy, for instance, disliked the Socs' control over school politics as well as their fashions. Norm said, "Often [the Socs] have their own incomprehensible and ridiculous styles which identify them as members of their group. In the Soc groups there are a lot of athletes, and in any school politics they dominate the whole thing entirely." A second boy, Carl, reports, "Frequently we would talk against individuals in the Soc groups but never against the [fraternity] club system and say that the clubs are bad. There is a sort of fear of them." Nathan, also an intellectual, simply observed, "The Soc groups have a power that is indescribable."

Self-Evaluations

Juxtaposed to all the opinions mentioned above are the judgements that the collective varieties apply to *themselves*. For instance, in the very act of derogating others, the streetcorner youth who belong to stable formations glorify themselves. In the company of peers, they look upon themselves with pride. The male Greasers, Eses, Dudes (or whatever else they may be called) have their own invidious lines of defense. They contrast themselves with "the others" who reportedly are forever climbing on top of one another; and, unanimously, they agree that "true" Greasers are "Men" who talk "straight out!" Moreover, they have discriminating taste and wear "nothing but the best."

Tony, a streetcorner youth, philosophized, "An Ese is more down-to-earth than a Soc. He doesn't beat around the bush when he talks." Besides earthiness, the ideals of streetcorner boys emphasize machismo, trustworthiness, courage, and honor, and, while it is admitted that some of their friends do not reach so high a mark, those are considered exceptions that prove the rule. (In this context, one boy candidly admits, "Some Eses are Punks too—but that don't mean anything.") Yet, there is also some dispute about what an Ese is really like. For instance, a sporty Ese announced, "We wear Sir Guy shirts and the Sir Guy shirt is the best shirt ever made!" However, his friends simply remarked: "We are just average, ordinary people.We're not like Socs. We wear what we can afford. We don't show ourselves off."

The same conflicting analysis applies to their standards of conduct. Cliff, the leader of a streetcorner group, proposed, "An Ese is not a Soc. There is only one [genuine] Ese and that is the guy that can take care of everybody else." However, his friend, who preferred to deal with conflict by "playing it cool," believed, "An Ese is not a guy looking for trouble or trying to pick a fight. An Ese is a cool guy."

The socialites also indulge in idealization. They, too, regard themselves as being friendly and trustworthy, and they emphasize being more sociable and interested in other people. The socs from petit bourgeois families, especially, see themselves ambitiously going about the business of "bettering" themselves. A Soc fraternity stalwart said, "What makes me different than an Ese or a Normal Guy? The club! If a person is in a club he wants to better himself."

Socialites, at times, counterpose their own "Soc way of life" against the "common" existence shared by "ordinary" peers, who take things as they are. A socialite put it this way: "It's almost impossible to define the word Soc. I think it is the person who is more—well, you can't say level-headed—but there are two ways of life and one of them is the Soc way. You have your friends, and your friends are somewhat like you. It's based on reputation. You want you possibly can to be well known and well liked such as participating in sports, running for a student body office or any participating in sports, running for a student body office or any office like that. Mostly athletics I think."

Socialite idealizations take the "facts of Sochood" quite for granted, including the placid acceptance of the shallowness and hypocrisy that these facts sometimes reveal. A Soc girl stoically observed, "Most of the people who go around saying hello to everyone are Soc even though I don't see how anyone could possibly like everyone. Because I know quite a few people who say hello to me and I don't particularly like to say hello to them, but in a way you feel obligated. You are a snob if you don't say hello. As far as athletics go . . . I'd say that half the people who go in for sports . . . do it for the glory."

A Soc boy echoed her remarks but made his point by contrasting Socs and Normals. He said: "A Normal Kid who says he doesn't want to be in a club is content with his own activity, say, getting good grades in school. He limits himself to a few close friends. Now if you are in a club [a high-school fraternity], you have to put out. You have to say hello to the girls you know or you are snob. A Soc, in a way, is a friendlier person than another person. You put out an effort to be friendly. *You don't act yourself.* If you act yourself you wouldn't say hello to half the people you say hello to."

The intellectuals are also recognized by traditional streetcorner and socialite prototypes, and, although opinions vary, they are usually seen as being comparatively less concerned with the status conflicts that preoccupy the others. A Soc girl made her observations about Intellectuals: "There are the ones who study all the time and all. They dress like Socs mostly—but really they are not acceptable from both the Soc point of view and the Ese point of view. They are outcasts. I really don't know what they do. We wouldn't go out with them. We call them 'Odd-Os'."

It should be recognized, however, that when it comes to the intellectuals' view, the feeling may not be reciprocal. Most intellectuals find the Soc's style of life, when compared with the Greasers', to be more compatible. As a result, one intellectual said, "You [actually] can't classify every Intellectual as not a Soc. There are some Soc Intellectuals. Every Intellectual is an individual and has a different attitude."

But the intellectuals do reflect unique standards by which they judge themselves. While others may label them as being socially or sexually retarded or physically deficient, they refer to themselves in more dignified terms, although sometimes with a hint of self-depreciation. Ernie remarked, "There is a group of us—the Intellectuals. We are different from the others. It means that you are not in a class—in the same way as the others. Intellectuals work for their grade. To do as well as you can as an individual." Phil admitted, "We are prejudiced in a different way than the Socs and Eses. They are prejudiced in the normal way. But if you define prejudice as 'prejudging others,' then we are prejudiced. We prejudge the Socs and Eses." Then he pointed up one difference: "We wouldn't take advantage of others, though."

"You ask if we would take advantage of the girl if she wanted to," says Peter. "There is a contradiction in that insofar as if the girl wants to be taken advantage of then you are not taking advantage of her. Even so, there are more Socs and Eses who will engage in sexual acts at the drop of a pants than in our group. The Intellectual group has a greater percentage of persons who have inhibitions built into them."

Some intellectual boys maintain that their broader social perspective also affects their relations with girls. Paul noted, "An Intellectual is aware of the way the world is and a person is. And he looks at a girl as more than just a sexual opportunity." On the other hand, greater sexual inhibitions do not mean that groups of intellectual boys are less sexist than other social types. Nor should their wider interests necessarily imply greater compassion. Intellectuals can be arrogant and mean, especially toward peers whose intellectual interests and abilities are not as well developed.

The statements above were made by streetcorner, socialite, and intellectual prototypes. Some of these youth lived in communities where the parents included unskilled and subemployed laborers, skilled blue-collar workers, shopkeepers, professionals, managers, and wealthy entrepreneurs. Such a divergent socioeconomic composition of families provides especially fertile ground for the emergence of all the varieties of youth.[3] In these communities, when one moves gradually from later elementary school to high school, terms for these adolescent types are filled with status implications. But these terms often incorporate highly discrepant meanings, and their referents shift, depending upon the standpoint of the speaker. In other words, complementing the basic structure of informal peer networks, there is a symbolic tapestry of social type images with conflicting conceptions of self and others.

These images and conceptions are also filled with accusations about fraudulent peer behavior and status usurpation. The justifications for these accusations invoke various commonsense *schemes of status gradation*, which rank people as being superior or inferior to others.[4] Thus, Socs grade Socs at the top of a status hierarchy and Greasers at the bottom, while, simultaneously, Greasers invert this order.

These schemes of status gradation are not the products of "emotional disturbances" or delusional processes. They are composed of folk categories and ethical standards that reify and evaluate social regularities in personal behavior. The socialite, streetcorner, and intellectual youth develop commonsense classification systems for identifying and comparing types of adolescents in their peer society. Emerging with these comparisons is the growing consciousness of the other social type standpoints from which their own status is being *judged*.

NOTES

1. The phrase, "Sir Guy," was derived from the name of a popular sportswear manufacturer.
2. The observations that follow were obtained from interviews of elementary-school girls and boys from a variety of communities. These observations were first reported in Schwendinger (1963).
3. Socioeconomic heterogeneity, however, is not necessary for the emergence of these types. They exist to one degree or another in homogeneous communities.
4. The concept of commonsense scheme of gradation is adopted from Ossowski (1963).

7

Relatively Autonomous Peer Groups

The jigsaw puzzle of networks and social types fits together into a significant pattern. Toward the end of 1959, we first encountered the interconnected crowds representing the largest networks of socialite and streetcorner groups. Not long afterward, the world of adolescent social types opened up to us.

Complementary, Intermediary, and Outside Types

While socialite and streetcorner youth were main perceptual anchors of the crowds in these networks, we soon observed that these youth did not account for all the social types. Within the crowds, there were complementary types, subtypes, and intermediary types. For example, whenever the socialites dominated status relations among peers, their networks contained complementary groups of Athletes called Soc Athletes. Similarly, when Greasers dominated status relationships, then Greaser Athletes appeared. Moreover, in many communities we observed an intermediary stratum originally organized by a subtype called "Low Socs." The adolescent networks, therefore, lost some of their simple outlines and gained in complexity. To deal with this complexity, we adopted the terms "anchor" and "end anchor" from studies of perceptual discrimination and social judgement processes (Sherif and Sherif, 1956). Peers identifying the composition of a single large crowd, for instance, would *anchor* their judgements in the higher status or dominant types such as socialites, even though these types sometimes represented only a plurality. (A plurality is illustrated when Socs actually compose only 40% of a "Soc crowd.") On the other hand, when peers considered the differences between networks of crowds, they woud *end-anchor* their observations in highly contrasting types such as Socs and Greasers. They placed Socs and Greasers at opposite ends of a peer status order and, in support of their judgements, referred to membership exclusion practices. (The Socs, they said, excluded the Greasers from membership in Soc groups. The Greasers, in turn, excluded the Socs.) End-anchoring introduced an added complication. When making status assignments, peers would also mention other types such as Surfers, who were "in-between" the Socs and Greasers. References to Soc Surfers, Surfers, and Greaser Surfers suggested that intermediary types might bridge the Soc and Greaser networks. The intermediary types implicated status groups linked together in highly extended network patterns.

Our study of adolescent status networks was also confronted with changes in social type compositions occurring over time. Between 1960 and 1963, in southern California coastal communities, the socialite junior-high-school formations were being totally replaced, especially among the boys, by new groups, composed of surfers. When this occurred, many junior-high-school youth accorded the surfers highest status. In the senior high schools, the surfers were also absorbed into the highest status networks, but the patterns were different. Some surfer formations nested themselves within socialite crowds, but for the most part surfers anchored the intermediary stratum formations. While this stratum had been previously established by Low Socs, at this time they were changing into surfers *en masse*.

Countercultural movements, taking place externally to preexisting adolescent status groups, also had an impact in certain communities and were responsible for later changes. Toward the end of the 1960s, the Flower Children and Hippies first formed distinctive groups *outside* the socialite and streetcorner formations. In some cases they replaced or merged with preexisting groups of outsiders composed of bohemian and artsy-craftsy adolescents.[1] A later development in this ever-changing scene was another variety of Hippies that appeared *inside* the networks composed of traditional status groups in the 1970s. For instance, Weis (1973:293–97), in a study of an upper-middle-class community, reported that some groups were called "pseudo Hippies" because they merely dressed and groomed their hair like Hippies and affected Hippie argot and rituals, which, by then, had become fashionable and highly commercialized among middle-class consumers. But these groups, unlike the original Hippies, were not committed to standards that countered the competitive and materialistic ethos of our society.

In our ongoing observations of the composition of groups of intellectuals, we also became more sensitive to differences between two types: Intellectuals and Brains. We found the term Brain being used on all class levels to signify academic overachievers; moreover, it was used much more frequently than Intellectual in junior high school.[2] On the other hand, all sorts of combinations of the two were also perceived. In addition to Brains who were not considered Intellectuals, and Intellectuals not distinguished as Brains, we found Brains who were also called Intellectuals. In fact, since the Brain and Intellectual types complemented each other in certain respects, it came as no surprise that they were usually not differentiated by peers. The words Intellectual and Brain were often used interchangeably, and, even when they were differentiated, they frequently had highly overlapping meanings.

Observations of these Brain and Intellectual types suggested various lines of development. Apart from possible membership in special interest groups frequently organized by adults, a number of the Brains did not develop the distinct styles of life and the larger peer networks of socially active groups. Pure Brains were especially prevented from energetically organizing such collective relationships by forces associated with their individualistic preparation for life.[3] Their social identities were overdetermined by their persistent striving for technical achievement; and the time devoted to this striving isolated them from other groups to some degree. Furthermore, while Intellectuals and Brains eventually became independent of adults, their interests and views on life were only partly due to youthful interactions. The initial development of these social types was closely interwoven with family, with educational and youth-serving institutions, and, in some cases, with social and political movements. Consequently, Intellectuals and Brains were often found together, and their groups were frequently skewed away from Socialites or Greasers. Even though the social-class backgrounds of Intellectuals and Brains were most similar to those of the Socialites, and even though some Intellectuals or Brains acquired similar tastes, manners, and political standpoints, they established circles of their own and gravitated toward institutions having only limited attraction for Socialites. Some Intellectuals and Brains did associate with Socialite crowds, especially in the final years of senior high school; but most formed networks *outside* the domain of Socialite groups.

Finally, in this complicated pattern of network relationships, we found still other types of individuals and groups who were not Brains or Intellectuals and who also stood *outside* the networks anchored in socialite and streetcorner groups. These outsiders were highly restricted in their activities by the institutions to which they belonged. Though many members of these groups indulged in ranking peers, and they might have shared certain invidious standards with the socialites or streetcorner youth, they were primarily oriented toward status arrangements within their own institutions. Here, they were governed by a multiplicity of institutional rules and programmed activities; consequently, adult controls sharply limited the sphere of autonomy left to them, and their group relations were channeled in different directions.

Peer Domains and Community Conditions

When we first encountered networks of socialite and streetcorner groups, we called them "systems of adolescent strata."[4] But as our research concentrated on quantitative methods for charting network patterns, we searched for categories that would facilitate the analysis of the extended networks formed by socialite and streetcorner youth. To deal with the complexities of network relationships, we gradually discarded the phrase "system of strata" and adopted alternative concepts for naming quantitatively differentiated groups. One of the terms we settled on was "domain of peer groups." This term denotes a *collection of peer networks* with common characteristics. For instance, gender domains might consist of three collections of networks consisting of all males, all females, or a mixture of both males and females. If age characteristics were added, then the domains would be divided by both age and sex distinctions. Other notable attributes capable of defining domains could be race, ethnicity, socioeconomic status, or social type composition.

Another domain characteristic worthy of mention is the variation in degree of inclusiveness. To illustrate this point, let us return to groups classified by gender. Every group in a peer society can be assigned to a domain based on the presence of gender characteristics; consequently, domains divided by gender are exhaustive. However, this degree of inclusiveness may not be true for other types of domains. Take for instance, a domain characterized by socialite, streetcorner, intellectual, or other social type groups. Most groups in peer societies are not members of such domains. Such groups may consist of individuals who are ridiculed and called Clods, Turkeys, Nerds, and so forth. Socialite, streetcorner, or intellectual groups therefore belong to *noninclusive* domains, and the quantitative procedures for identifying these domains are described in our expanded research edition.

A very important dynamic is the effect of larger social conditions on the expansion of specific peer domains. This effect is frequently mediated by family, school, and other community characteristics such as the types of families in a community, the degree of racial and ethnic segregation, recreational and employment opportunities, and school policies toward fraternities, sororities, and streetcorner groups. For example, the national and international flow of capital into southwestern cities stimulates urban growth and the competitive ethos of economic individualism. When these conditions interact with communities predominantly composed of bourgeois families, socialite formations rapidly expand and their conspicuous consumption becomes particularly pronounced. If this flow of capital also stimulates the growth of occupations much more devoted to accumulating wealth than serving humanity, then socialite domains may further expand. The socialite groups seem to derive their members disproportionately from families headed by entrepreneurial, managerial, and commissioned sales persons. These occupational groups are directly integrated into the control and circulation of commodities and money. They signify occupational experiences and ideologies that cultivate status relationships resonating with the ethos of the socialites.

Finally, the proportions of adolescents in peer domains are affected in several ways. A reduction in the number of adolescents who are in socialite (or streetcorner) groups may be influenced by social policies that encourage high-quality education, organized recreation, and employment programs. Such programs can diminish these groups (or at least weaken the effects of their antisocial norms) by absorbing some of their members into school activities, youth-serving agencies, or satisfying employment.[5] Domain sizes are also influenced by the socioeconomic composition of families in a community. Carol, an Intellectual who lived in Beverly Hills, a very wealthy community, pointed to this possibility. She said, "In our [wealthy] school there aren't many tough guys. Some of the guys are rich and they are regular guys, but they go out of their way to act tough. *But there aren't many of them.* We call them Jo-Bads. You'll find more of them down in the poorer schools in Santa Monica or Culver [City]. The Socs in our school are like playboys."[6] Judy, an Intellectual who lived in a depressed working-class community, referred to East Los Angeles, where we find the other half of the socioeconomic equation. She said, "In my school, the only in-people are the Tough Guys. Like [a high school in a poor community] on the East Side, there are some Socs and Intellectuals there but *the bad kids are the largest group* and most of them are in clubs." On the East Side, the large number of economically marginal families reinforces the marginalization processes in the school and establishes the conditions that generate a higher proportion of streetcorner youth than socialites. Therefore, the proportion of streetcorner youth becomes larger than the socialite proportion where families having lower socioeconomic status are concentrated.[7] But the proportion of socialites grows larger under the opposite conditions.[8]

Yet family resources and occupations are not absolutely necessary to the achievement of individual success in emulating a Soc style of life. Success, for instance, can be due to such highly personal resources as athletic ability, physical attractiveness, and personal charm. Consequently, when the effects of community conditions on group relationships are considered, the most decisive socioeconomic factors are those that objectively limit adolescent discretion in friendship choices—whatever the options afforded by peer standards or personal qualities. These conditions create economically segregated communities and put a lid on the possible styles of life as well as the variety of friends selectable by any given individual. For example, fairly poor girls are frequently acceptable to Soc peers because of their physical attractiveness and personality. To be acceptable, these girls must often make their own clothing in order to keep up with Soc dress standards. However, even to make this clothing, their financial resources must be above an absolute minimum level. They need to have regular access to a sewing machine and the money to buy stylish patterns and fabrics. If their families are destitute and have no sewing machines or money, their chances of emulating socialite styles of dress are near zero. If most peers in the community are impoverished, then it is also unlikely that they would validate this kind of emulation; peers acting like socialites would be ridiculed.

In extremely wealthy communities, on the other hand, the marginalization processes of the school are weakened by the extent of family resources. Here, the possibilities of establishing distinguishable streetcorner styles of life are minimized. Stable Greaser formations are the exception and not the rule. Streetcorner formations with a qualitatively distinct style of life may not, in fact, appear at all when these well-to-do communities are homogeneous. If they do appear, they will probably emerge in later adolescence. On the other hand, distinguishable socialite formations may not appear in extremely impoverished slums and ghettos; and, if they do appear, it is likely that they will emerge later when the possibilities for greater discretionary buying power and conspicuous consumption among peers increase.

Local relations involving ethnicity also have an impact on the relative sizes of socialite, intermediary, or streetcorner groups. While the numbers of intellectuals may not seem to bear any relationship to the size of the socialite formations, in some communities such a relationship exists because of the interaction between class and ethnic traditions. Consider the traditional emphasis on academic achievement which encourages the development of Intellectuals and Brains in Jewish families or among highly educated families in general. Since highly educated families usually have bourgeois identities, large numbers of these families in a community may also cultivate crowds of Intellectuals and Brains that attract peers who would otherwise join Soc groups. The increasing number of Intellectual crowds and the concomitant drain on Socialites will thereby diminish the number of Socs relative to Greasers. The proportion of Socialites will be diminished.

When examining the relative sizes of peer domains, it is also important to note whether some peer networks are segregated because of racism, ethnic chauvinism, religious bigotry, or other factors. Where racial segregation sharply separates the black from the white youth networks, for instance, the relative proportions of the black socialite and streetcorner groups are sensitive to the class composition of black families *alone*. Therefore, in many communities, there may be a higher proportion of black youth in streetcorner formations, because the socioeconomic statuses of the black families are lower. The following can occur where whites and blacks are segregated. If the black families in a community are extremely depressed, the stradom formations of young blacks will be anchored preponderantly by streetcorner youth. Black socialites may appear elsewhere; but, in these particular communities, black socialite formations may not appear at all. However, if the class composition of the white families in the community is heterogeneous, a fully elaborated "community" of status groups centering around socialite, intermediary, and streetcorner groups will appear among white youth.[9]

We have mentioned changes in domain sizes that are especially apparent under contrasting class conditions, but the relations between adjacent class fractions may contribute to other domain variations. In some communities, for instance, considerable social interaction develops between the fractions composed of petit bourgeois families and those headed by skilled workers. Both of these types of families may identify themselves with an all-encompassing "middle class." Behind this identification are communal relationships that soften the invidious comparisons between the two class fractions and distinguish both of them from those higher or lower in social status. Therefore, when the families of the petit bourgeoisie and skilled workers are numerous in a community, the largest and most popular Soc formations may be drawn primarily from adolescents in these families. Moreover, these adolescents might even develop invidious standards that discourage higher-status bourgeois peers as well as lower-status working-class peers from joining their formations.

Stratified Domains of Groups

Peer status groups are relatively autonomous entities. Their styles of life and relative positions within peer societies cannot be readily predicted from the social-class characteristics of individuals. Social-class processes influence the ideological parameters of the adolescent subcultures, but they cultivate socialite or streetcorner standards among youth in all classes. Consequently, subcultures often adopt styles of life that are incongruous when compared with the class backgrounds of their individual members.

This relative autonomy contradicts classical community stratification theories, which use the phrase "social strata" (or "social class") for layers of networks that include *all* the adolescents (and adults) in a community. Warner and Lunt (1942:112), for instance, present a geometric figure containing 18 cliques arranged vertically to denote differences in status. They add, "our interview material attested to the fact that all cliques fell into an interlocking vertical hierarchy which cross-cuts the entire society." In Hollingshead's (1949) study, the stratified peer networks also include all youth, and they correspond directly to class divisions in a community. We rejected these uses of "social strata" (or "class"), because we observed a great variety of informal groups whose social-class and socioeconomic relationships were far more complicated than the classical theories suggested. To avoid any confusion with the conventional terminology, we finally adopted the term "*stra*tified *dom*ains," or simply "stradoms." The use of this alternative concept was motivated by a similar need to that of geologists for the category "terrane." "Terrane," a fairly new word in geology, is made to sound like "terrain" but to mean something special. A terrane (like terrain) is also a piece of land but with a history unrelated to its neighbors. A terrane's geological origins differ from the surrounding terrain. (Parts of Alaska and much of the Yukon, for instance, appear to be assemblages of terranes that over millions of years traveled thousands of miles from separate birthplaces to gather near the Arctic.) For parallel reasons, our analysis of extended peer networks required a similar choice of categories. We chose the word "stradoms" to designate something special. Stradoms (like strata) are informal groups with certain socioeconomic statuses; however, they differ by having distinctive social type compositions. Also, unlike strata, stradoms are not exhaustive: they are embedded in larger informal networks. Finally, stradoms should not be placed one on top of the other merely because dominant class standpoints automatically assign the highest status to the socialites and the lowest to the streetcorner youth.[10] Their peer status is subjectively determined, and disagreements exist about their relative worth. One can readily imagine that groups of Socs and groups of Greasers do not uphold the same scheme of gradation. In addition, some of the status standards supported by socialite and streetcorner groups are firmly rejected by intellectuals who judge peers on the basis of different criteria.[11]

Contextual relationships often determine how the word "stradom" is being used. Even though most intellectual groups are highly stratified, we will usually restrict the terms "stradoms," "stradom formations," or "three stradom formations" to the socialite, intermediary, and streetcorner groups. This practice will be adopted because our discussion primarily applies to these groups. When exceptions to this practice are made, we will point them out. Finally, it is sometimes difficult to distinguish either socialite or streetcorner formations from all the groups in a peer universe on the basis of socioeconomic variables alone. This difficulty stems from the fact that there are unrelated groups (without distinctive styles of life), whose socioeconomic statuses are comparable to these stradom formations. Consequently, when discussing the socioeconomic characteristics of groups, our comparisons are usually restricted to the stradom formations. When exceptions to this practice are made, we will also point them out.

Returning to the point of relative autonomy, the three stradom formations are also somewhat autonomous with regard to socioeconomic status—a category that is different from social class. Before giving examples of this, we would like to make a point about socioeconomic status itself. This status in our theory does not refer to social class because the latter is based on the relations to the means of production.[12] Rather, socioeconomic status signifies the relative worth of family resources based on parents' income, occupations, education, and property. While family resources are influenced by social-class relationships, they have a somewhat independent effect on adolescent types and group formations. Therefore, regardless of the class composition of families in a local community—in either middle-class or working-class communities—individual socialite youth are more likely to belong to families whose socioeconomic statuses are *relatively* higher than families of intermediary or streetcorner youth in the same community. Streetcorner youth, on the other hand, will generally be drawn from *relatively* lower-status families. Similar differences in status characterize the socialite, intermediary, and streetcorner groups.

Examples will make this last point clear. We can see this relationship between the two statuses reflected in the following response by Chuck, a boy from a petit bourgeois family in an affluent community. Chuck is, himself, a member of a formation of streetcorner youth.

"You know, Chuck," we remarked, "they say that only poor kids are delinquent. That isn't so. Look at your club. All the guys are getting into trouble with the Man [the police] even though they are well off. They all live in substantial houses."

Chuck responded indignantly: "What do you mean? We're not well off! You should see the Jaxons's houses. That [fraternity] club is the one that is well off. We live in dumps compared to them!"

Our allusion to well-off families was in the context of the city-wide socioeconomic gradient that included communities with poor and destitute families; however, Chuck only legitimated a gradient that referred to the types of families in his immediate community. The majority of streetcorner youth in his community lived in houses that, by current standards, are worth between $150,000 and $250,000. The styles of life of such bourgeois streetcorner youth are often copied from the larger formations of working-class streetcorner youth in the poorer sections of the city. Moreover, these youth frequently gravitate toward these larger formations especially when the latter exist in adjoining communities Interestingly, there is a parallel trend of socialite youth moving in the opposite direction. Two examples illustrate these trends. In one predominantly petit bourgeois community, we noted that a YWCA agency provided a meeting room for a Soc girls' group from an adjoining predominantly working-class community. Simultaneously, a group of streetcorner boys from a much wealthier community frequented a "drive-in" restaurant south of their area that was popular with the streetcorner groups in the relatively poorer petit bourgeois and working-class community to the south.

These examples connect voluntary conduct and mobility with peer networks. Whereas some bourgeois streetcorner youth leave their own community and slide downward, some socialites travel out of their poorer community and climb upward. Taken together, these opposing trends provide the first significant evidence of the voluntaristic peer developments affecting both social and geographical mobility and occurring within the lifetime of a single individual.

NOTES

1. Our early ethnographic observations suggested that the bohemian groups are especially distinguishable whenever families headed by artists, musicians, poets, and similar types of "cultural" workers and artisans are concentrated in a single community. Also, individual bohemian types may develop in families where parents emphasize art, folk culture, etc.
2. We found that both working-class adolescents and younger adolescents are much more likely to use the word "Brain" instead of "Intellectual" (and mean the same thing as "Intellectual") in instances where bourgeois adolescents (especially from highly educated families) would readily differentiate between the two. Poveda's (1970) study also indicates the use of the word "Brain" (not "Intellectual") in a predominatly working-class high school.
3. Weis' (1973) study provides insights into the changes in the division of labor that differentiate the Brain from the Intellectual. Perhaps another distinction that might differentiate among Intellectuals or Brains is somewhat reminiscent of C. P. Snow's "two cultures." Intellectuals and/or Brains interested in literature, music, arts, or political life may form networks that are distinguished from those interested in engineering and in computer, managerial, or physical sciences.
4. These networks were also called "noninclusive systems" because they did not include many youth in a community; and, although we adopted the term "Outsider" (a common term used in Southern California communities), "the

system of strata" and networks of Outsiders overlapped to some degree. Social systems theory would consider them "weakly ordered" systems because variant status attitudes regulate the interrelations among persons in different parts of the system. (No single integrative mechanism regulates these relationships).

5. The integration of some Soc formations into school activities differentiates their moral conduct from other Socs, as Weis (1973) points out. Also, employment programs such as the Job Corps may affect streetcorner youth and help move them away from delinquent activities into the job world earlier than they might without such programs (Schwendinger and Schwendinger, 1983a).
6. Carol's reference to "poorer schools" in Santa Monica or Culver City is highly relative, because these communities at the time had major concentrations of bourgeois families; and, by contrast, the socioeconomic level of both communities was much higher than that of communities in East Los Angeles.
7. We are referring here to proportions (based on the total number of socialite and streetcorner youth) rather than the absolute magnitude of group formations. (The latter may be affected independently by other factors such as the density of adolescents in a community.) Also, however small, a proportion of bourgeois families may be important for the stable development of socialite domains. Poveda (1970) notes that in his study of a predominantly blue-collar community, the proportion of white-collar families among the socialite adolescents—who are called Upper Class or Elites—critically distinguishes these socialites from the streetcorner youth, even though both derive most of their members from blue-collar families. This relationship may hold for other blue-collar communities. Furthermore, after we had estimated the number of socialite and streetcorner youth from his data, we found the proportion of streetcorner youth to be greater than that of the socialites.
8. This generalization assumes that a peer society has not been substantially altered by new social type developments. The next chapter describes the impact of the surfing movement on peer societies in southern Californian coastal communities. In one community in Greater Los Angeles that was affected by this movement, the reputedly most prestigious (i.e., hegemonic) formations among girls in junior high school remained socialites in 1963–1965. However, their counterparts among the boys were centered around surfers, especially in the seventh and eighth grades. In high school, on the other hand, the socialites had no successful rivals for this hegemonic status among either girls or boys. These changes are still evident, according to our 1983 interviews.
9. The propositions about the variation in proportions of socialites and streetcorner youth (in communities with a heterogeneous or homogeneous socioeconomic composition) were originally indicated in Schwendinger, 1963.
10. Studies that tacitly use a single scheme (based on the standpoint of the socialites) as the ordering principle include Hollingshead (1949) and Schwartz and Merten (1967). In many communities there are "hegemonic" gradients that originate in particular social type and social class standpoints. But these subjective gradients should not be used as "the" ordering principle. Also, it should be understood that the composition of stradom formations usually consists of more than one social type. (This generalization applies more to larger groups such as crowds rather than cliques.)

11. Our concept of "stradom formation" here is centered on informal peer relations that are generated by the macroscopic forces mentioned in Part I. It is important to recognize that these forces are not restricted by any institution identified with a particular social class. Our concept takes for granted that peer groups also emerge within specific types of institutions (such as family, church, and youth-serving agencies) that are stratified by social class relationships. Finally, it recognizes that nonspecific neutral terms such as "Regular" or "Neutralite" are more likely to identify youth who have a somewhat higher socioeconomic status than nonspecific derogatory terms such as "Clod" or "Lame." (The meanings of these social type metaphors will be clarified in Chapter 9.)
12. Class relations are therefore concerned with whether people own the factories and other means of production or whether they sell their labor power to the owners.

8

Athletes and Surfers

There are many youth who consider themselves athletes, but only few have Athlete reputations. The same is true for surfers. Furthermore, both types epitomize subcultural variations produced by educational and recreational activities. Certainly, the commercialization of sports should be considered when such variations are explained; however, the development of independent peer formations, organized around a special interest, is usually based on an active rather than a passive engagement. Though spectator sports have their afficionados, the autonomous groups of athletes and surfers represent youth who are actively proficient in their sport. In fact, youth are often not even certified as Athletes unless they are official members of a team.

Although much can be written about athletes and surfers, our primary concern here is not with the types themselves. We can only devote space to the relationships between these types and the stratified domains anchored by socialite, intermediary, and street-corner groups. Also, before examining these relationships, there are some stereotypes about Athletes that should be challenged because they involve the stradom formations. For instance, the value of athletic activities among peers is recognized by Coleman (1960).[1] But Coleman suggests that high-school athletic stars are more popular than brilliant students because sport encourages peer solidarity. (It therefore compensates for the divisive effects of academic competition.) His conclusion, accepted by many, is that the social functions of athletics and academic study are often antithetical.

On the other hand, Coleman (1960:344) claims that giving athletics such high regard undermines scholarly pursuit. He says, "When high schools allow the adolescent subcultures to divert attention into athletics, social activities, and the like, they recruit into adult intellectual activities many people with a rather mediocre level of ability and fail to attract many with high levels of ability."

To prevent diversion from academic pursuits, Coleman (1960:346–47; 1962:317–29) recommends integrating academic and athletic activities by having competitive games in drama, mathematics, music, and debate. Presumably, such competition would redirect the content of games in an educational direction yet maintain the enthusiastic identification with the school that athletic games would ordinarily provide. He concludes, "Through such means it might be possible to transform schools back into the educational institutions they were intended to be."

At first glance, Coleman's claims appear to be borne out, and we would agree that educational games might motivate students to learn solid subjects better. In our own research, however, we have observed many youth who valued both athletics and academic achievement. In addition, there does not seem to be any intrinsic conflict between athletic aims and scholastic goals; in fact, good athletic programs support scholastic values. Where conflict exists it is largely due to the exploitative manipulation of athletic programs geared to enhancing the social status of peer groups, academic institutions, and college alumni. This manipulation is frequently accomplished by people whose class values embody a strong dose of anti-intellectualism. The real key to any endemic antagonism between athletics and intellectual pursuits in society at large lies in the class organization of sports and the crass exploitation of athletes.

The Athletes

Yet, even though the antagonism between athletics and intellectual pursuits is often due to larger forces, when conflict between these two pursuits occurs in peer societies it is usually grounded within the stratified domains. The three stradom formations place far greater value on competitive athletics, especially on spectacular, aggressive sports like football, than on intellectual achievement. While Socs and Greasers view the Athletes as celebrities whose friendship enhances their status, intellectual achievement is regarded instrumentally or with indifference or disfavor. The converse is also true. Youth outside the stradoms usually do not foster the conflict between athletic and intellectual activities. Intellectual groups, for example, who are usually not considered important by those in the formations, frequently value *both* intellectual and athletic activities.

Furthermore, the Athletes themselves do not originate within the stradom formations. Generally, socially validated Athletes originate in institutions and programs established by adults. Although most peers accord high status to Athletes and the latter usually associate with higher-status adolescents, their athletic careers are, nevertheless, directly controlled by recreational and educational programs.

The Athletes parallel the adolescent subcultures that comprise the basic structures of informal peer relations, since they have an autonomous base within adult-regulated institutions. On the other hand, they also interpenetrate these subcultures, and, even though Athletes usually associate with Athletes, most of them also associate with other types. For example, outside their concentration on sports, some Athletes associate regularly with Socs, Greasers, or Intellectuals, and their age mates classify them by combinatorial terms. The word Athlete is combined with the other social type metaphors. Thus, the Socy Athlete or Soc Athlete, for instance, is usually accorded a dual identity because he is integrated into both Athlete and Socialite formations. Other combinations of types such as Intellectual Athletes and Brainy Athletes also come about. Where Greasers are involved, two observations have been made: Greasers and Athletes establish dual identities, especially when the Greasers dominate a peer society. However, if these Greaser Athletes reside in communities that have substantial socialite crowds, then they become "Soc-ally mobile." They leave their old streetcorner crowds to move into "higher" status circles.

In addition, sexist norms powerfully affect the sexual composition of groups of athletes, their informal relationships, and their relations with stradom formations. A much greater number of boys than girls become athletes, and the stratified domains are more likely to accept male athletes than female. (Hopefully, the struggle for sexual equality will change this traditional pattern.)

Athletic activities do not receive equally high ratings by members of the stratified domains. Socialite and streetcorner youth consider almost all sports important; yet, they discriminate between types of activities. Fencing, while an established form of athletic contest, does not rate highly for evaluating social superiority. Debating and chess tournaments are competitive but they are not sufficiently aggressive and violent to be used for status purposes. Therefore, it is not merely competitiveness in games themselves that is deemed most important. While there are regional and class variations that account for the relative importance of football, basketball, baseball, tennis, and track and field, the primary athletic contests that galvanize reputations usually include only the aggressive, fast-moving, male-centered, mass spectator sports like basketball and football. Football is especially valued because it appeals to the violent male-supremacist standards held by Socs and Greasers.

In this social context, the popularity of athletics has nothing to do with compensation for scholastic competition, as Coleman believes. Rather, athletics are important because they symbolize (to certain peer formations) male supremacy, power, social status, and violence. If competition in mathematics, dance, drama, and poetry could be wrenched into a form that symbolized these values, then this competition would also become supremely popular. But if they cannot draw blood in the struggle for supremacy, those who usually dominate peer societies will continue to organize their rivalries around old-fashioned aggressive athletic contests.

On the other hand, the primacy of the formal requirements for athletes imposed by physical education programs cannot be disputed. Athletes must subordinate themselves to these requirements if they wish to remain Athletes.[2] The Athlete's participation in wild sprees is discouraged by physical education programs, except on weekends or during vacations. Consequently, many considerations are given to Athletes by nonathletic peer groups who welcome their membership. Socialite and Greaser formations, for example, recognize that Athletes find it difficult to remain on a team unless they abstain from smoking, drinking, and persistently late party-going during their sport seasons. Whenever these restrictions are validated by peers, the Soc Athletes and Greaser Athletes are exempted, to some degree, from the peer standards ordinarily imposed on members of Soc and Greaser formations.

Thus, individual groups of Athletes may bend the rules, but their full absorption into the life of stradom formations is checked nonetheless. Though a Soc Athlete does not have two mutually exclusive identities, he must juggle the requirements of independent scenes of action, and this necessity is recognized widely by peers.

Surfers and Gremmies

But these restrictive conditions do not apply with equal force to special-interest groups such as the Surfers, since they develop outside the rules of any formal organization headed by adults. Whether or not they are recognized by a formal organization devoted to sports, the identity of Surfers is validated by peers on the basis of their own criteria, which often refer to a style of life as well as specialized knowledge and skill. As a result of Surfer autonomy, by comparison with the system of Athletes, there has been greater interpenetration between the stratified domains of peer groups and surfing networks. Because of the complex nature of this interpenetration, we shall examine surfing in greater detail.

Surfing is another social regularity that both interpenetrates and parallels the basic structure of the peer society. Surfing in the United States reaches back to 1907 when a Hawaiian, George Freeth, demonstrated the skill in order to promote resort properties at Redondo Beach, California. However, not until the 1930s did surfing attract devotees who helped each other carry the only board available at the time, the 100-pound "monster" redwood surfboard. The surfing movement took place in a limited number of coastal areas. Like most sports activities in the United States, surfing was an all-male sport, even though wives and girlfriends of the early surfers camped with them at the beaches on weekends or during vacations. Soon, Surfers were organized with other groups of water enthusiasts into the Southern California Paddle Board Association. Clubs of Surfers were formed at Santa Monica, Venice, Manhattan Beach, Palos Verdes, and San Onofre. In time, surfing gained all the earmarks of a special-interest activity.

On the other hand, accounts indicate that styles of life expressed by those who surfed varied somewhat. With respect to the Palos Verdes Club at the time, Irwin (1964), a sociologist, reports, "approximately half of the club members were college age and the rest held jobs. . . ."[3] Irwin suggests that the interest in surfing was subordinated to academic and vocational aims. Thus, these Surfers did not "let surfing conflict with their jobs, school and other phases of their lives. . . . when one of the members took a leave from school and devoted six months to nothing but surfing, the others criticized him and threatened ostracism because they disagreed with his sponging, lack of direction and non-productiveness." These particular Surfers seem to have been quite conventional.

By contrast, Jerry Ringerman, a California youth camp director, informs us of his small group of surfing enthusiasts in the early period who hung around Santa Monica and Venice, beach cities in Los Angeles. Members of the local population called them Beach Bums because they promenaded in old denim pants with large gaping holes and nondescript, ragged cotton shirts and blouses; they could be seen wearing partly unravelled straw hats and hats of every other description and color. The boys kept their pants up with frayed ropes instead of leather belts, and the girls wore men's faded blue jeans instead of dresses. These Surfers ranged from fifteen years of age to their early twenties, and they seemed to express the freedom and informality of young people, not hard pressed for economic survival, who could spend a great deal of time on the warm beaches in southern California.

The diffusion of surfing among high-school populations began in the middle 1950s with the commercial development of the light polyurethane foam and balsa surfboards. Lighter boards of balsa and fiberglass had been developed previously by Bob Simmons, a legendary figure in surfing lore. (Simmons took to surfing after an auto accident in order to exercise a paralyzed arm and save it from amputation. He is reputed to have searched the world for new beaches and surf to ride, until, in 1954, he finally drowned off the coast of La Jolla.) His surfboard designs were incorporated into later boards using polyurethane foam. This development enabled teenagers to purchase boards that could easily be carried, and therefore the younger surfers were no longer restricted to beaches where the waves suited only the heavier boards. For the price of a board and transportation, adolescents could ride the waves most of the year on numerous beaches along the southern California coast.[4]

The diffusion of surfing among adolescents was also reinforced by the mass media. For instance, a 1959 Hollywood surfing movie called *Gidget*, starring Sandra Dee, attracted the attention of thousands of preadolescents and adolescents.[5] Though it was constructed according to the standard Hollywood formula dealing with parental anxiety about a teen-age daughter becoming involved with boys, the setting of the film was unique. To become accepted by a crowd of peers anchored among male Surfers at Malibu Beach, the daughter attempted to become skillful at surfing. Malibu was indeed an important surfing area, and it is reputed that *Gidget* was actually written by an author who vacationed there one summer with his daughter. This film was followed by a series of "Gidget films" including Gidget Goes to Hawaii. The romantic portrayal of the life style of the surfing crowd led many more adolescents to reevaluate surfing as a recreational activity. The diffusion of surfing accelerated sharply, and within a few years small manufacturers of surfboards began to emerge in order to keep up with the demand.

Soon, films about surfing made by older surfers were being marketed regionally. Famous surfboard personalities turned to manufacturing surfboards designed and merchandised under their own names. With the broadening interest and market, popular song groups and recordings of surfer-style music, skateboards for elementary-school children, surfer's "baggies" (blousy male surfer underpants with gaudy decorations), and wooden Tikis (Hawaiian or Easter Island fetishes hung by a thong around the neck) were produced by mass media, toy, clothing, and other manufacturers who capitalized on and stimulated the diffusion of surfing.

In the early 1960s, thousands of adolescents along the southern California coast were carrying their boards down to the sea. By the summer of 1964, it was reported that every weekend an estimated 100,000 Surfers frequented the coastal areas. Surfers were also appearing on the east coast and in other countries.

Consequently, as early as 1960, we came across small, isolated groups of Surfers while observing adolescent formations. These groups occupied their own areas in school lunchrooms and at the beaches; and we noted that the Socs and Greasers reacted at first with astonishment to their raggedy jeans and cut-offs (trousers cut off above the knees), to their open sandals or the abandonment of any footwear altogether. Especially distinctive was the unusually long, unkempt hair of the boys. Surfer hair styles predated and perhaps paved the way for long hair among Hippies in the later 1960s. But when it first appeared, very long unkempt hair was rarely ever seen on males.

To the Greasers, the Surfer boy's hair style was effeminate. Furthermore, bleached hair for girls was acceptable, but male Surfers sometimes peroxided their hair to simulate sun-bleached hair, and this custom was a particular object of ridicule. The Greaser's general response was: "Surfers walk around with T-shirts cut to ribbons, no sleeves, hair hanging down. All Beach Bums. Like Fags!" However, the Surfer boy's hair style was due far more to status than sexual factors. In some cases the extended exposure to the sun did bleach their hair but not dramatically enough. Moreover, some Surfers did not ride the waves with sufficient frequency to become noticeably blond. For these youth, peroxide and artificial tints created a sun-bleached effect overnight, and the bleached hair conspicuously distinguished them from other social types.

In this early period, the Surfers' cavalier attitudes towards nudity when changing clothes at the beach also surprised other adolescents. Sexual prohibitions were becoming looser in the early 1960s, but the content of this freedom varied considerably. The Greaser, for instance, was hardly a paragon of sexual virtue, but he did have some prohibitions. Though he sometimes jutted his pelvis forward and grabbed his crotch or sexual organs to show great contempt, he rarely ever committed this act without his pants on. Least of all was it done in full view of girls, or at girls, for that matter. Surfers, on the other hand, not only offended Greasers at the beaches by changing their clothes in public, but there were numerous stories of undressed Surfers who actually grabbed their sexual organs to show contempt for adults who complained about their nudity.

Equally astonishing in these early days was the "brown-out"—that is, the exhibiting of one's "bare ass" through a car window to startle the occupants of another car or the crowds of people exiting from a movie theatre. This particular stunt may not have been invented by Surfers, but it was certainly identified with them, and, as far as social types like the Greasers were concerned, "only Fags dye their hair and show themselves off like *that.*"

Some of the first adolescent Surfers were also distinctive, because they readily adopted a romantic philosophy about the harmonious unity between surfing and nature. That philosophy was shared by earlier surfers with many other out-of-door enthusiasts who idealized the characteristics of man-in-nature while attributing his downfall to the harshly competitive and machine-dominated urban society. This philosophy was later disseminated widely among adolescents in surfing films and magazines.

Yet, whatever their philosophy of life, the single most important thing that brought adolescent Surfers together was their great joy in the act of surfing itself. They lived for the thrill of balancing themselves precariously on a surfboard while it moved at increasing speeds diagonal to and atop the larger incoming waves.

They would ride a wave, just as it broke off-shore, almost all the way up to the sandy beach.

Since enormous speeds can be attained on high, fast-moving waves, Surfers also delighted in racing each other, in displaying their prowess by performing stunts on the board, or by guiding the board skillfully while it moved at high speed between partially submerged rocky crags or wooden pilings. At times, the sport proved dangerous to life and limb because of the possibility of falling off the board and sustaining severe cuts from its prow or stabilizing fin. Yet this very element of danger added to the exhilaration of the sport.

In the late 1950s, the crowds of adolescents using the beaches of Los Angeles, Santa Monica, and Venice for swimming and sunning were clearly stratified by age, sex, community, and social type composition. For example, certain beaches were hangouts for crowds of Socialites, while Greasers clustered at others. However, from 1960 onward, many of these crowds were scattered like the sand by the great conversion to surfing. Large masses of youth fanned out northward and southward toward Zuma, Carillo, and Malibu beaches where there were fewer bathers and where the waves were more conducive to surfing. Crowds of adolescent Surfers, then as now, could be seen on beach after beach by passing motorists driving along the Pacific Coast Highway from San Diego to Ventura, California.

Effects of Surfing on Peer Societies

Where did all these adolescent surfers come from? Probing for the social type origins of the major recruits into the Surfing style of life, we made an interesting discovery. We concluded that young Surfers were initially drawn from the *less* prestigious socialite crowds (e.g., Low Socs) or from those youth often held up to ridicule who had no distinctive style of life. (Of course, many athletes, especially those interested in water sports, also took up surfing early.) Because of the allure of this exotic new activity, youths were flipping from their older social roles to surfing. To signify this identity changing, peer groups rapidly adopted the religious term "conversion," and, with the increasing popularity of surfing, representatives of *all* social types "converted" to the sport.

There were also youth who took up surfing who were neither Socs, Greasers, nor Intellectuals. In some cases, their families supported their initial exploration of this new sport and helped them seek out prime surfing conditions. These families transported their youngsters to the beaches and anxiously observed their novice Surfers from piers, walkways, or the sand. Later, these youngsters moved off on their own with small groups of surfer enthusiasts in their old sedans or their vintage "woodies" (wooden-sided station wagons that had seen better days).

The lack of representation in surfing by poorer working-class youth, especially by nonwhites, was also discerible. By 1962, coastal lifeguards at the beaches informed us that for the first time a small number of black youth were seen to be surfing. In 1963, we interviewed and observed a small group of Surfer-Hodads from a poor Chicano community along the coast. But surfing was taken up overwhelmingly only by white adolescents.

The sport of surfing was difficult to master and enjoy for those who did not possess certain advantages. To the observer, these advantages were rather clear: Surfing was not accessible to people who had to rely solely on mass transportation or walking to get to entertainment. Surfers were in a position to buy a board, obtain automotive transportation for themselves and their boards, and also had money to eat out. Their groups consisted chiefly of youth who had the leisure to surf fairly regularly on weekdays, on weekends, and during summer vacations. The financial situation confronting very poor youth and work obligations for youth with steady jobs conflicted with such requirements.

Perhaps this is why we felt that the surfing "style of life" initially took hold in fairly affluent bourgeois communities and diffused downward. Naomi Robison checked out our impression, using "nonobtrusive" measures of the diffusion patterns.[6] She found that the commercial sale of surfing clothing and accessories occurred first in stores for the affluent and that it took place later in time in communities composed chiefly of petit bourgeois and skilled workers' families.

Consequently, conversions to surfing exerted greater influence on formations anchored among Socialites than among Greasers, unless the latter lived quite near the beach or belonged to families with adequate incomes. In other words, surfing was concentrated in communities of bourgeois and/or well-paid workers' families. For a while, in these communities, the Surfers usurped the higher prestige that had been accorded previously to the Soc formations, and their groups nested within the "main crowds" of high-school youth.

Why did adolescents in these communities readily adopt surfing, and what, if any, was the effect of their rapid conversion on the stradom formations? With regard to its adoption, the hedonistic character of surfing and especially its open sexuality provides fuel for psychoanalytic explanations. However, speculation about causes and effects might consider more obvious relations based on its individualism, its status mechanisms, and the consequences of its adoption by younger adolescents. First, surfing is a highly individualistic sport, and it does not make the same kind of demands for cooperative activity that are required of Athletes who are on track and field teams. One is not recruited or pledged according to standards set by others for membership. Surfing can be chosen by an individual regardless of skill or the opinions of more proficient surfers or recreation officials.

Second, the outward symbols of "surf-hood" met the status needs of adolescents regardless of their proficiency as surfers. Numerous attributes associated with surfing, such as dress, grooming, carrying a surfboard on a car, hanging out at the "right beaches," and using the "right" argot, provided status for the adolescent who decided to be a surfer. Also, despite the sexist restrictions on athletic activities, girls as well as boys could be identified with surfing by adopting a style of life rather than engaging actively in the sport itself. The style of life was itself very attractive to young people because of its assocation with pleasurable beach activities, Hawaiian costumes, "luaus" (parties), and exposure of the body to the sun and to each other. Finally, unlike the adoption of automobiles and motorcycles, one could enter the "world of surfing" early in adolescence because the adoption of surfing is not regulated by law.

During the junior-high-school years, tens of thousands of adolescents chose to become surfers. Since the stratified domains of groups usually coalesce on a large scale during these years, these domains are more sensitive to disturbance than the senior-high-school domains, which are stabilized and well established. Consequently, the widespread adoption of surfing by younger adolescents was highly disruptive, and its disruptive effects, especially on the styles of life expressed by the stradom formations, continued into the middle-adolescent period.

From 1961 to 1962, in one virtually all-white junior high school, Surfer formations expanded rapidly and, in the eyes of most youth, acquired higher status than any other social type. In fact, we observed that most of the eighth- and ninth-grade girls and boys were galvanized around one big complex of overlapping surfing crowds, a sort of melting pot within which, it was said, "almost everyone is surfing." (Actually, in these grades, the boys were virtually the only *active* surfers.) Indeed, none of the distinctive Soc or Greaser cliques was visible, even though they had previously been plainly evident. A nearby senior high school experienced the same degree of conversion, leaving only a handful of Socs behind. Nearly all the preexisting Socs had either graduated or converted. The Greasers "still hanging around" were slightly more numerous than the Socs, but their number was also somewhat diminished because of conversions. No formations "in-between" the Socs and Greasers remained, and other youth, such as the Intellectuals and Squares, who had not converted, were believed to make up approximately half the school. Since many from this latter group were also surfing, the main cleavage in the largest peer formations (apart from those based on ascribed characteristics like age or sex) appeared to consist of Surfers and non-Surfers.

Probing for signs of differentiation among crowds of Surfers produced further impressions. First, those who were both competent and actively engaged in surfing were entitled to be called Surfers, but those who "look like Surfers yet don't know how to handle a board well" were called "Gremmies." Second, some youth simply adopted the Surfer style of life—the music, dress, argot, and grooming—but did not surf at all. They were also called "Gremmies" or "Sand Surfers."

Eventually some girls surfed, but at first a girl Surfer was a rarity; riding the waves, she attracted everyone's attention. Since most of the girls only adopted the style of life but did not surf, they were called "Sand Surfers" or "Surfer Bunnies," not "Surfers."

Toward the end of 1962 and into 1963, other divisions among Surfing crowds became apparent. Groups of Social Surfers became increasingly noticeable. These groups engaged in surfing but were also "socially active," holding many more parties and dating more frequently than the others. Consequently, their distinctive activities did not reflect the priorities assigned to surfing itself or to its philosophy of nature and traditions. The Social Surfer development occurred especially among the older adolescents. In Jack's high school, the Social Surfers were unquestionably more popular than the other Surfers, and Jack, one of the oldest students, remarked, "You know, the Social Surfers act *just like the old Socs.*"

Crowds of Surfers that acted like Greasers also appeared in the high school, and they were called Hodad Surfers. (The metaphor, Hodad, was derived from the Surfer peer greeting: "Ho! Dad!") These groups were known for their rowdy behavior at the beach, and quite often Surfers were heard commenting that the Hodad Surfers "were giving surfing a bad name."

As indicated, economically deprived youth did not usually surf, and this meant that, by comparison with other Social types, Greasers converted less often. However, in beach communities there were still many streetcorner youth who finally did convert.[7] For a year or two, their conversion obliterated the recognizable styles of life that had characterized streetcorner formations.

From these observations, we have concluded that the massive conversion to surfing in certain communities virtually demolished the subcultural standards identifying preexisting peer relationships. The older relationships were replaced with new standards largely organized around a surfing style of life. Some of the traditional networks organized by stradom formations were also somewhat destroyed. Out of this destruction, the formations were partly reorganized around crowds of Surfers and Gremmies. However, within a short span of time the older collective relations began to reassert themselves *within* the crowds of surfers and Gremmies. Surfing styles of life did not disappear but were maintained by plain Surfers in formations of their own. Most of these formations of Surfers located themselves within the most prestigious or intermediary *stradom formations.* Eventually, the Surfer styles of life were absorbed by the collective developments that reflected far more enduring social class processes.

NOTES

1. Coleman (1962) conducted an important, extensively quoted study of peer relations in high schools. Gordon (1957), however, is the first scholar who noted the half-world of frequently nonrecognized and nonapproved cliques, factions, and fraternities.
2. The Athletes share certain qualities with the large numbers of "special interest buffs" who devote their time to stamp and coin collections, airplane modeling, and other special-interest activities. Some of these latter may be devoted to much more individualistic pursuits, but their identities are also organized around specialized knowledge and skills. Moreover, the normative standards that govern their pursuits are quite independent of their peer relations and are frequently maintained by local or national institutions that sponsor such groups as the Eagle Scouts or 4-H Clubs. Comparing these institutions with athletic teams in physical education programs may seem incongruous, but such organizations are also regulated by formal rules, and an adolescent's peer status or loyalty to a peer group is not a formal qualification for membership in them.
3. From Irwin's unpublished report prepared for our study; see also Severson (1964).
4. This was not the first time that technological innovation and the commercialization of special products strongly influenced the organization of informal relations within the local peer societies. After World War II, Detroit's commercialization of small sports cars, specially designed power plants, and

other customized parts contributed to the rapid development of Hot-Rodders and car clubs. Again, southern California was a center of this development.

5. The movie was based on a book of the same title, published in 1957.
6. This study of surfer styles is reported in Chapter 30 in the research edition of this book.
7. This conversion even included some of the older streetcorner youth. Oscar, a 17-year-old Ese, remarked, "We think the Surfers are fags. They bleach their hair blond and are nothing but Surf Bums. Their whole life is surfing. They even have old Eses who are good surfers and set up a *class all by themselves*."

9

The Nonspecific Metaphors

Each collective variety of youth has its own standards for defining individuals as good or bad, better or worse, superior or inferior. The Surfer degrades Socs because the latter are reputedly "afraid of water." The Intellectual derides the Athletes as "ignorant Jocks." The Greaser, shaking his head in sham wonderment, remarks: "They may be Brains but do they have balls?" Thus, virtuous Surfers are fearless when facing the sea; authentic Intellectuals are highly intelligent; bona-fide Greasers are courageous fighters: They're Men!

The competitive ethos spares no one. Every collective type engages another to some degree. And even though the invidious comparisons among compatible identities may be muted, the comparisons made with others often erupt into violence. The periodic clashes between socialite and streetcorner youth illustrate the potential for violence erupting from their rivalry for status.

The Nonspecific Derogatory Metaphors

There are more subtle forms of violence in which people express their contempt for others. In the midst of the never-ending jockeying for status, and as an important tool for ridiculing age-mates, one also hears the derogatory metaphors: Square, Spaz (Spastic), Clod, Plastic, Misfit, Lame, Nerd, Crud, Weirdo, Turkey, Simple, Fool, and Wimp. We call these words *nonspecific derogatory metaphors,* because the referents being derogated are not explicitly specified. Squares are not square people, Lames have nothing wrong with their legs, and so on. In other words, terms with denotative referents that are potentially descriptive are usually employed *without* reference to the original defining criteria for the word. These denotative meanings, if pertinent to the derogation, are only treated as metaphorical extensions. Since they do not actually signify clumps of earth, smouldering substances, geometric patterns, or paralyzed people, they cannot be taken literally.

The nonspecific derogatory metaphors are used on a widespread basis early in adolescence and are, in fact, most widely used during the formative stage of peer networks. Their use is prompted by the extraordinary intensity of the competition that molds the general structures of informal relationships. Through the end of elementary school and into junior high school, this competition spurs an endless number of conversations marked by peers holding each other in contempt. Though the nonspecific derogatory metaphors become quite faddish, changing with the times and with their users, they never seem to go away.

In grasping the social significance of these derogatory metaphors, it may be helpful to locate them, for now, on a simple evaluatory gradient with a top and bottom perceptual anchor. As indicated previously, an evaluatory gradient is usually implicit when adolescents using certain standards rank themselves and others in their daily conversations.

Two analytic features characterize the gradients implicated in the use of the derogatory metaphors. First, the bottom anchor of the gradients is symbolized by either a nonspecific or a specific derogatory metaphor. Second, the top anchor is characterized by a metaphor symbolizing one of the social types with distinctive social behavior. Types such as Soc, Greaser, Intellectual, and Athlete can represent top anchors, and they provide distinctive sets of standards underlying some of these gradients. We will show that other types can also serve as perceptual anchors.

When group standards regulate conversations, the meaning of a frequently used derogatory term such as Weirdo cannot be interpreted without knowing the typical standpoint being employed in making the derogation. In some cases it is impossible to grasp the term Clod unless you are familiar with the term Surfer; or the word Punk without Hood; or Spaz without Athlete. Of course, these derogatory words are so nonspecific that they can also be placed on any other evaluatory gradient constructed by a collective identity.

The implicit attributes being derogated in any one usage of the metaphor may vary greatly from the attributes in another usage. However, it must be kept in mind that these terms are only important insofar as they point to the derogatory status of the referent being named. Consequently, the words Clod or Crud are good examples of nonspecific metaphors, while the word Clown is not if it only signifies a person who is "always joking around" or playing practical jokes. The word Clown, in these particular usages, may be sheerly descriptive, and it does not necessarily connote ethically evaluated characteristics of individuals.

Sociologists and linguists have made use of the verbal derogation as an indicator of differences in class relations, economic conditions, and personal aspirations. (Hollingshead, for instance, indicates that "lower-class" adolescents in Elmtown are called Grubbies; and, while Labov's descriptions suggest a more varied population, he clearly identifies certain ghetto Lames—who are labeled by streetcorner youth—with conventional aspirations and enhanced social mobility.)[1] Nevertheless, in addition to such characteristics, there is an indeterminate number of other relationships that can affect the use of the derogatory metaphors. Any social type can be derogated with nonspecific words: for example, a person can be identified as a *Cloddy* Soc or a *Cloddy* Greaser. Their nonspecific derogatory attributes enable these words to express many different points of view and to characterize any number of negative referents.

In this particular analysis, we are primarily concerned with the viewpoints of the three stradom formations and their use of nonspecific metaphors. However, other types of youth may construct gradients with top anchors consisting of the same or different moral standards than those held by stradom youth. Such standards might include the virtues held by some Intellectuals—principled political action, for example—rather than the virtue of being "a sharp dresser" or a "popular person" in a "fast crowd."

Still other identities can serve as the top anchor of a gradient. The identity substituted may be a nonspecific metaphor such as Cool. The word Cool, or "he acts cool," can replace a top anchor, because a Cool person is virtuous. Cool, moreover, implies the existence of a set of vices. Both Cool and any contrasting conception, such as Misfit, are often employed as generalized symbols of virtuous and nonvirtuous behavior.

We further suggest that the enormous frequency with which derogatory statements are made encourages the adoption of metaphors with a minimal number of phonemes for a wide diversity of persons. We have indicated that at no time are these minimally codable terms used among peers with so great a frequency as during the formative stages, when the general structures of peer societies are developing. This usage decreases in later stages, however, because the metaphors are steadily replaced by other social type names. The new names, with their own morally evaluated usages, carry additional meanings that make the nonspecific metaphors inapplicable or semantically redundant.[2] Consequently, once the stradom formations have become relatively stable, the names for their members increasingly stand by themselves because their descriptive referents often include the moral status of a social type.

On the other hand, there are frequent occasions when the moral status of certain peers cannot be based on the evaluation of their collective relationships because these relationships are not known. When this happens, conversationalists can choose either a nonspecific metaphor alone or a more specific term that can be invested with a sense of moral repugnance. This latter term might be based on descriptive attributes of the repugnant individual, like height (Shrimp), obesity (Fatty), or the length of his or her nose (Bird Beak).

Very often, the different classes of derogated youth are defined by reference to (1) diverse attributes negatively reflecting the virtues of the collective varieties themselves, or (2) youth having virtually no positive characteristics. Youth with such negative attributes are seen, for example, as being unpopular compared to the least popular Socs, physically incompetent compared to the worst Athletes, retarded compared to even the dumbest Intellectuals, or a cream puff compared to the gentlest Greasers. Furthermore, from the standpoint of the collective varieties—especially the socialite and streetcorner youth—large numbers of boys and girls are reified as having no highly correlated sets of virtuous or descriptive characteristics that they share collectively, aside from their negatively reflected attributes. Consequently, for classifying these youth, nonspecific terms such as Clod, Nerd, Turkey, Lame, or Wimp have a clear monopoly for general usage.

We pointed out that social type names may be combined with derogatory names. Of particular interest, however, is the use of these derogatory terms for adolescents (or adults) who are usually called by *no other name* than Clod, Punk, Square, or Spaz because they lack *any* of the positive attributes attached to important peer reputational identities. When such terms are used alone, adolescents may call an individual "just a Clod." This usage contrasts with calling someone a combined name like Cloddy Intellectual or Punk Greaser, for example. Moreover, this conditional relation is more complex than relationships based simply on socioeconomic characteristics or on a specific attribute such as personal aspirations. It suggests that certain individuals are *outside* those collective relationships important enough to be classified with a positive name by members of the same "speech community."

If we refer to the "social distributions" of such typifications, we can perhaps discover some of the general conditions affecting the use of derogatory metaphors such as Clod. Social distributions are influenced by the variation in standpoints of various types of labelers. The actual locations of the labelers and labeled persons within the general structures of informal peer relations are also important. For example, because of social pressures to validate their own identities by downgrading nonstradom peers, the stradom youth tend to use a derogatory metaphor alone more frequently to classify adolescents outside their clique and crowd formations. Since there are no substitutes available for peers with highly ambiguous or unrecognizable social identities, these particular peers are very likely to be classified by an uncombined, nonspecific derogatory metaphor alone.

Apparently there are several corollaries about the receivers of labels that characterize this singular use of the derogatory metaphors. Low-status youth, but not necessarily low-income youth, for example, are the most likely to be recipients of these derogatory terms. In many communities, peers acknowledge the socialite's status but reserve derogatory terms for streetcorner youth. In addition, individuals on the fringes of crowds in the stratified domains, those who do not dress in a consistent fashion, or those who are introverted and therefore are not well known, have a higher probability of receiving a derogatory label from formation members.

When the stradom formations are set at their highest point of development, the following relationship is produced: an individual has an increasing probability of being labeled with a nonspecific derogatory metaphor the further he or she is located from the centers of these formations. From the standpoint of these formations, those who are on the rim or those who are completely outside have little social status. They have no valued social identity.

Most of the youth whose *sole* label is Square, Clod, Turkey, Lame, Spaz, and so on are outside the domains anchored in socialite, intermediary, and streetcorner groups. But we do not simultaneously regard them as a collection of atomistic beings somehow left over after all the other reputational identities have been accounted for. Instead, if inquiries are made into the social relations that enfold these youth, it can be seen that they have identities of their own—diverse as these may be—which are often far removed from stradom identities. While some of these youth are loners, most are firmly associated with peers and adults in family and extended family relationships, in special interest groups, religious organizations, community centers, civic groups, extracurricular school groups, national service organizations, and political movements. Some of these youth generally live their lives apart from other peers because they are more strongly regulated by families, individual activities, and traditional youth-serving organizations. This is just one more reason why they are given nonspecific names by the very "sociable" youth within the stradom formations.

The Nonspecific Neutral Metaphors

The nonspecific derogatory metaphors are not the only nonspecific metaphors that exist. Here we will refer to nonspecific neutral metaphors. The first point to make about them is that their usage is extremely variable. For example, after the stradom formations emerge, further differentiation takes place, and some altogether new nameless groups start to operate. These groups may span the gap between the socialite and streetcorner formations; consequently, they may be called In-Between—a nonspecific neutral metaphor. Sometimes the new groups are partly composed of lower-status members of the original formations. Thus, for instance, we have the Low Socs who take the name of Socialite for themselves but modify it to Low Soc to acknowledge their status differences. For example, early in our research we discovered youth who were classifying themselves as both Low Socs and In-betweens.

There was logic in this. From the Socialite standpoint, a Low Soc's status was "in-between" Socs and Greasers. The term Low Soc seemed appropriate because their styles of dress and grooming were akin to the Socs' even though they were not as preoccupied with the latest fashions. Moreover, if they were, in fact, a Socialite variant, then the designation In-between was also plausible.

The ambiguities associated with metaphors such as In-Between are extensive. Strange as it might seem as first glance, we did not find universal support for the interpretation of In-between. "In-between" could also signify a peer's position in an intermediary formation outside the Soc-Greaser formations. Instead of locating themselves on a gradient anchored in the Socs and Greasers, some of the In-betweens positioned themselves between Socs and *Clods*. They called themselves In-betweens; but the scheme of gradation from Soc to Clod, implicated by their metaphorical name, was unexpected. Additional meanings further complicated the ambiguity of In-between. For instance, responding to our questions about its meanings, one youth remarked: "I would say that an In-between is a Neutralite, like a Regular, Ordinary Person." Our questions to this youth and others elicited word groupings or collocations that merely substituted one ambiguous metaphor for another. To say the same thing in different ways, the additional metaphors, like Regular, Ordinary, Average, Normal, Neutral, or Neutralite, were being grouped with In-between. But their meanings were equally baffling, because their referents were not really being specified by the added words.

Consequently, we seemed to be confronted with a linguistic problem that was similar to, but not the same as, that concerning the usage of the derogatory metaphors Clod, Lame, Spaz, and so on. Words like In-between, Regular, and Neutralite also seemed to be nonspecific, but they were not generally used as derogatory labels. We finally called these words "nonspecific neutral metaphors" and, after analyzing their structurally relevant usages, classified them by differences in meaning and function. For instance, the most elementary usage refers to the sheerly descriptive nonevaluative connotations that place an adolescent "in-between" other peers without referring to invidious status distinctions. In this context, an In-between means an adolescent who is *merely* "in-between all the other groups" or "someone who belongs to a group that is in-between all the other groups."

More complicated usages are based on an honorific value—the In-between's honoring a nonpartisanship or neutral stand. For example, in this sense one is somewhat involved in the social scene but "does not take sides" regarding invidious status distinctions. Wally, an In-between youth, insists that the In-betweens occupy a neutral social terrain, not taking sides in the conflicts among stradom formations. He says, "The In-Betweens are those that are trying to have a lot of friends. When they like someone as a friend, they like them because they are a person. Not because they are popular. That's why we have friends with the entire bunch—Soc, Ese and so on. We don't join with either crowd."

Many youth do not have to "take sides," because they themselves are integrated into status groups *outside* the three types of stradom formations. (While these groups are substantially outside the stratified domains, there is some degree of interpenetration, since some non-stradom youth have friends within stradom formations.) Large networks of socially active nonstradom youth support the In-between's status neutrality. Such groups frequently belong to youth-serving agencies, and, because their activities gradually become popular, their members are not derogated by the stradom formations. Instead they are assigned a neutral space ambiguously located "in-between" the stradom formations or between the stradoms and the totally derogated peers outside these formations. On the other hand, these "in-between" formations recognize the schemes of gradation among the stradom groups, while not *fully* legitimating them. They have their own status community and their own centers of social activities, and this difference enables them to reflect on stradom behavior in a noncompetitive manner.

The gradients underlying such neutral standpoints can be anchored in a variety of social types. The social types with distinctive styles of life end-anchor the tops and bottoms of the gradients, while the more ambiguous and residual types, such as nonspecific types, are reserved for the middle positions. For instance, in Peter's definition of the In-betweens, the metaphor is positioned at the mid-point of a gradient end-anchored in Socs and Greasers. Peter says, "In-betweens? They are in-between, I guess, the Socs and the Greasers." It should be noted that Peter does not explicitly talk about Clods, Surfers, etc. in his placement of the Neutralites. Nevertheless, while adolescents in any given instance do not validate the neutral metaphors by comparing every social type, the connotations of the neutral metaphors are influenced by such comparisons over time.

Status gradients vary in scope, and therefore a neutral metaphor can be phenomenologically grounded in a gradient composed of more than just two social types. Bill says, "Neutralites are active but not too active. They have their own groups of friends and they conform with the styles. They don't act like Clods. They are kind of above the Clods and a little below the Low Socs." These remarks explicitly position the social types within a descending status order: Low Socs, Neutralites, and Clods. However, Bill's reference to the Low Socs probably brings in the higher status Socs, too. Therefore, implicitly, the Neutralite in his response is actually located on a gradient composed of Socs, Low Socs, Neutralites, and Clods.

In addition, Bill is using at least three behavioral indices in his definition of the Neutralite. The standards are (1) degree of social activity ("active but not too active"), (2) peer associations ("they have their own groups of friends"), and (3) style of dress and grooming ("they conform to the styles"). Such standards are employed separately or together in any given scheme of gradation, suggesting that the positioning of neutral social types may require greater perceptual discrimination. Frequently, the In-betweens are differentiated as persons "who get pretty good grades, but not the highest grades," "look sort of neat but not the neatest," "hang around in their own groups but not the largest groups," or "sponsor parties but not the biggest parties."[3]

Depending upon the definer, numerous behavioral criteria play important roles. Adolescents employ criteria based on athletic interests and prowess, heterosexual activities and parties, peer popularity or social distance, and styles of dress and grooming. Ability to get along with others, group inclusion/exclusion standards, and moral conduct are also used to identify In-betweens and their status relationships. For example, with the importance of athletic and heterosexual activities in mind, Peter said: "An In-between is not a Clod and it's not a Real Popular Person. He goes to dances and goes to football games." In this use, the nonspecific neutral metaphor functions as a generalized midpoint of multiple gradients that are based on varied social types and behavioral criteria.

There are still further complexities in using the term In-between. Typically, the In-betweens are located on a gradient *between* other social types; however, under certain circumstances, they may themselves anchor a gradient. When adolescents refer to In-betweens as less snobbish, less exclusive, and more friendly than Socs, they imply that the Socs' conduct is illegitimate and downgrade the Socs. Thus, the In-betweens are positively reflected against the Socs; moreover, this reflection frequently inverts the dominant gradient by anchoring the In-betweens at the top and the Socs at the bottom.

Also, the neutral identities can be elevated in status by contrasting them with an unspecified number of other depreciated types. "The In-betweens are in-between everything. They can be popular and likeable. There is nobody against them. They have nothing to do with a Clod," said Lisa, an In-between. From her standpoint, the In-betweens are especially meritorious because they are nonpartisan and not, like other social types, "against all other groups." (She also takes for granted that this neutrality refers only to Socs, Surfers, and Hodads. Depreciating Clods doesn't seem to count, because they are indisputably unpopular.)

As indicated, some In-betweens are nonpartisan partially because of their involvement in youth-serving agency peer networks. Their social and athletic activities and the status that these activities acquire become significant. Earlier we discussed Low Socs who called themselves In-betweens. Now we see that some In-betweens may be called Low Socs. As these In-betweens increase their social activities and status during the middle adolescent years, their leading cliques are sometimes tacitly compared with the leading Socialites, and then, regardless of being outside the stratified domains, they may be called Low Socs. This metaphorical choice is appropriate because of its contrasting status referents. Compared to the other In-betweens, the members of these particular groups have enough prestige to be seen as some sort of socialite even though their prestige is not as high as the "genuine" Socialites in the main senior-high-school formations.

In sum, it can be stated that the social types implicated by the nonspecific metaphors function as the background of a complex figure-ground relationship. Phenomenally, the nonspecific metaphors—the derogatory as well as the neutral—are like a forest framing various species of life. These species—the socialites, streetcorners, intellectuals, athletes, and surfers—exist against a backdrop of innumerable unspecified adolescent social types.

NOTES

1. See Hollingshead (1949), *Elmtown's Youth*; and Labov (1973), "The Linguistic Consequences of Being a 'Lame'." In Elmtown, the name "Grubby" (for protomarginal youth) was sharply determined by the standpoint of socialite youth. William Labov's article deals with the labeling of black youth who are outside the streetcorner formations (and who are either isolates or affiliated

with institutions in the community). Labov locates the source of this labeling in the vernacular terminology of black streetcorner groups. The average socioeconomic status of the Lame is usually higher than that of the streetcorner youth; and, in ghettos, this difference may make a positive difference in mobility and conditions of life. However, from our observations in more affluent working-class or middle-class white communities, the differences between "Lames" and other types may sometimes implicate the reverse—namely, lower average socioeconomic status and relatively less mobility. Generally, however, the nonspecific metaphors refer to adolescents exhibiting fairly large variations in school performance and occupational aspirations.

2. For instance, each collective variety interprets a social type name from its own standpoint, encapsulating both moral and descriptive implications in the name. As a result, for many purposes, there is little point in adding any derogatory terms to a social type name unless special emphasis is needed. When status rivalries intensify, a derogatory metaphor, such as Punk, is frequently coupled with other names such as Soc, even though the polylexeme, Punk Soc, may be composed of words that overlap in meaning. Therefore, once Greaser formations, for example, develop highly standardized linguistic usages, a label for such status rivals as "Punk Socs" is somewhat redundant since the usage of the term Soc alone can readily signify people already regarded as Punks. (Today, of course, "Punk" is sometimes used differently in the context of "Punk Rock" developments. However, our comments above refer to its traditional "street" meanings. These meanings remain very much in evidence.)
3. We have noted, for instance, that the derogatory metaphors are often defined through negative reflection ("A Clod is simply not a Soc"). A similar usage characterizes the neutral metaphor: "You could almost describe a Neutralite as a person who never quite made it," said Jannete. In her statement "making it" is implicitly equated with the popularity enjoyed by the Socs, and the In-between is being downgraded by negative reflection.

III

IDEOLOGY AND ETHICAL BEHAVIOR

10

Introduction

Part II described the three stradom formations. We will now focus on their ethical standpoints and delinquent activities. We will continue to employ an analytic strategy that distinguishes different levels of social reality. This strategy "progressively concretizes" the causal analysis: it moves the reader from broader social relationships to more concrete patterns of life centered around peer networks.

Once again, therefore, we will begin with broader causal relationships, specifically the ideological standpoints that characterize our society. Economic individualism is one of these standpoints. It subordinates social interests to personal interests, because it reflects private property relations based on the capitalist mode of production. This individualism is cultivated by the schools and mass media and is recounted in numerous biographies and films about rugged individualists. Adolescents, especially males, acquire this ethical standpoint as they learn to be competitive, possessive, and interested primarily in their own welfare.

On the other hand, while thriving on education and media reinforcement, this ideological standpoint actually originates in commodity relationships. Contrasting capitalism with very different societies that are not dominated by economic individualism will illustrate this point. In certain nomadic and agrarian societies, people gather food, tend animals, and prepare meals on the basis of a simple division of labor. Specific tasks in these societies are assigned to particular children and adults, yet each member works for all the others. Since everyone works for everyone else and all items are produced for their useful values rather than exchange values, the labor of each individual is obviously social labor, and the moral obligations to serve the *social good* fall unambiguously on *every* person. In such a society, the productive relations between all individuals are direct, and each person is expected to provide for the others' welfare. In our capitalist society, however, the labor of each commodity producer is transformed into social labor only through the circulation of goods in commodity markets based on *private* exchanges. Since market relations intervene between the productive activities of individuals, their contributions to each other's welfare are indirect. Moral obligations, outside particularistic groups such as the family, largely present themselves to people as *exchange* relations among independent commodity holders. Consequently, the dominant ethical standards are necessarily individualistic, and each person is expected to provide the things that other people need only when profitable or when money is exchanged for labor. Thus, the ethics of capitalism are affected by the way commodity relationships present themselves to people. These relationships direct all eyes toward the market, that is, toward the sphere of commodity circulation. In this sphere, service to society is considered a mere by-product of service to self; therefore, social service is not the ultimate end toward which economic activity aims. Instead, the economically productive activities of individuals are gilded with money. Each person provides service to others because it is personally advantageous. Market relations, therefore, provide social connections that *limit* the scope of moral obligations emerging from the economic structure of society.[1]

This limiting effect is expressed as *indifference* to other people's welfare unless self-interests are at stake. Such indifference, however, is not immediately apprehensible, because it is usually taken for granted and therefore operates as an unconscious determinant of choice-making behavior. Furthermore, indifference is not expressed by highly emotional states such as love, compassion, anger, or hatred. Instead, this indifference tacitly minimizes obligations to others. In the normal run of things, time is money, and, unless money can be made, people have no time, interest, or the energy to ameliorate other people's suffering. Despite feelings of compassion and sympathy that are expressed even among strangers during emergencies, market relationships cultivate an impersonal attitude that places the welfare of most people outside the realm of individual responsibility.[2]

This indifference gives full reign to the contradictory and conflicting moralities based on the interests of kinship, friendship, occupation, class, and national groups. Such moralities, as opposed to indifference, are immediately apprehensible. They are especially evident in the "war of all against all"—one family against another, one company against another—in class societies. Moral contradictions, for example, are sometimes expressed in the language of individual rights (or "entitlements") because the material conflicts created by social class and private property relationships provide little support for clearly deducing particular rights from general moral obligations (Asch, 1964:86). For example, under capitalism, do poor children have the same or even greater rights to public resources than middle-class youth? Do workers and their families have a right to an adequate standard of living if this right conflicts with capital's right to make profits? Do poor people have the same right as wealthy people to security in old age, even though they have not accumulated enough for retirement and they are no longer employed? In these conflicts of rights, what is the role of "society" when it is made up of these same contending groups? The main point is: when class interests and private property are at stake, political and economic power, not moral principles, determine what most people really are entitled to. Moreover, under these conditions, moral principles reflect contradictory interests and provide conflicting and hypocritical standards of conduct. Such standards exist even among people who hold the highest positions of public trust. Research shows that men who move from high government positions to private corporations alter their expressed attitudes about the public interest like chameleons (Seider, 1974). They adopt whatever standpoint is advantageous to their current organization, even though such a standpoint completely contradicts statements made previously when they occupied government positions.

The extensiveness of moral contradictions based on economic individualism can be seen in people who persistently speak of bettering the "human condition" yet justify indifference to laws and practices affecting human suffering. Such people condone child labor among migrant workers while mouthing platitudes about strengthening "the traditional family." They wax indignant about solitary homicides at home but studiously ignore genocidal crimes in imperial wars. They support humanism in the abstract but passively disregard the oppression of racial minorities. Because such discrepancies are widespread, our dominant rules for individual conduct are a morass more closely resembling the ethics of Hobbes' "jungle" and the indifference of Camus' *Stranger* than the highly principled social order that idealizations of our society proclaim it to be.[3]

Moral Antinomies and Eligibility Principles

A deeper understanding of moral contradictions requires further examination of their expression as antinomies—that is, as antagonisms between two conceptions of right or between one ethical rule and another. Students in philosophy of ethics courses discuss antinomies very abstractly when they consider the familiar ethical dilemmas posed by conflicts between individual and society, work and family, or duty and pleasure. For example, antinomies arise from the right of capitalists to exploit their workers as much as possible and, on the other hand, from the right of workers to reduce the terms of this exploitation by increasing wages or reducing the workday. The capitalist, for instance, asserts his rights as a purchaser of labor power when he tries to obtain as much work as possible for as little money as possible. The worker, on the other hand, asserts his rights as a seller of labor power when he tries to increase the price at which this power is sold anew. Consequently, there is here an antinomy, right against right, and both rights are justified by the principle of equal exchange, of value for value, that legitimates the terms under which commodities are exchanged. When equal rights conflict, however, ethical standards based on the same principle often cannot provide unequivocal guidelines for deciding who is right. When this serious moral contradiction must be dealt with, force or the threat of force may decide the issue.

Conflicts between individual rights are even more apparent when they are caused by widely diverging ethical principles. Examples of such antinomies frequently include circumstances in which political concepts of right (which are called "human rights") conflict with principles derived from market relationships. Labor and welfare rights movements, for instance, insist that the unemployed have a human right to a decent standard of living, which means higher standards than they now have. Justifying such standards, however, collides with a market principle—the principle of eligibility—recognized by economists and moralists as far back as the seventeenth century. This principle dictates moral judgements about standards of life based in part on the equal exchange principle, which is expressed by the exchange of "value" for "value." Therefore, a person is only entitled to the standard of living he or she can earn. A related principle, the principle of "less eligibility," is applied to welfare recipients; and it restricts recipients to a very low standard of living. It is said, in accordance with this principle, that the unemployed may have a right to be supported by the government. But, to maintain competitive pressures on the sale of labor power, these people are entitled to *less* than the least valuable forms of labor power can earn, regardless of how little this may be. (If they cannot exchange earnings for an equivalent standard of living, then they are only entitled to a standard lower than that of the average lower-waged member of the work force.) In this example, therefore, conflicting concepts of right are defined by qualitatively different principles. From the standpoint of labor and welfare groups, the right of individuals to a higher standard of living is conceived as a human right and asserted in political demands for economic equality. From the standpoint of the eligibility principle, this right is defined in accordance with principles based on commodity exchange and competitive market requirements.

Further conditions *undermine* the principle that people have no right to a higher standard of living than they can earn. In industrial societies, a higher level of productivity, which results from increasing levels of economic development, yields vast numbers of commodities for personal consumption, but it also yields an ever-constricting proportion of the population needed for work. It quickly becomes obvious that numerous contradictions and antinomies accompany this reduction of the minimum labor time necessary for society. These contradictions are especially sharp in the face of the expansion of wealth, which, on one hand, fosters the scientific and artistic cultivation of individual personalities and, on the other hand, creates consumer goods available for everyone, but only at a price. Under these conditions, the credibility of the equal exchange principle is undermined. New needs arise whose legitimacy is validated and reinforced by marketing practices and credit policies geared to high consumer-goods production. People are under great pressure to acquire commodities, regardless of personal income. They hesitate to say they do not need what they cannot afford. Especially where there are very large discrepancies in standards of living, such antinomies intensify feelings of relative deprivation and undermine the legal conformity to, as well as the moral legitimacy of, the principle of living within one's means.

These relationships also apply to youth, even when their purchasing power is totally determined by their parent's income. Among youth, in addition, the equal exchange principle is further weakened as peer groups establish invidious modes of personal consumption to distinguish themselves from one another. These invidious modes, moreover, become more influential with increasing amounts of leisure time. The expanded production and the increased availability of time outside work precondition the modes of consumption among both working-class and petit bourgeois youth. With the decline of adolescents in the labor force, these youth are able to engage each other for longer periods of time, developing distinct modes of consumption (i.e., styles of life). The increase in free time heightens the rate of change in the production of status tokens—clothing fads, hair styles, mannerisms, and so on—that are merchandised for less affluent adolescents by magazines, newspapers, television media, and manufacturers.

The free time and high pressure marketing practices encourage a social individualism that extends the spirit of economic individualism to everyday life. Socialite, intermediary, and streetcorner groups are particularly affected by this individualism, and among their striking characteristics, therefore, there is an indifference to the welfare of others and a restricted set of interests. Such groups, for instance, frequently regard devotion to social ideals with cynicism. They are preoccupied with peer status, sensate delights, and conspicuous consumption. Their narcissism is so uncontested that its particular forms of individualism seem to be derived entirely from the immutable human nature of the adolescents themselves.

By comparison, personal consumption patterns often have totally different effects on youth outside the socialite and streetcorner groups. Peer groups in our society are not cut from whole cloth, and they include, as indicated, groups interested in the pursuit of science, art, technology, theatre, music, and other activities by which individuals fulfill their creative potential. Such groups are encouraged by schools, churches, and youth service organizations that employ whatever resources they can to support the development of such activities; and, while these groups frequently mimic the status orientations characterizing professionals and semiprofessionals in highly competitive commerical institutions, the programs that channel their conduct and accomplishments moderate the impact of marketing efforts. In addition, these programs usually make demands on conduct that may be in conflict with the three stradom formations. Of course, youth who apply themselves to the disciplined achievement of artistic, scientific, and technical accomplishments usually have less need of external regulation, because they have already internalized habits and motives, voluntarily moving their group formations in approved directions.

There are yet other adolescent groups whose patterns of self-regulation oppose commercial values, but these groups, because of their political orientations, frequently conflict with such institutions as the school and government. In Berkeley, California, around the end of the 1970s, for example, a research study of high-school youth by Dagnais and Marascuilo (1972) found a group of political activists. The study showed that the scholastic ability of the members of the group was very high. It also revealed some background information about the group, which had been gathered by questionnaires. However, the researchers had not been personally acquainted—as we were—with the group members and their parents for the entire high-school period. Some members of the group were involved in extracurricular school activities such as the high-school theatre group, but all were devoted to struggling for civil rights, freedom of speech, "student power," and an end to the Vietnam War. This devotion led them into repeated conflict with school authorities including the school principal and the Board of Education. For some members this meant being forcibly suspended from school for conducting a "theatre of the absurd" spectacle mocking the student election in the main auditorium; and some were arrested and temporarily jailed in a Juvenile Detention Center for allegedly failing to disperse, as ordered by police and state militia, after an antiwar demonstration.[4]

Despite their status as high academic achievers, this group of adolescent activists was by no means controlled by school authorities. There was constant friction between the youngsters and the school, because the group's political activities, such as distributing leaflets, were repressed on school grounds. It could also be said that this group was beyond the control of the criminal justice system. (At the Juvenile Detention Center, for instance, members of this group were told by juvenile justice personnel that their release was conditional upon their signing unconstitutional statements promising that they would never demonstrate against the war again. They refused to sign the statements and were not released until their parents intervened.) Despite this apparent lack of social control, it was inconceivable that this group would engage in the street crimes characterizing other peer formations in the community. These high-school student activists were paragons of virtue and conformity when it came to thievery or interpersonal violence.

Certainly, family relations played an important role in encouraging group members' participation in cultural and political activity. Most parents were middle-class professionals, and some were noted civil libertarian lawyers. Some parents had "old left" backgrounds, and most of them were either liberals or socialists. Some of the parents themselves were actively involved in the struggle for civil rights and against the war. But group norms did not simply reproduce parental values. The group was strongly influenced by the new left, and it exemplified both the anarchic and creative trends encouraged by this leftist development. On occasion, the group's actions horrified the parents. This was especially true whenever the group's newspaper rolled off the printing press. The *Pack Rat*, as it was called, was superb technically considering that it was produced by adolescents, but it always shocked the parents because of its flagrant use of vulgar sexual language.

The group's rejection of common delinquent activities cannot be attributed merely to parental influence. This rejection also had its locus in the moral standards developed by the group itself. The standards were humanistic and encouraged moral outrage against the social harms entailed in the common forms of delinquency. Most important, these group standards mandated each member to live up to humanistic principles; and departures from these principles were rapidly met with a round of social criticism.

On the other hand, adolescents can refrain from delinquency in other ways. They do not have to acquire articulated humanistic values that consistently oppose delinquent victimization. The development of interests that habitually galvanize their lives around family activities or youth service programs can also keep them within the law. Family relations and youth programs may buffer the moral contradictions, the individualistic standpoints, and the status conflicts that arise spontaneously in society at large. Delinquent behavior can be minimized if these institutions encourage alternative values or if their resources are adequate to motivate and capture sufficient numbers of youth in challenging activities. Individual adolescents without these family or community resources often fail to develop their personal capacities. They become attracted to modes of consumption adopted by stradom formations, either because this is the only satisfying culture readily available or because parental status attitudes and cultural standards reinforce the attractiveness of these formations.

In a broader sense, the attractiveness of the stradom formations reflects the antagonism between the hopes for human fulfillment emerging from the increasing productive capacity of a society and the parasitic styles of life encouraged by the commodification of social relations. Ironically, the amount of surplus labor produced by working people becomes the condition for the development of schools, youth programs, mass media, and culture and therefore expands the general power of the intellect. However, the cultivation of the powers of the individual in these peer status groups is devoted to narcissism, invidious worth, and manipulation; and in this context a humanity realizing its collective potentialities unencumbered by private property and exploitation is yet to be fulfilled.

NOTES

1. For the materialist use of individualism in criminology, see Bonger (1915) and Buchholz et al. (1974). As a large body of writings attests, market relationships focus attention on money and other things that people own and thereby generate a materialistic view of reality that reinforces this individualistic standpoint (Ash, 1964; Bonger, 1915; Buchholz et al., 1974; Marx, 1959; Rubin, 1972). Money, for instance, is a "generalized" commodity because it is exchangeable for other commodities; nevertheless, it is merely a thing and not a human being. Yet, even though *people*, not money, make commodity values and *people*, not money, rule other human beings, it is often said that "Money makes money" and "Money is the God of this world." This peculiar form of consciousness is called the "fetishism of commodities," and it is expressed by ideological images of social relationships. In commodity fetishism the relations between people are defined by their relations to commodities or relations between commodities themselves.
2. Attention to the suffering of others is relegated to the sidelines where "altruistic" (not "self-serving") philanthropists operate, because business cannot be devoted to philanthropy and "survive."
3. Our focus here—and in the book as a whole—is on causal relations developing under capitalist conditions. We do not thereby suggest that some of these relations automatically disappear in "market socialism," "mixed economies," or other socialist societies. The topic of delinquency and socialism requires a complex analysis of the variation in socialist economies and the degree to which they differ from capitalist societies. Parts of our theory with modification should apply to delinquency in socialist societies.
4. In actuality, the adolescents and adults in the demonstration did disperse, but they were forcibly prevented from leaving via the streets adjacent to the demonstration by a cordon of armed militia. The mass arrest that took place following this criminal action by the police and militia appeared to be aimed at acquiring names of demonstrators; providing an opportunity for testing portable fingerprinting and photographic equipment; and trying out methods of transportation to be used by the criminal justice system and military agencies for processing large groups of political dissenters.

11

Delinquency and Moral Rhetoric

Our theory now requires familiarity with the ways in which adolescents justify criminal acts. We find that these justifications are frequently organized around particular kinds of moral statements or rhetoric. To describe these rhetorics, we use a number of analytic concepts derived from the work of May Edel, an anthropologist, and Abraham Edel, a philosopher of ethics. The following description of these concepts is brief yet sufficient to indicate our approach to ethical discourse in peer groups. We then continue to explore ideological patterns underlying delinquency.

The Edels (1959:120–48) note that different cultures have different styles of moral utterances. They say, "moral discourses of the Navaho, Winnebago, or Zuni are each characterized by different levels of generalization, operative rules for conduct and linguistic patterns of organization" (1959:125). In some cultures, common proverbs that simultaneously express "ideals and goals and principles of justification" prescribe situated conduct. In other cultures, these elements may ordinarily be expressed separately. But all cultures have some body of standardized moral discourse containing "sets of principles commonly referred to, explanations of some order of generality and easily adduced lists of appropriate behavior for different situations." We find that in our culture adolescent subcultures share similar styles of moral rhetoric with adults, but we shall see that these styles are affected by peer relationships.

Mode of Moral Rhetoric

A general and important point in the Edels' analysis is that an apparently unsystematic moral discourse, adopted by any collectivity, may actually be organized around a "mode of moral rhetoric." For example, on first appearances, medieval moral discourse might seem unsystematic. Edel and Edel (1959:128) observe, however, that medieval morality "found no difficulty in looking upon every moral rule as a command; it was able even to assimilate laws of nature to commands . . . because plants grew and stones fell only by God's will." How might this imperativistic mode translate into everyday life? "Who commands whom? Is it just parents ordering children, or is the whole social structure a highly authoritarian pecking order?" In this case, systematic moral thinking may be achieved through analogies. For example, all forms of authority (between kings and subjects, masters and slaves, men and women, parents and children) can be regarded as an expression of God's commandments or as analogous extensions of the relation between the creator and the universe. (Since the universe is ruled by one creator, subjects, slaves, women, and children must also have rulers.) With these examples, the Edels imply that the feudal social structure gave rise to an imperativistic mode of moral discourse that justified authoritarian relations in a number of feudal institutions.

A mode of moral rhetoric acquires its systematic expression because it is based on similar "organizing principles," "guiding principles" or "ordering principles." These principles may themselves be organized around various kinds of interests such as sex, power, and property; obligations such as kinship duties; moral rules or authority such as the Golden Rule or God's commandments; certain aspects of the social structure such as inequalities in wealth; or major institutions such as the patriarchial family. Sometimes moral discourse can be influenced by beneficent political authorities whose hegemony forces political accommodation and whose guiding principles are captured by the ideal of following the mean, of avoiding extremes. Goodness, in this context, is attributed to political accommodation and moderation but not to revolution.

Operative Rules and Standards

A mode of moral discourse also includes operative standards, rules, and procedures. Operative standards and rules are frequently applied when resolving antinomian conflicts or in circumstances where adherence to one moral precept will threaten another. Often we can discern these standards and rules in references to alternative courses of action and the relative priority or weighting assigned to different obligations or values. In moral discourse, the Edels (1959:141) note that "relative weightings are sometimes made explicit. We talk of 'man's highest duty' or his 'first duty' (these need not be the same: first duty may be to family, highest to conscience or God or country), and we make use of comparative expressions like 'better' or 'more important'." An example of this weighting comes from a businessman who, while comparing better and more important values, admits: "Religion and the 'finer things of life' are our ultimate values and the things all of us are really working for. But: A man owes it to himself and to his family to make as much money as he can" (Lynd and Lynd, 1937:61).

Operative rules also include "phase rules" such as: "for-the-most-part" rules and "I-do-this-only-with-regret" rules, which are used when people realize that attaining certain values under a given set of conditions threatens equally or more important values. The "for-the-most-part" rules are simply probability statements that roughly indicate the frequency with which an action will become a duty in a particular circumstance. (They are expressed, for instance, when people say that on the whole it is wrong to exhibit anger, but there are occasions when it is *perfectly right* to do so.) When these rules are used, there is no regret in a particular case, because duty is found to lie in another direction. On the other hand, "I-do-this-only-with-regret" rules suggest a very different attitude toward a moral precept which is associated with regret when the moral category cannot be supported. Many people, for instance, do not deny that there is some sense in which killing is universally wrong, but they frequently believe that wartime conditions require killing if other values are to be maintained. Consequently, they invoke an "operational universal" or rule of reckoning that says: in every situation in which a moral reckoning is taking place, the killing aspect is reckoned as wrong. This is a universal statement, but it does not imply that the act of killing will be excluded in every situation.

> "Killing as such is wrong" tells us that whenever the situation includes a killing its value will be much less than it would have been if, other things being equal, the same relevant result had been secured otherwise; but it does not say that the act of killing cannot under special circumstances rescue greater values (e.g. many lives). It may even then be one's duty (based on the results of reckoning) actually to kill or risk killing, as in certain wartime situations. (Edel, 1955:46–47)

Taken-for-Granted Ethical Ideas

Frequently, styles of moral discourse tend to make explicit either the general *principles* that govern conduct or the operating *procedures* by which these principles are applied to concrete situations. When one of these, such as general or organizing principles, is explicit, the other, the operating procedures, are usually taken for granted.[1] Let us examine, in general, the way these principles and procedures can work. Moral prescriptions in our society are often expressed as universals, but this does not mean that people believe they should be applied to every situation (and that they therefore always have priority over all other values or prescriptions). Therefore, when people mention universal precepts, such as "Thou Shall Not Kill," they usually take for granted operating rules such as phase rules that specify the conditions under which the precepts can be limited. On the other hand, in the more particularistic moralities, it is the organizing principles that are in the background (Edel and Edel, 1959:129).

Sometimes reformulations (in theological or philosophical writings) make written reference to basic axioms and guiding principles of moral rhetorics. But, even though teachers and theologians interested in ethical education may codify or formalize such moral principles as the Ten Commandments, the use of codified principles for clarification of everyday moral discourse is an exception rather than the rule. Usually, moral principles are either taken for granted or expressed in a shorthand version. Moral tenets may therefore be indicated in folk expressions, adages, and proverbs summing up and evaluating common experiences and then prescribing action. These folk usages also vary from one culture to another and from one subculture to another. Again, Edel and Edel (1959:124) write, "One culture may prefer pithy allegorical summations, another long proverbs, with or without stated moral. Still others may go in for a good deal of prosy moralizing, on the order of copy book maxims."

Multiple Modes of Moral Rhetoric

When referring to the modes of moral rhetoric for the analysis of adolescent conversations, we should not assume that any given peer group employs only one kind of moral rhetoric consistently. Our observations suggest that *different* rhetorics may be adopted by the same persons especially when social contexts change or in times of stress. Depending upon the circumstances, they may invoke one rhetoric when speaking to judges or teachers and another when conversing with peers. As a result, their moral utterances may appear to be highly inconsistent.

However, despite their inconsistencies and taken-for-granted universe of ethical ideas, it is vitally important to recognize that adolescents are not aliens recently immigrated from another planet. They speak the same language as adults who also frequently alter their rhetoric, unaware of doing so. Like others, these youth on occasion feel pressured by their groups or circumstances to adopt rhetorical devices that hide the petty, mean, or insecure quality of their lives. They adopt perspectives that assume certain social relationships exist simply because they ought to exist. Yet, we reiterate, they are not alone. Other kinds of people, such as public officials, lawyers, and salesmen evidence numerous contradictions between their utterances and their social behavior.

Contextual Shifts in Moral Rhetoric

Depending upon the context, rhetoric may shift. Research by Short and Strodbeck (1962:189) describes responses illustrative of the contradictory expression of moral utterances by the same group of youth. They found a discrepancy when older adolescents and young adults were asked questions about marriage and about family responsibility.[2] Fairly conventional responses were expressed confidentially in private interviews with researchers, but the responses given in a setting dominated by peers were quite different. In the interviews, these youth expressed the desire to support their obligations to their girl friends and illegitimate children; however, in the setting dominated by peers, they adopted an extremely chauvinistic and irresponsible standpoint. Their statements in the latter context were organized around male supremacist principles that justified abandonment of any obligation toward the girl friends and children. Moreover, this peer rhetoric (and not the rhetoric expressed in the interviews) reflected the attitudes that squared with how they were, in fact, actually behaving.

Early in our investigation of delinquent behavior, we became aware of the fact that adolescents often adopted different moral rhetorics in the company of peers. Some of these rhetorics supported delinquent behavior, but, since relationships among delinquents are never wholly unconventional, there were shifts between different modes of discourse characterizing their public and private conversations. As a result, our use of individual questionnaires, a form that is frequently employed to survey adolescent attitudes, was abandoned. We substituted the "thematic dialogue," based on sociodramatic techniques, which enabled us to study moral rhetoric expressed in the context of adolescent groups (Schwendinger and Schwendinger, 1965). The dialogues were obtained by recording arguments (between members of peer groups) about whether to commit an act of theft or violence.

Egoistic Rhetorics

As indicated, the Edels suggest that sometimes an established philosophical system helps clarify the basic, but not evident, ideas behind a moral rhetoric. In fact, a philosophy may be useful because it actually codifies commonsense rhetorics developed by people within a particular institution, such as the Catholic church, or a social class, such as the bourgeoisie. Insofar as it does codify commonsense rhetorics, such a philosophy can provide abbreviated statements that might be useful for developing a *model* of moral rhetoric. A model of a rhetoric is a description of a particular mode of rhetoric—that is, the model provides a brief summary of representative ideas, which functions as a short-hand guide to the mode.

What philosophies are embedded in the rhetoric used by juvenile delinquents as well as other adolescents? The models of moral rhetoric adopted by delinquent youth include, first of all, *conventional* utterances based on the rhetoric of egoism. If we look at the philosophical perspectives in Thomas Hobbes' *Leviathan* or in Jeremy Bentham's utilitarianism, we can see elements of the delinquent's moral rhetoric. Hobbes' and Bentham's writings reformulated ethical precepts cast from a similar social-class viewpoint and applied these precepts to many areas of life. On the other hand, while they expressed the ethical standpoint of the bourgeoisie as a whole, they especially reflected the so-called "market mentality," "possessive individualism," and utilitarian attitudes of the petit bourgeoisie.[3] This petit bourgeois morality and its egoistic rhetorics continue to provide the most conventional mode for structuring moral utterances in our society. At the center of this morality are individualistic standards. Taken-for-granted interests in money, property, family, friends, and national identity are associated with these standards. Certain assumptions about how society *ought* to be are also central to petit bourgeois morality; for instance, life outside the family is considered an infinite series of multilateral exchanges whose general form should be an acquisitive laissez-faire society. Since the ethical weight of any person's decision is seen to rest on free choice, individuals are morally responsible for their conduct.

There is a large number of people whose commonsense standpoint toward the sources of moral relationships has changed little since their reformulation by philosophers centuries ago. These moral relationships take the form of social rules, criminal laws, and "contracts." (Hobbes referred to them as "covenants," while modern sociologists call them "norms"). According to this view, when resources are scarce, people become amoral and selfish; consequently, social order and stability cannot survive unless some "power" is voluntarily given up by individuals to the state, which, in turn, controls people's selfishness. "Men" (but not "women") are by nature highly acquisitive and self-interested; and their relationships therefore tend to be anarchic and destructive, unless an "outside force" regulates their conduct in the common interest. In this perspective, forceful moral regulation is strongly warranted by reality. Moral universals are usually grounded in the image of society as a collection of atomistic entities with a supraindividual agency (such as the family or the state) to mediate or integrate conflicting interests.

In its secular form, however, the moral ideals in this egoistic model of moral rhetoric are not necessarily good in themselves. The goodness of honesty as a secular ideal is not generally founded on spiritual commandments. Honesty is simply good because it is the "best policy" for most people. In the long run, dishonesty leads to mutually disastrous consequences, and hence honesty is good because it "pays off" egoistically for most people. Also, moral acts are frequently acts of compromise representing adjustments between the individual ego and the demands of "society." In fact, the extremely moral man is "altruistic" because he has completely surrendered his egoistic interests to the interests of "society."[4] Such surrender is necessary because of the alleged *universal* contradiction between the interests of the individual and those of society.

Thus far we have described some of this rhetoric's basic axioms, which have been formulated by philosophical discourse. But, again, it should be kept in mind that the commonsense counterpart to this formulation is not so tidy and consistent; also, people who use this rhetoric are usually not aware of the processes by which its underlying perspective has been developed. They take it for granted. They do not reflect on the logic of the rhetoric but rather see other things through it; and it structures their moral discourse despite their lack of awareness. A discussion about an illegal course of action, for instance, rarely gives voice to these taken-for-granted assumptions. The feeling that the risk of personal harm and mutual destruction vastly increases in a society without obedience to legal norms may only be expressed in conversation by one or two phrases. Consequently, when youth object on moral grounds to propositions from friends to commit delinquent acts, they may simply demand that their friends should "play fair," "go by the rules," "keep up their obligations," or "act right" simply because "if everyone acted wrong then where would *we* be?"

The rhetoric of egoism is likely to be used by delinquents who still feel guilt about delinquent acts. Often new criminals or delinquents have not yet developed a dispassionate attitude toward their offenses, and therefore their verbal reflections are still largely dependent on conventional moral concerns. They use egoistic rhetoric to neutralize the moral stigma associated with their unlawful activity. Delinquents, for instance, might define their thefts as a sanction against greed and immorality by saying that theft enables them to get even with store owners who charge unfair prices. But this kind of justification cannot be taken at face value, because it often represents a need to compensate for a sense of guilt and to preserve a sense of moral integrity, even though this integrity is inauthentic.

Instrumental Rhetoric

Let us now look at a distinct variant of the egoistic rhetoric that also structures the accounts and justifications of socially harmful acts. This variant, called the instrumental rhetoric, seems to apply egoistic operating principles to a particular set of conditions, but it disregards egoistic standards of fairness. Philosophical peers who adopt the instrumental variant claim that most people abandon their responsibilities when they can to advantage. The instrumental rhetoric justifies such abandonment in terms of cunning or power, and it considers parity between individuals to be exceptional. Too many people can use deceit or power to make others serve their desires, violently if necessary, for parity to be the norm. Adages generated by older delinquents actively engaged in illegal markets offer superb illustrations of this world view. "You know, man, everybody's got their little game," says Whitey. Mousey agrees and wisely adds: "It's fuck your buddy week, fifty-two weeks of the year." When asked about the legal implications of his crimes, Dodger responds: "What difference does it make? If I don't cop it [steal it], *somebody else* will."

The general conditions taken for granted by the instrumental rhetoric reflect a drastic shift in assumptions about the nature of social reality, especially regarding the inequalities in power. It is assumed that people are not really autonomous individuals or formally equal to one another. The formal equality established by law veils an unending struggle for power in which the stronger and usually unscrupulous person wins out. Since the forces that divide society into powerful and powerless people are actually uncontrollable, it is perfectly proper to take advantage of others or to engage in fraud and deceit when "opportunity knocks."

Whether or not the victim is dishonest sometimes influences the moral utterances structured by the instrumental rhetoric. It certainly influences a speaker's tactical responses toward potential victims. For example, the confidence game is sometimes dependent upon whether the victim has a "little larceny in his heart"; and, since the character of the victim regulates the Con Man's responses, the assessment of the victim is an intrinsic part of the victimization as well as its justification. Since, at bottom, every human being (including oneself) can serve as a justifiable victim, such character traits as the greediness or gullibility of the victim are regarded opportunistically. One even finds predatory delinquents remark that they are too trusting and gullible. Then these youth painfully admit that they *deserved* being victimized by others because of these "weaknesses." In this parlance: "*Anybody* that's stupid deserves to be swung [conned]!" However, in the instrumental view of things, the illegal act need only be justified on the basis of the personal needs of the criminal and the opportunity to commit the crime. The opportunity may merely consist of the victim's inability to prevent the act from happening.

The instrumental rhetoric, and the interpersonal conditions that generate it, are not restricted to streetcorner groups in the United States. The autobiographical account of Manuel Sanchez, in Oscar Lewis' *Children of Sanchez*, is filled with this rhetoric. His observations of streetcorner groups in his barrio make this same point. "If a guy shows weakness and has tears in his eyes, and begs for mercy," exclaims Roberto, "that's when the others pile on him. In my neighborhood you either are a *picudo*, a tough guy, or a *pendejo*, a fool" (Lewis, 1961:38).

Thus, a guiding principle of this rhetoric assumes people to be engaged in a vast power struggle, with the weak and the powerless as legitimate victims. In this view of reality, the images of humans are virtually stripped of meaningful moral qualities, and individuals are seen primarily as instruments for egoistical ends. Often, moral qualities are not even present in the consciousness of the criminal or in the criminal's selection or definition of the victim. The selection of victims, in this context, seems entirely fortuitous. The metaphors for characterizing victims adopted by delinquents and criminals clearly reflect these cognitive relationships. The sexual victim, for instance, is a Piece of Ass, Box, or Cunt, and *nothing* more. Of course, it may also be assumed that some women—potential wives or sisters and mothers—possess special moral qualities that exempt them from victimization, but these particular women are the exceptions that prove the rule.

While such metaphorical images are also adopted early by adolescents (especially where the ideological relationships have been supported by stable forms of domination such as male domination relationships), the numbers of these amoral conceptions increase significantly among delinquents during later adolescence. The justifications that increasingly employ these conceptions of people as "things" tacitly shift their references to events and relationships external to the victim's person and center on the "way things are." Under these conditions the rights of the victim are meaningless, and such wholly egotistical accounts as: "I beat him up because *I* needed the money," or "If *I* didn't rob him, somebody else would've done it," become sufficient.

Delinquent Rationalizations

Let us now use the concepts indicated above to evaluate contemporary approaches to delinquent rationalizations. The sociology of deviancy, for instance, repeatedly reminds us that rhetorical devices (usually based on operating rules) are used by delinquents and criminals to neutralize any sense of personal responsibility and blame. Delinquents, on occasion, say that they stole money from people but deny that they really hurt anyone because their victims had more money than they needed. Delinquents also say that a victim of violence deserved to be hurt because he acted wrongfully; therefore, by implication, the violent attack actually upheld moral standards because it righted a wrong. Sometimes gang members express regret at engaging in gang warfare but claim that their higher loyalties (to the honor of their gang, for instance) mandate their engagement in violence.

Sykes and Matza (1957) call such rationalizations "techniques of neutralization." They claim that delinquents actually subscribe to "the dominant moral norms" but have learned rationalizations that "bend the moral implications of the delinquent act." Since the moral implications are only neutralized by the rationalizations, these scholars propose that delinquent youth have the same moral commitments as nondelinquents. Our research into adolescent rhetoric has refuted Sykes and Matza's theory, and it has pointed out that rationalizations, which deny responsibility and guilt, are much less important throughout the course of a delinquent's career than is assumed by the sociology of deviancy.[5] Our analysis of "thematic dialogues" (produced by asking members of a peer group to debate whether to commit a crime) found that few rationalizations were directed at the reduction of guilt due to the subscription to "dominant moral norms" (Schwendinger and Schwendinger, 1965). The rationalizations overwhelmingly appealed to minimizing risks or other tactical considerations; therefore, they could not be understood on the basis of the "techniques of neutralization."

However, there are added considerations that counter the logic behind Sykes and Matza's way of thinking about moral norms and delinquent rationalizations. Do these rationalizations necessarily "neutralize" moral responsibility and guilt? It depends. Leaders of delinquent groups, for instance, may "appeal to higher loyalties" when they call upon members to break laws and resort to violence in defense of their group. But this kind of appeal may have nothing to do with assuaging regret caused by committment to legal norms. Leaders may, in fact, have no legal norms in mind when they make these appeals to higher loyalties. They may make this appeal simply because the members are afraid to fight or because they promised their parents or girl friends that they would not. On the other hand, they may also be concerned with being sent back to a correctional institution by probation officers. And even if this appeal is made because they want to persuade a few morally concerned members to fight, such an appeal by itself actually provides no information about the circumstances under which these members consider violence a proper response. Consequently, it cannot be concluded (as Sykes and Matza's theory would lead one to think) that delinquents subscribe to the legal norms simply because rhetorical devices for justifying illegal conduct are used. All that can be concluded is that leaders have adopted a phase rule to justify a course of action; but such a rule, by itself, provides no information about the kinds of values or duties being upheld in conversation.

Perhaps further scrutiny of this matter, in the context of our previous discussion about phase rules (such as I-do-this-only-with-regret rules) and killing, will make our objections clearer. Any support given by the I-do-this-only-with-regret phase rule to the prohibition against killing leaves enormous latitude for the feeling that killing is necessary in given circumstances. Therefore, regret can be felt about illegal (as well as legal) killings without implying agreement with the legal norms distinguishing between types of killing. Moreover, people's differences about killing, even when they kill with regret, cannot be explained by merely noting their use of the same phase rule to justify the act. Varying social contexts make all the difference. Explaining the differences requires identification of the social circumstances, personal attitudes, and group norms lying behind the use of these rules; otherwise it would be possible to claim that Allende, a democratic Chilean socialist, and Pinochet, a fascist, shared the same moral attitudes about killing merely because each asked his supporters to fulfill "higher loyalties" when Allende's government was overthrown by Pinochet's fascist junta.

Consequently, awareness of rhetorical devices and operating principles, such as phase rules, directs our attention to the particular *contents* of the "higher values" or moral precepts people believe to be threatened unless they are defended violently. With regard to delinquent formations, coming chapters show that "higher values" are denoted by the specific codes upheld in certain delinquent groups, and that these values frequently do not represent the same values and codes of honor supported by nondelinquent formations.

The Formal Organization of and Necessity for Rationalizations

Some sociologists have attempted to create theories of criminal behavior by searching for causes in the systematic features of criminal accounts. Thus, some of the imprisoned embezzlers studied by Cressey (1953), for example, indicated that they felt justified in abrogating their fiduciary trust because they were treated unfairly by their employers. The embezzlers construed their act as "a way of getting even" for unfair treatment; consequently, by implication, the theft was committed by an unjustifiably injured person; and it was not "really" immoral. According to Cressey, these accounts operate as one link in a causal chain. After analyzing the embezzlers' accounts, he proposed that violation of a position of trust will not take place unless people currently have a financial problem that cannot be shared with anyone; therefore, they have no one who can help them resolve their problem legitimately. These people also recognize that violating the trust can resolve the problem. The embezzlement then takes place once the offenders have finally been able to neutralize their feelings of guilt by rationalizing their acts to maintain their own images as authentically trusted persons. We also studied embezzlers, but our study was based on embezzlers who were not apprehended by police and who trusted the people who interviewed them. Our research completely contradicts Cressey's findings. We found embezzlers admitting that they stole money or property even though they had no financial problem. Some embezzlers shared their problem with their family and friends. We also found embezzlers who did not bother to rationalize their crimes to maintain their image as trusted persons because they were indifferent to the moral status of their crime. We have stated that the embezzlers interviewed by Cressey were using egoistic rhetoric to account for their actions. While this rhetoric can help us understand how some criminals structure the accounts of embezzlement, it reveals little about the etiology of this crime (Schwendinger and Schwendinger, unpublished).

Further, it is important to reiterate that rationalizations are not absolutely necessary for the commission of illegal acts. When people are *conditioned* to act illegally, the cognitive requisites for their acts may not involve a rationalization process. Their motives can be acted out directly without reflection in the heat of the argument or when opportunities for gain present themselves. We grant that the rationalizations and accounts of delinquent or criminal behavior have greater importance for coordinating collective action. However, even in a collective context, other kinds of rhetorical devices—words like Punk, Chump, Mark, and Motherfucker—incorporate sufficient meaning to justify illegal acts, especially personal victimization, all by themselves. Finally, there are some delinquents and criminals (as well as "respectable" citizens) who are so indifferent to the ethical dimensions of the harm they cause that even a model of moral rhetoric cannot be used to understand their justifications. These persons do not rationalize their guilt when committing particular crimes because guilt is not part of the subjective reality associated with these. Their conversations may not be influenced by any ethical principle for organizing rhetoric other than indifference. Indifference can operate in isolation from egoistic, instrumental, or any other ethical conceptions of persons and society. Once the obligations toward victims, social groups, or society are excluded from ethical consciousness, what is there to talk about besides maximizing the opportunity to do harm with impunity?

Does Delinquency Result from the Inability to Reason Morally?

Numerous social scientists agree with Kohlberg (1970) that delinquency results from an adolescent's inability to reason morally on the same level as other youth. In the very early 1960s we entertained similar ideas because of our reading of Piaget's work, an important source for Kohlberg's theory. We constructed various experimental apparatuses to test whether delinquents were deficient in the ability to reason about cause-and-effect relationships. We abandoned this line of investigation rapidly when it became clear that delinquents were no different from other types of youth and that differences in causal reasoning were simply due to their lack of adequate education. We concluded that ideas based on Piaget's work, like all the other "arrested maturational state" theories, could not help us understand delinquency.

In recent years, the research contradicting Kohlberg's thesis is beginning to mount.[6] This research shows that cognitive abilities among delinquents improve with maturation yet they remain delinquent; therefore, an arrested state of cognitive development cannot account for the ethical standpoints of delinquents.

An Evaluation of the "Survival" Rationalization

We have indicated that delinquents often use the rhetoric of egoism to structure their moral conversations. Conversely, we have insisted that the rhetoric by itself does not *necessarily* encourage delinquency. What implications does this have for the familiar "survival rationalization" that researchers find among poverty-stricken and racially oppressed delinquents?[7] Delinquents who use this rationalization justify stealing, pimping, or hustling drugs in order to survive oppressive social conditions.

The so-called "survival" rationalization merely reflects the adoption of operating rules derived from the rhetoric of egoism for legitimating criminal behavior. We have indicated that operating rules provide relative weightings for deciding which values or obligations justify courses of action. (Thus, one speaks of "better" or "most important" values or of "first duty" or "highest duty.") The survival rationalization operates by justifying any course of conduct solely on the basis of "paramount" or "most important" individual needs. The emphasis on individual survival achieves this end because, in the rhetoric of egoism, it denotes an ultimate standard for comparing values. (There are no values or obligations more important to individuals in this context than their egoistic "survival.") Consequently, the notion of "survival" automatically discounts all rules of fairness, which are threatened under certain circumstances if this value is to be achieved. Moreover, since the standard of "paramount" or "most important" survival needs can be used by anyone who shares the assumptions underlying the rhetoric of egoism, it is adopted as a rhetorical device by people throughout our society. It is not used exclusively by streetcorner criminals or delinquents to justify their crimes on the basis of deprivation. It is also used by wealthy entrepreneurs to justify victimizing the public. (Businessmen often say that tax violations, bribery, false advertising, and other violations of the law are necessary for "survival" in the economic jungle.) This attitude toward "survival" is even given unwitting credence by scholars who attribute crime and delinquency to economic circumstances that make "paramount values" unachievable by legal means.[8] Such theories, however, would hardly be credible without taking the rhetoric of egoism and its commonsense logic for granted.

The sociology of deviance literature abounds in typologies of rationalizations for committing crimes that depend upon the rhetoric of egoism for their plausibility. The reason for these typologies is no mystery. To credibly justify their conduct or account for their actions, everyone, including sociologists, must learn to use the guiding principles and operative rules of this extremely conventional rhetoric, whether the reasons produced are sincere or not. On the other hand, these typologies do not justify the degree to which such reasons are considered causal agents, in the absence of understanding the collective lives that people lead and the norms and values they uphold within their groups. Without these additional elements, the rationalizations structured by this rhetorical mode provide very little insight into delinquency or any other kind of deviancy. These rationalizations simply cannot be placed all by themselves in little positivist bottles that are labeled "drink me" or "eat me," which, when consumed, produce an adolescent Frankenstein or Joan of Arc.

NOTES

1. Thus, the Edels mention the taken-for-granted" nature of moral discourse and conclude that, in our culture, "the operative procedures . . . for applications of universal ethical statements are usually taken for granted." Because of these taken-for-granted relationships, ethnomethodology (Garfinkel, 1967) can contribute greatly to the analysis of delinquent rationalizations and personal accounts of delinquent behavior.
2. Short, Strodbeck, and Cartwright (1962:189) note: "the group norms [expressed by gang members in a *group* interview] clearly were not consistent with the attitudes and expectations expressed in the individual interviews."

3. This is not to say that larger-scale mercantile and manufacturing developments were exempt from the development of these perspectives. See, for example, Shumpeter (1955:121, 133).
4. This concept of altruism can be found in writings by such sociologists as Emile Durkheim or Talcott Parsons.
5. See, for example, Pfuhl (1980:65–68).
6. For one of the studies that also summarizes this line of research, see Morash (1981).
7. For example, see Krisberg (1974). Such an ethic is implicated by "opportunity structure" theories, including those utilizing the concept of relative deprivation. On the other hand, Krisberg provides an excellent account of the "hustling ethic."
8. Merton's theory of anomie utilizes such reference to paramount values because it relies for its psychological dynamics on the commonsense "survival ethic" (and rhetoric) mentioned previously.

12

Delinquent Rationality and Sense of Rightness

In this chapter we discuss further theoretical issues centering around the rhetoric adopted by delinquents to justify their conduct. We will also explore the rationality behind unreflexive delinquent conduct—that is, conduct that seems irrational because it is not accompanied by verbal justifications or self-conscious thought. (While we assume that most forms of delinquency are rational, we are aware that there are delinquent youth who have unstable personalities, and their instability is reflected in unlawful behavior.) It is not our intent to develop a comprehensive or integrated approach to these theoretical issues. However, the development of such an approach might consider some of the ideas expressed here, and it might reflect on the valuable insights in such works at Matza's (1964) *Delinquency and Drift.*

Group Contexts and Changing Discourse

The forms of rhetoric used to justify illegal acts are important in the development of antisocial standards. But we shall see that these rhetorics play their developmental role in group contexts. In other words, this role does not originate in intrapsychic processes. Furthermore, once the behavioral standards of crowds, cliques, or clubs are established within a stratified domain, specific kinds of intragroup processes orient, justify, and coordinate the attainment of these standards. These intragroup processes are usually centered around the leaders of peer groups, because group norms coalesce in those having the major responsibility for maintaining group identities and coordinating collective activity.[1]

It is well to recall, in this context, that not all members of groups, strata, classes, or institutions—including the family—share equally in, or are equally capable of expressing, the ethos of their collectivities. For this reason, Halbwachs (1958:16–17) believes, "there must be in every society a gradation through those who are most sensitive to general ideas and feelings and who best manifest them, to the more indifferent." Leaders of delinquent groups, like leaders of other groups, learn to justify themselves, in their own eyes, through their fulfillment of group standards. This is less true for most of the other group members. The ethical influence that groups exert on their members is therefore mediated by those particular leaders who are adept at supplying "good reasons" for engaging in delinquent behavior. The supplier of these good reasons is analogous to the journalist, public relations man, or Madison Avenue huckster. Sometimes, among streetcorner youth, these hucksters are the philosophers of "the street" who reputedly "always know the score" and serve as experts providing sage advice or news about "what's happening." The influence of leaders is especially important during the formative stage of group life, when many antisocial standards are developing.

Just as the early socialization of children is largely dependent on their relations to their parents within the family group, members of stradom formations are primarily influenced by the most prestigious and powerful members in their adolescent groups. Their leaders help them come to terms with their personal values and with the moral implications of conduct being enforced by group norms. (Coming to terms is necessary here because the personal values and the group norms are often contradictory.) The members come to terms with themselves when they rationalize the contradictions between their public and private moralities. Once again, the leaders are frequently suppliers of rationalizations while working relationships are being established between themselves and the members. Furthermore, the contradictions between public and private attitudes may be modified at any given moment in the group process when leaders compromise with followers in hopes of maintaining group cohesion and the integrity of major group goals. This process may be less smooth than is implied. For example, the contradictions, in some form, usually remain in the background, where they exert a gnawing anxiety. This anxiety is only relieved when the members in conflict can transform their public standards into private ones and thereby adopt attitudes that respond readily to group demands. (Some members, who never undergo this transformation, engage in delinquent activities with considerable ambivalence.)

Consequently, in their collective discourse, streetcorner youth begin to justify their acts with a language of interests and obligations legitimated by peers. These justifications represent the process by which the group's ethos shapes the individual's operative view of others. During the earlier phases, the younger streetcorner youth, aware of the status conflicts around them, give credence to peers who advise them that "others" are perpetually violating the rules of the game. Because others violate them, these rules are considered useless, and new guiding principles are substituted to meet the exceptional circumstances. The empirical warrant for these new principles does not always have to be experienced personally; it can be acquired from older Dudes "who know the ropes" and whose advice is avidly grasped by admiring younger streetcorner youth. This is how Sam learned that Socs were not trustworthy. "I tell you how it started off with me," said Sam. "They started talking about Socs and telling me how bad Socs were. And I started disliking them from what I heard because then I still didn't know the difference. After a while I started watching them. I'd run around with a couple of them to see how they acted, and they act like goddamn little children—as old as they are! They acted like Punks! I finally caught on to what the hell my friends were talking about!" We asked Sam whether he had heard about the Socs while he was in junior high school. Sam replied, "Yeh, a lot of guys I knew were older than me and had already found out about them. And the guys I had already gone with—they had gotten in with the Socs more than I had and told me about them and I finally began catching on to it." In addition to learning from others, the new delinquents, when coordinating actions with peers, must also support their peers' reasons with reasons of their own for "tearing up the town" or "stealing some stuff" or "looking for a fight." And they must have "cool reasons" if they value their relationships with friends. At times, adolescent "cool reasons" for improper behavior may be referred to so often that an abbreviated term will be adopted to signify them. Thus, at first, a delinquent might put things together and say: "I'm going to con Jim out of his bread [money] because he is gullible and too stupid to know what's happening and anyone who is too stupid to know better deserves to be fucked." Later, the statement might simply be, "I'm going to swing [con] that chump, Jim." All the justificatory meanings associated with the act of victimization are now taken for granted by the use of the word "chump."

The increasing adoption of these victim words signals the gradual acquisition of a working ethic, of motives, rationales for action, images of victimizers and their victims, and assumptions about reality. This *instrumental* ethic is eventually integrated into the collectivity, even though it is not shared equally among all members of streetcorner formations. However, when they linguistically coordinate their behavior, even dissenting streetcorner youth learn conformity to group standards by habitually applying the operating principles of their working ethic. In this way a climate is created in which no serious challenge, on broader ethical grounds, can be made by members to achieving group goals illegally. In the company of peers, such challenges are considered nonsense, a sign of hypocrisy; or they may be attributed sarcastically to temporary insanity.

There are some delinquents who learn to perceive a world of "chumps" and "cool" people consistently from childhood. These youth have been prepared for delinquent activity prior to adolescence through family discourse and experience. Parents exhibiting the behavior that seems to encourage delinquency in children have been described by Glueck and Glueck (1959:144–45) as "two-faced," "evasive," as having an "excessive interest in themselves," or, as persons who are unable to give "their love with no strings attached." The child becomes delinquent by following the "warped feelings of his parents." Despite the value judgements underlying these observations, the authors indicate certain kinds of ethical conduct in families of children who are delinquent in their earliest years. In the psychoanalytic descriptions, the idea of manipulation for personal ends often appears. In conceiving themselves primarily as instruments, in the eyes of significant others, these children generalize such expectations, and their view of the world is filled to overflowing with highly manipulative people.[2]

Although instrumental perspectives among streetcorner youth are, usually, situationally delimited, we should note that the relationships among these youth are never absolutely separate and independent of the so-called "respectable" and "law-abiding" world. We draw this conclusion even though their youthful patterns are balanced precariously with this so-called respectable world. Once again, leaders play a role in making the separation. To swing the balance toward law-breaking, leaders may employ terms that assuage anxiety and achieve cooperation from peers who feel morally uneasy. For example, when ambivalent members ask why questionable courses of action should be pursued, leaders sometimes invoke an operational principle of the rhetoric of egoism. They define the motivation of their escapade as "kicks," "play," or "fun" or give any possible motive other than one explicitly implicating deviant intentions. They thereby undermine the empirical warrants establishing moral responsibility for conduct, because the harmful consequences of their conduct seem inadvertent. Consequently, they can strike an innocent pose: "We only fooled around to have fun . . . not to hurt anybody." In this interpretation, delinquency is the result of "accident," and no one is to blame. Such justifications (of delinquency as play) are therefore likely to be employed to reduce feelings of guilt. On the other hand, sometimes there are no feelings of guilt aroused by the delinquent act, and in such cases these justifications may be taken at face value by members or fulfill very different functions. They are not adopted in these cases because they neutralize personal blame.

Peer ideology also influences *violent* behavior. Ideological processes within the group build upon prior conditioning that to some degree inures much of American youth to violence. Extreme forms of violence are partly related to the incidence of violence in families and in a community as a whole; and these forms of violence can become habitual without support from highly elaborated justifications. On the other hand, ideological processes within peer groups may provide additional cognitive elements that feed back on violent emotions and generalize these emotions to circumstances other than those evoking them previously (for instance, family relations or contact with the mass media). Group ideology, therefore, links the emotions to intergroup relationships that occur during the ethnocentric phase, for instance, and encourages self-regulation of violent emotions in accordance with group standards. Peer discourse tops off this social learning by providing the cognitive meanings that connect violence with group interests and goals.

The use of the rhetoric of egoism to comprehend and justify their evolving patterns of violence has important consequences. By invoking the operative rules that allow them to justify violence on the basis of situational exigencies, streetcorner youth usher in a process that initially suspends the legitimacy of the common fighting codes restricting certain forms of violence. (These codes consider individual "dueling" or fighting without weapons to be legitimate when there is ample provocation. Since weapon use against people is relegated to police, fighting with weapons, especially in groups, is not legitimate regardless of the provocation.) In time, however, the influences that stem from this suspension of fighting codes transform unrestricted violence into a symbol of virtuous behavior. Winning a violent encounter at all costs becomes a legitimate end in itself. Consequently, as we will presently see, the very process of rationalizing violence among streetcorner groups helps habituate the use of violence.

Unawareness, Self-Consciousness, and Delinquency

Young delinquents can hardly grasp the long-range changes taking place in their behavior even though they may be aware of the specific reasons for committing each individual act. Understanding the more general changes requires the ability to think abstractly and to make some theoretical sense out of their own behavior. Consequently, comprehensive ideas about their own motives are only adopted as youth grow older. In fact, comprehension may appear years after they begin to engage in delinquency.

Looking back over the years, older adolescents sometimes say they fight or steal because they were deprived in some way or another. But there are many reasons why the expression of such causal ideas cannot be accepted at face value. First, the use of motivational terms to characterize long-range personal developments signifies that people have taken a reflective standpoint toward themselves and their own activities. To take this standpoint, people usually view themselves in relation to an ordered series of personal events. They also decide that this ordering is created by some causal mechanism such as imitation, frustration and aggression, or the force of circumstance. For instance, the delinquent's awareness that violence often compensates for frustrating experiences shapes such explanations as: "I punched him in the mouth because I ain't taking no lip from nobody. I've had enough of it from my Dad." Thus, commonsense explanations of behavior may not say that "frustration leads to aggression"; yet adolescents often associate similar ideas with their personal justifications for violence.

Once delinquents have learned such justifications, they may, in fact, sincerely believe that these ideas explain their biographical changes. It is sometimes difficult, however, to tell where their beliefs leave off and where their manipulations of other people (or themselves) begin. Most personal behavior occurs without the need for causal evaluation. Such evaluations are acts in themselves, often brought about when problematic situations or questions from others require a reflective stance toward one's own behavior (Mills, 1940). But the knowledge that particular notions are given greater credence by people is often used to control the responses of these people. Adolescents know that the kind of treatment they will receive at the hands of a judge, for instance, may depend on the reasons they give. Therefore, they may adopt particular explanations chiefly because they make sense to people who demand an accounting.

As indicated, the type of questioning that prompts these youth to consider the most general reasons for their actions can be raised by parents, teachers, police, social workers, probation officers, or even peers. However, during the first years of their adolescent development, peers rarely ask each other why they became delinquent. Moreover, when such questions are raised by adults, they are most often asked after delinquent activity has become habitual. Therefore, it is not unreasonable to assume that many young boys and girls did not really know why they became delinquent prior to the questions being first asked. When they finally do respond with an answer, their explanations are likely to be more heavily determined by their relations with the questioners than with their actual biographies.

When investigating delinquent activities among youth during the formative yeas of the stradom formations, we were struck by the absence of reflective awareness. This lack often manifested itself in the younger teens' inability to construct theoretical reasons for generally acting the way they did. Instead of self-conscious theorizing about personal behavior in general, we found such truthful remarks as: "I don't know why I did all these things."

Hal, a 12-year-old Greaser, provides an illustration. Thinking back to the previous summer, he recalls: "We all hung around State Beach. *Suddenly* the guys were all gloving cars [stealing items from glove compartments]. It was like a fad. *I don't know why I did it.* I just went along with the guys. Everybody was doing it."

Gorgo, a 13-year-old who was unsure of the causes, said: "I met the guys in classes. *I really don't know why.* I suppose I went around with them because I liked them. Half of the guys didn't fool around in class because they got good grades. The dumber guys cracked up in class because we wanted to have a good time."

The same admission of ignorance appears in relation to inquiries about sexual activities, fighting, and drinking. Often the only generalization indicating an attempt to become aware of the causes of personal behavior is a reference to the magnetism of "bad company." Such a reference, however, begs the question of why the company was chosen in the first place.

Interpreting these statements confronts us with a crucial decision. We can probe for the "hidden motives" psychoanalysts find to be laden with guilt and repressed into an unconscious reservoir. We might then conclude that these youth are really afraid of knowing why they act delinquently. But, then again, there may be no repressed hostile motives. Or, we can look for older youth or adults who provide criminal role models. But, what if these same boys also inform us (as they did) that many of the older delinquents and criminals they knew were immoral and depraved and therefore they rejected them as role models. How deep must one plumb for hostile motives? Where are the role models to be found?

We became convinced that the younger delinquent's ignorance was not a sign of the repression of childhood pain and frustration. As far as the vast majority are concerned, such complex personality dynamics have little to do with their ignorance of the major determinants of their life patterns. When the researcher shifts to probing motives behind *specific* delinquent acts, these motives are easily found. While delinquents may not know why they engaged in stealing for an entire summer and have no general explanation for thieving activity, they do know why they went along with others in those specific situations when stealing was a means to a variety of ends. There were attractive items being stolen; they feared being considered cowards or joined the thieving crowd because they "wanted to be one of the boys."

Perhaps motives can be discovered if we consider the character of the acts and the types of youthful explanations. That these stolen items belonged to other people seemed to be far less important than their desirability. Therefore, frequently, the concerns that delinquents do *not* express, because such concerns are *not* really considered important, symbolize the mobilization of bias toward a particular set of egoistic standards.[3] These unexpressed concerns are at times more significant theoretically than the expressed concerns. Researchers who are present during, or not long after, delinquent incidents will also find that the egoistic character of these specific acts is readily expressed by the actors. Therefore, after a shoplifting caper, even the more sophisticated Greaser will admit, "We stole mainly clothes. We're not kleptomaniacs. We used most of the stuff we stole. The majority of the guys do a little shoplifting—like if we want a coke we'll lift it." "What is the reason I stole?" Jack asked rhetorically. "Well, I didn't want to spend my money and the guy wasn't looking." On the other hand, the particular situation in which delinquents find themselves may affect the character of the explanation. By contrast with these egoistic reasons, we heard a very different explanation after a boy was caught by the police. In such a case, we find a crude attempt to generalize the motives for theft in a more conventionally acceptable form. Andy generalized: "Me and my friend got busted for taking shirts. Me and my ingenious plan! I don't know. We saw these good shirts . . . you know . . . they were in the hallway . . . on racks . . . about 40 of them. We figured we would take some of them, keep the tough ones and sell the others. You know, it's mostly temptation."

An outstanding feature of the explanations uttered to delinquent peers or nonjudgemental researchers is the indifference toward the legal codes or moral issues involved. Also, for most youth, feelings of remorse in reference to these acts usually arise only because of failure or punishment.[4] Yet, even if they are apprehended by the police, it apparently does not occur to young thieves to blame everybody or society in general for their delinquent biographies (as one might assume from reading various interpretations of delinquent behavior).[5] Particularly during the initial phases of stradom development, a young delinquent is likely to admit to peers: "How do I feel about it? I did it and it was my fault. I don't blame anybody for it." And if the stealing stops for a while, moral reasons are also not likely to be expressed in peer company. While adolescents may invent all sorts of reasons to explain their conduct, it is chiefly fear, shame in the company of peers, and various other interests that play the most prominent role in shaping their explanations. Such explanations also include reasons for not committing crime. For example, implying that his change of heart was actually due to the power of women and not the law, Chuck, a Greaser said, "After a guy gets busted he always looks down on himself. If he gets away with it, everything is fine. Babes also look down on you. That's one reason why I stopped, because babes always look down on you."

The sources of rationalizations and individual values are also of interest. Crowd and clique relationships provide youth with new rationalizations and accounts that confirm the rightness of their decisions. The presence of numbers reinforces the commission of questionable and risky acts. "You're different in groups," said a Greaser. "If you're in a group you have more security and you feel that you can do more things like crashing parties, or choosing someone off [picking a fight with someone]." Because risky consequences frequently accompany delinquent acts, group support for these acts is important. As stradom youth move through the formative stages, they become increasingly tangled in a web of obligations with close pals or with members of larger groups; and such group relations further intensify the influences that encourage delinquent behavior. Group norms even pressure those exceptional members of the group who are morally concerned about their acts to "go along with the crowd." Frequently, adolescents say, "We want to be part of a crowd. If one guy fucks up—everybody fucks up." If group identity is prized above the victim's rights, a youth goes along with the crowd regardless of personal ambivalences.

Rational or Irrational Motives

Let us now discuss whether delinquent behavior should be viewed as irrationally motivated. Some forms of delinquency, such as joyriding, might be considered irrational even though peers regard them as "play." Other forms, such as victimizing peers who cannot defend themselves, might also be considered irrational. The laughter of peers who cruelly provoked a mentally ill boy to fight someone far more alert and powerful demonstrated that the tormentors lacked any deep sense of guilt or sympathy. Such an act took place among bourgeois youth who were members of an intermediary stradom formation. We have seen almost the same act recreated in the incredibly pathetic victimization of a boy with Downes' syndrome who was being repeatedly frightened and humiliated by the local streetcorner boys while foraging among garbage cans in an urban slum. This act, too, was rationalized as "just fooling around." Are these acts rational reflections of individualistic attitudes and lack of sensitivity toward a potential victim's rights to dignity, life, or property? Or are they irrational acts motivated by unconscious desires such as aggressive instincts or emotional problems?

There are scholars for whom such acts have no rational character. For instance, Healy and Bronner (1936:22) suggested long ago that since money is not the goal of a number of thefts, these acts are driven by irrational motives. (Sometimes delinquents playfully steal objects without any interest in using them, throwing away the items or giving them to their friends.) Other acts are said to be irrational because they seem to be committed "for no apparent reason." Cohen has classified such acts as irrational and non-utilitarian." When a youth says, "We did it for kicks" or ". . . for the hell of it," the reasons are considered irrational.[6]

But the contextual analysis of justifications and accounts reveals the rational character of delinquent acts. Objecting to Cohen's imputation of irrationality, Bordua (1961) points out:

> If . . . a group steals from freight yards, peddles the merchandise to neighbors for movie money, and so on, this can hardly be considered non-utilitarian. The behavior makes sense as instrumental behavior, however, only after one has a picture of the general life by the group. . . . youngsters may, of course, spend the two dollars gained from selling stolen goods entirely on doughnuts and gorge themselves and throw much of the food away. I think this largely indicates that they are children, not that they are non-utilitarian.

However, certain other motives that have little to do with what money can buy or the irrationality of children also enter into the motivated character of delinquent acts. Some of these motives are produced by stradom developments, and they center around group standards and peer status. Many acts are due to the honorific codes that emerge among stradom members. For example, destruction of public property such as burning park benches contributes to a reputation for fearlessness among peers in the neighborhood. Other acts contributing to peer status are smoking with "cool" sophisticated mannerisms in the company of older mates; or drinking heavily at club parties; and pressuring a girl to engage in sexual intercourse, not just for sexual gratification but to achieve status in the eyes of companions.

Socs are quite aware of the status motives and delinquent acts that accompany their drunken bouts, yet they frequently hustle themselves and others with their claims of playful motivations or pride in "holding their liquor." Joshua says, "A lot of guys go through with this kick to drink to impress people. Now I feel that, in our fraternity, when we drink we don't try to impress one another. We don't act like a bunch of babies. You can see some guys shitty drunk like 'Now I'm drunk I want the world to know it. I'm high! Now I'm gonna take a piss out in the middle of the street!' or some shit like that. Now most of the guys—everybody who is in our club—they drink [only] to drink. To enjoy it. They have a good time and they can handle themselves. They are not gonna say I was drunk [or] I am gonna break a window because I can get away with it. We are known as heavy drinkers and for handling our liquor."

Delinquents classify their acts and motives in varying ways. They discriminate between those acts engaged in "for money" and other concrete goals and those committed "for the fun of it" or "for kicks." Delinquent vocabularies of motive often employ such metaphors as "kicks," because youth differentiate the acts from the original goals. After this differentiation has become habitual, only the enjoyable feelings in experiencing the acts tend to be remembered, and thus they did it "for kicks."[7]

During the early development of the stradom formations, thievery, conning, and fighting are viewed as justifiable means to various ends, and the ability to use these means (stealing, being deceitful, fighting successfully) becomes highly valued as well. As a result, at that time, many delinquent acts can be seen as being instrumental to the possession of personally valued items or useful in acquiring honor in a system wherein deviant acts themselves are positively valued. In due time, the acquisition of the knowledge and skills necessary to carry out such acts successfully are considered virtues. Successfully engaging in fighting or thievery, especially when risks are great, is highly valued, regardless of the ends served. One illustration is the often repeated example of three boys going from store to store merely exchanging the stolen hats they are wearing on their heads. These forms of delinquency are not irrationally motivated, nor are they likely to reflect imitative processes in which deviants strike "a chord of solidarity" with older criminals, as suggested by Cloward and Ohlin.[8] A successful caper of this sort validates superior ability and discriminating humor. The sources of this validation are all in the present, because the capable thief or fighter is amply rewarded by the admiring glances of his friends.

We have heard and seen such stunts while observing delinquent groups. In one incident, a group of boys was intensely involved in tire stealing, from which they realized considerable sums of money. One night, a "competition" was held in which four teams of two partners each raced to steal a top-grade automobile tire in the shortest time. Speed was essential in this task, and partners were chosen primarily on the basis of their ability to work fast. On the night of the competition, four teams of boys rolled stolen tires down the middle of the street in a race to reach the time-keeper. The deep humor in this event and the activity itself may seem absolutely irrational in light of the risks taken by these boys. However, when one compares this seemingly irrational event with the enormous risks taken by riders at small rodeos organized by local ranchers for token prizes, then the transformation of instrumental activities into games of skill and fun do not seem so unusual. Frankly, running the risk of a police arrest seems to be a lot less dangerous than riding an enraged steer in a rodeo.

Although the rationality of such a caper can be found by inquiring into delinquent values at any given time, the attitudes of researchers affect this kind of inquiry. Healy and Bronner believe that theft for monetary reward reflects the activity of rationally motivated human beings, while other kinds of acts, on the surface, appear to be committed "for no apparent reason." But why are immoral acts obviously rational only when they pursue money? Why should pecuniary motivation be a preeminently self-evident category, while other delinquent motives mirror irrationally motivated behavior? Perhaps the tendency to label acts as irrational and nonutilitarian, if they are not aimed at economic gain, reveals more about the bourgeois perspectives of theorists than it does about the motivated character of delinquent behavior?

Sentiments and Habituated Conduct

Thus far we have argued that psychoanalytic theorists ignore reality when they explain delinquent self-awareness and the motivated character of the delinquent act. Certainly, some delinquent youth are emotionally disturbed personalities, but even the most violent acts committed by delinquent youth are usually not irrational. The motivated character of these acts is frequently apparent to people who understand the language adopted in peer conversation. On the other hand, it should also be recognized that there are delinquent acts whose motivations are so taken for granted they are not usually accompanied by highly reflexive activity. Instead, in such cases the motivational and ethical character of the acts is primarily due to personal sentiments, "feelings," or "emotions."

Sentiments are emotions associated with the thought of an object or relationship, and they are produced by psychosocial processes that condition the higher nervous system. They can be expressed to some degree when people are asked, for instance, how they *feel* about such things as male supremacy, narcotics consumption, or American foreign policies. However, sentiments are important because they often operate below the level of immediate awareness, and they replace the necessity for contemplating alternative courses of action. Instead of requiring people to make an effort to think actively about conduct, sentiments regulate conduct emotionally because personal reactions to circumstance have been habituated through prior experiences. Sometimes individuals are not fully aware of their sentiments because the modeling that cultivated the sentiments occurred without any reflection on the modeling process itself. Thus, children often model their aggressive behavior after their parents, and as a result they acquire a low threshold for violent reactions. However, these children are not likely to be fully aware of the identification processes that created these reactions. Nor are they likely to develop very active modes of self-conscious thought that would strongly regulate their aggressive reactions. Consequently, they respond directly to threat or frustration with violence, and their acts are rarely mediated by elaborate symbolic processes calling for self-scrutiny and rationalizations.

Such direct responses are important because they imply another level of behavior dynamics, which can occur independently of peer conversations. We have indicated that persuasive conversations may figure importantly in the beginning phase of social experiences that lead to habitual delinquent behavior. They may play an important role in cultivating the kinds of sentiments likely to encourage participation in delinquent situations. But once these sentiments are established, there is no longer any necessity to discuss and rationalize further delinquent behavior unless new circumstances require additional reckoning and justifications. Furthermore, since some youth may have acquired similar sentiments in the family, they may not even bother to engage in conversations encouraging the sentiments to begin with. They simply act according to the way they feel about the situation. Such socialization is implicated by older adolescents, who report they "snap it right up" whenever an opportunity for illegal gain presents itself. Two 18-year-olds whose delinquent careers we had followed for three years remarked in an interview (that took place a few hours after the crime): "We weren't planning a robbery but we seen the [clothes cleaning] store and said let's go and do it. We did it because it was close [to the place they were rooming at the time] and close to where we could get away." While discussing the events leading to other thefts they had committed, one of the boys remarked: "It's just like you were in a family and you got up *to get a drink of water* because you feel thirsty. You just get up and do it."

Some peers become involved in delinquency habitually because they internalize sentiments based, for instance, on loyalty, which support pragmatic accommodation to group standards. While they may internalize the loyalty, they may not necessarily internalize sentiments that legitimate the standards themselves. However, other peers (and especially the more powerful group members) usually internalize sentiments pertaining to group standards. This internalization results in a *sense of rightness,* which displaces the need to engage in ethical discourse unless the moral character of their acts is called into question by peers or adults. Although it may not be expressed verbally, this sense of rightness is sometimes made explicit when delinquent youth support their victimization with derogatory social type names or phrases that are charged with moral indignation.

Finally, the most egoistic forms of individualism operate at a deep level of consciousness. In addition to being readily supported by peers, they are reinforced by ethical standards that impart a sense of rightness to the narcissism and indifference characterizing so many adolescents in our society. Among delinquent youth, the sentiments that support illegal acts can also be acquired in childhood or adolescence, with peers, parents, or other adults. Whether these youth rationalize their acts on any given occasion depends upon their previous experiences. It depends on whether they have already acquired a sense of rightness, making the moral implications of the act irrelevant and tacitly mobilizing peer conversations toward ways of committing the act without guilt. If the sense of rightness is acquired, then the act may also take place without the expression of any moral justifications.

NOTES

1. The general orientation for our view is contained in C. Wright Mills (1940).
2. The development of such instrumental patterns in early childhood may have correlative effects that psychoanalysts mistakenly isolate as causes. Both the personality disturbances (reflected in diffuse anxiety or hostility) and the child's highly generalized instrumental definitions may be the effects of the peculiar ethical relationships observed by the Gluecks. The personality disturbances in this case may not necessarily be the cause of instrumental attitudes on the part of the child. Both the disturbances and the attitudes may arise because the child has not yet learned to, or is unable to, symbolically specify the persons and situations in which manipulation is likely to occur.

Adolescents are able to specify these relationships more readily because of discourse with peer-group members.

3. The concept, "mobilization of bias," is derived from Bachrach and Baratz (1970). This concept refers to the selection of some issues or topics as important and others as not important. The bias is therefore demonstrated by the absence of issues or topics in conversations. It is not only shown by the issues that people talk about because they consider them important.
4. Merton (1938:136, n7), however, believes that violation of the legal norms evokes a sense of guilt. For example, "It is unlikely that interiorized norms are completely eliminated. Whatever residuum persists will induce personality tensions and conflict. The process involves a certain degree of ambivalence . . . manifestations of this unrelieved tension . . ." Also, concepts such as "attributions of legitimacy" and "moral implications of the act" in other sociological writings fulfill the same function as guilt in psychoanalytic usage (Cloward and Ohlin, 1960:130–39; Sykes and Matza, 1957). Obviously, we differ from these standpoints because we do not believe that the alleviation of guilt is necessary for committing delinquent acts.
5. See, for example, Cloward and Ohlin (1960:111–12). They say that frustrated working-class boys who attribute the "origin or personal failure to others" become delinquent. The psychoanalysts have also referred to delinquent "psychopaths" in a similar fashion. See, also, the section on "Injustice Collectors" by Berger (1948:48).
6. "There is no accounting in rational and utilitarian terms for the effort expended and the danger run in stealing things which are often discarded, destroyed, or casually given away" (Cohen, 1955:26).
7. Again, vocabularies of motive, such as "kicks," "for the fun of it," or "for the hell of it," also have other usages.
8. The original source of this example is Shaw (1933:8). It is used by Cloward and Ohlin (1960:164) to illustrate how "delinquent role preparation and role performance may be integrated even at the 'play group' stage of illegitimate learning." Cohen (1955:26) uses the same incident to illustrate a very different point about the "negativistic" or "malicious" character of delinquent behavior.

13

Sexism, Masculinity, and Virtues of Violence

While capitalism has not invented violence, it gives birth to conditions that reproduce violence anew. Furthermore, these conditions generate the existential realities that link masculinity with violence and femininity with nonviolence.[1] Under these conditions, women undergo early childhood experiences that reduce their engagement in most antisocial forms of conduct. The differential in regard to violence, however, is most significant. Women act far less violently than men, whose character structures are more closely aligned with the exploitative requirements and industrialization of the capitalist mode of production. Also, men retain a monopoly over weapons and training for war, and these relationships reinforce male aggression. Consequently, it is not surprising that with respect to crimes based on personal victimization, such as robbery, assault, and rape, female criminality can hardly be compared to criminality among men.

Sexual Fetishism of Violence

The synchronization between masculinity and violence and femininity and nonviolence is cultivated ideologically. Everywhere in the United States, for instance, the mass media display the archetypal images of men whose innate violence is presumably acted out in myriad situations. These media portrayals also leave a lasting impression: male aggression, rather than socioeconomic relationships, appears to be the fundamental source of violence in general.

Furthermore, in everyday life this synchronization appears to be firmly rooted in biological differences. Two sets of conditions create this appearance. First, the relationship between violence and gender may be perceived first-hand within one's family relationships, while the sociohistorical determinations of this relationship are not experienced directly. That is, the face-to-face relations are readily observable, but the historical relationships are understandable only by theoretical reflection; they simply cannot be understood on the basis of daily life.

Second, the weight of our cultural traditions favors biological explanations of social relationships. This is true especially whenever sexual, racial, or other biological traits seem obviously correlated with social relationships that are seen day after day—women and kitchens, blacks and menial jobs. Thus, the personal appearances of things are influenced by preexisting interpretations of reality, and under these conditions it is not surprising that the relationship between violence and gender seems to validate natural facts of life established from birth by genetic differences between men and women.

Such relationships underly what we call the *sexual fetishism of violence*. At the earliest level of religious evolution, fetishism was expressed by the deification of various things or objects (fetishes) to which mysterious supernatural forces were attributed. Male idols, for instance, were attributed vast powers of destruction, and female figures were associated with fertility and the force of life. Modern-day fetishes have similar qualities, although they do not necessarily involve religious symbols. In the case of the sexual fetishism of violence, the powers for determining war, crimes of violence, dictatorships, and colonial oppression are attributed to the nature of man, often in contrast to the nature of woman.

Thus, in this context, human relations are fetishized when social facts are collapsed or converted into natural ones. Fetishism is involved when complex social relations are explained on the basis of natural or supernatural laws "governing" the power of people or things. When people take for granted that nature has made men predators toward women or, for that matter, made them predators toward all other living things, violence is itself fetishized sexually. Here, the category of gender substitutes for the real social determinations of violence in general, as well as sexual violence in particular.

Finally, since people have fetishized violence sexually for thousands of years, their sexual stereotypes operate as archetypal reference points for self-identity. Today, many men actively represent themselves and are emotionally conditioned by these symbolic relationships. Regulating their behavior stereotypically, they believe in ready-made axioms and other "essential truths" about sexual relationships. They feel an obligation to act benevolently toward women who submit willingly to their "innate desire" for mastery, but they easily find justifications for violence when women are "ungrateful." They believe, too, that when women submit willingly, it denotes a natural passivity; although, on occasion, women can be dangerous. And, despite the logical contradictions, they are equally convinced that whenever women do become their enemies, the Machiavellian tendencies lurking deep in their feminine hearts are revealed.

Such stereotypic notions characterize the fetishism of violence. But again, since many forms of violence are fetishized sexually in everyday life, the words "man," "masculinity," and "machismo" stand for more than male domination of women. In the grammar of motives, these words serve as master symbols of male violence in general. In all sorts of circumstances, these words associate masculinity with violent power and domination: thus, they glorify violent sports, glamorize war, and idealize ruthless businessmen. Violence is even separated ideologically from its myriad ends and conditions; and, in this context, it appears to validate masculine ideals all by itself.

This sexual fetishism helps us understand why some men also define sexual violence against men as an affirmation of "manhood." Davis (1968:15–16), who studied homosexual rape in Philadelphia jails and prisons, for instance, says, "A primary goal of the sexual aggressor, it is clear, is the conquest and degradation of his victim. We repeatedly found that aggressors used such language as 'Fight or fuck,' 'We're going to take your manhood,' 'You'll have to give up some face,' and 'We're gonna make a girl out of you.' Some of the assaults were reminiscent of the custom in some ancient societies of castrating or buggering a defeated enemy."

Davis (1968:15–16) suggests that these sexual assaults are not primarily caused by sexual deprivation. He concludes: "They are expressions of anger and aggression prompted by the same basic frustrations . . . [which] can be summarized as an inability to achieve masculine identification through avenues other than sex."

Denied other avenues for expressing their "manhood," male prisoners displace their frustration in rape. Davis' observations, in our opinion, are valid, yet his psychoanalytic, causal explanation is not.

Whatever its form, rape and other forms of violence are mediated by socially acquired attitudes; and even though it can be catalyzed by a sense of frustration, it is vitally important to recognize that this violence occurs regardless of whether or not men are experiencing any deprivation at all. The validation of personal "manhood" through violence is conditioned by the social experiences underlying sexual inequality and by the sexual fetishism of violence. Its expression is not necessarily restricted to frustrating conditions and defense mechanisms. Furthermore, as we have noted, the degree to which this fetishism is actually used by individuals to justify violence is strongly influenced by personal motives that are supported by definable sets of economic, political, and ideological conditions (Schwendinger and Schwendinger, 1983).

Social scientists are aware that delinquents equate manhood with toughness and the monopoly over violence, but there is ambiguity about whether this attitude toward manhood is centered only in the working class. For instance, Miller (1958), among others, indicates that "lower-class" boys are concerned with being "tough," "hard," "fearless and undemonstrative"; conceptualizing women as "conquest objects"; and favoring "masculinity" and not "effemininity." He attributes these concepts of manhood to centuries-old working-class traditions. But Adorno, Frenkel-Brunswick, Levinson, and Sanford (1950) also report a strikingly similar "masculine component" in "Ethnocentric" adult respondents who were drawn almost exclusively from the *middle class*. These respondents denied any "tender feelings" toward others, and they defined the woman's role "as one of . . . passivity and subservience" (1950:476–77). They perceived themselves as "active, tough, powerful, masculine," as opposed to "weak, soft, passive and homosexual" (1950:855–57). If such similarities undermine Miller's attribution of "masculinity" and "toughness" to singular working-class traditions, what should be said about Thorstein Veblen (1953), who equated masculine domination primarily with predatory exploits by *ruling-class* men?

The same points should be made about adolescent formations. More extreme forms of violence can be found among working-class streetcorner groups than among middle-class socialite groups. However, although the streetcorner formations are somewhat more violent than the socialite, the latter are certainly more violent than members of nonstradom formations. In fact, members of socialite groups share attitudes about masculinity and femininity with members of streetcorner formations. This brings us to the related topic of sexual exploitation. Let us further compare the formations regarding attitudes toward girls.

Sexism in Stradom Relations

The male's instrumental and sexist views of female peers further illustrate the similarities between these types of youth. The tendency to justify exploitative sexist relations in stradom formations is revealed by the frequent use of the familiar stereotypes that broadly divide females into "good" girls or "nice" girls. Among youth observed by us, these types were frequently operationalized by youth who differentiated "good, clean girls" from "the girls who have been 'made' by a lot of guys." Such a definition is aphoristically represented in this sarcastic verse uttered by a Soc boy:

> A "Good Girl" goes on a date, goes home and goes to bed.
> A "Nice Girl" goes on a date, goes to bed and goes home.

Victimization of the girl who treats the boys "nicely" is seen as justifiable; moreover, in this case, sexual exploitation adds to a boy's sense of honor among the brotherhood. When "steady dating" becomes as established mode during high school, Soc boys remark: "When you take out a girl you think about two things. Either you think the girl is a whore and you can get her. Or you can take her to a disco and get something to eat and just have fun."

Soc boys frequently look upon the streetcorner girls as the "Nice Girls" who like to go on a date, go to bed, and go home, although not all streetcorner girls are perceived this way. "You can spot a whore Ese girl from the other Ese girls right away," says Bob, a leading Soc, "They wear long silver earrings and tight clothes and usually they are pigs. You can't tell the difference with a Soc girl. You have to work on her to find out."

To many Soc boys, the line between "Good Girls" and "Nice Girls" often becomes tenuous, and the former may become transformed into the other "overnight." "It doesn't hurt a guy's reputation," says John who is in Bob's club, "but if a girl does it one time and the boy has a big mouth—she's typed. That means she's fair play for everybody." The fact that the newly "ruined" girl may have serious problems because of this change in reputation does not seem to matter greatly. She becomes "fair game," and that is all there is to it. In a roughly similar fashion, Greaser boys type girls they respect as "women" or "chicks" and girls they don't respect as "boxes" or "cunts."

Perhaps more fundamental is the tendency to define love as well as the girl in instrumental terms. Let us take as an example a dispute about this matter by three Soc boys: George, Harvey, and Paul. The boys were arguing about "how far" a girl should go in meeting their sexual needs. George flatly claimed that "If a girl loves your ass she will do anything for you." Harvey agreed and emphatically declared: "That's right! If she is in love with you." But when Paul objected and said: "I know some girls who won't," George countered: "Then those girls probably never *loved* anyone. A virgin has to love to go down on a guy but a whore loves to go down. There's the difference!"

In such hard-nosed and egotistical interpretations of a loving relation, a girl is obligated to conform ultimately to a boy's sexual desire. As Harvey said, "If two persons are going to get together for a long period of time, then any girl, no matter how virgin, is going to go for it." Further, the girl is defined in this light as placing a greater premium on sexual relations herself. "It's my theory," Harvey exclaimed, "that girls like sex more than boys do. But they can't do it because they are scared. They are worried about their reputation and they are ignorant."

Whether there is any truth to such speculation is far less significant than the facile and self-serving attribution of fear, ignorance, or inability to love for understanding why girls withhold their sexuality from boys. Inability to "perform" adequately in this regard is seen as "her problem," since the girl is defined by her so-called "natural interests." However, contrary to psychoanalytic premises that are guided by similar sexist biases as to what constitutes the nature of female desires, male supremacy and the instrumental attitudes among stradom boys determine such definitions of the girls. Under these conditions, there is a rational and practical quality about George's rule of thumb: "Before you break up with a girl you try all you can to make her. If you don't like her anymore." As long as no other desirable interests are in conflict, she is "fair game."

Such terms do not exist in isolation from the antinomian conflicts that pervade adolescent relationships. For example, after accommodating to male domination, the girls are under great pressure to organize their personalities around themselves as objects that are valued as sexually attractive things. However, this organization develops in conflict with other values. As a result, the girls experience anxiety because they are forced, on one hand, to conform to standards that estimate personal worth on their clothing and physical appearance, and, on the other hand, they must cultivate personality characteristics that encourage noncompetitive, trusting, and compassionate relationships with other girls as well as boys.

An instrumental view of females is similar among streetcorner boys. In its most extreme form, adolescents in the peer formations evaluate the desire for love on the part of a girl as a sign of weakness. Her desire is seen as a manipulative handle to be used for sexual exploitation. An example of this view is apparent in an incident related by Billy, a streetcorner boy. He exclaimed one evening: "You know that stupid broad, Helen? She's crazy about me. She will do *anything* for me. I scored with her last night in the car and when we were just finished, Mike came by and said that he was stood up by his Chick. I saw that he was feeling bad and asked Helen to help him get his gun off. At first she didn't want to go for it, but I said that if she really loved me she would do me the favor. She finally did it."

Alongside conceptions of women that imply quite different social relationships based on respect, friendship, and love, the sexist exploitation of girls is common to all stradom formations. However, the girls themselves, to some degree, resist this exploitation, although their success varies depending on stradom conditions. For instance, during junior high school, the groups rapidly developing into female socialite formations frequently exert greater control over sexual relationships with boys than do groups developed by streetcorner girls. Never developing anything comparable to the complex sorority club systems that anchor socialite formations among girls during high school, the girls from streetcorner formations have less effective support from peers. Lacking such group support, the streetcorner girl's relations with the boys are much more determined by the boy's interest in sexual by-play and intercourse. By middle adolescence, sexual by-play and promiscuity also exist among the socialites, but it continues to be more extensive and exploitative in the streetcorner domains. Like many other conditions that are outside their personal control, such relations become interpreted by the girls as the "way things are," and even as a sign of acceptance and status by others.

Not only do the socialite girls feel the pressure to resist exploitation from club sisters who are their status equals, but the boys in Soc domains are sometimes influenced as well. Boys can also develop a reputation for "going too far" and be turned down systematically by girls with regard to dating or invitations to parties. By middle adoescence, an entire fraternity can be ostracized by popular girls' groups because individual members are not "kept in line" by the boys. Group support of this sort among girls is highly infrequent and short-lived among streetcorner girls. The streetcorner boys do not have to accommodate to the girl's interests to the same degree, and they can be unscrupulous in their relations with girls to a greater degree.

Heteosexual relations are varied in the stradom formations. Besides exploitation, they also include romantic love based on friendships that grow from solving problems together, from compassion, sympathy, and sexual gratification, which is perceived as a mutually satisfying event by the boy as well as the girl. However, under certain conditions this perception fades as exploitative relations with women become significant. Especially for those girls classified as "pigs" or "whores," the boys feel entitled to sexual favors on demand.

Class, Community, and Violence

We have discussed similarities in conceptions of masculinity and sexually exploitative practices among the stradom formations; however, we have also indicated that the streetcorner male formations are usually (but not always) more violent than other formations. This section will discuss some of the ideological conditions that support the very violent conduct developing, especially among streetcorner groups, in certain kinds of urban communities.

A few caveats are in order here. First, we must emphasize again that the violence in question should not be attributed to working-class traditions. Unfortunately, in the media, physical violence is frequently equated with a mentally deficient "ape"; and, often as not, he wears a "hard hat" and a "blue collar" and has a pick or shovel in his hand. While working-class families may have a higher incidence of physical aggression and may even rely more than middle-class families on corporal punishment in child-raising, any deductions made from this behavior should avoid the common stereotyping of working-class males. Some aggression, of course, is cultivated in many working-class families, but extreme violence is not. On one hand, the ability to fight during boyhood is encouraged by working-class fathers who teach their sons how to defend themselves more effectively. The contact between sons and fathers is often physical contact when they playfully wrestle on the living room floor or test and admire each other's strength lifting heavy objects or flexing their arm muscles. This fighting and wrestling is supported by a large complex of manual occupational and sports activities that is greatly valued by working-class men. Middle-class men also place important emphasis on body contact, especially in sports, even though physical prowess may be less important for their occupational activities.

Regardless of their own aggressiveness, most adults attempt to restrict violent behavior. Socialites usually refrain from extreme forms of violence because, for the most part, adult sanctions effectively restrict violence in their immediate communities. Thus, it is in circumstances where adult controls are weakest that socialite formations become more aggressive, physically engaging in sporadic fights and drunken brawls. For instance, aggressiveness heightens when these youth are away from the community at beaches or other vacation spots in summertime. Also, they sometimes engage in "spontaneous" riots with boys from other schools after highly competitive sports events, when emotions are peaked. But these "riots" are rare compared to the violent conflicts between streetcorner groups occurring in communities where adults are less able to restrict violent behavior. Under these conditions, violent manipulation often dominates all the other ways in which stable forms of reciprocity can be maintained. (There is no more persuasive argument than the use of a fist.) Unless the weaker boys can form alliances with those more powerful, even their ability to speak well in their defense is ineffective, and violence or its threat preempts the field. When this happens, the weight of regulatory influences is shifted from rule-governed conduct to regulation by power alone. Group stability under these conditions becomes dependent upon the ability to establish defensive alliances and attract more powerful members. When such developments accompany the evolution of stradom relationships, they provide their own impetus to the growth of violence.

Thus, the ideological factors (such as the fetishism of violence) that support physical aggression by males are part of the life experiences that affect adolescents outside as well as inside the stradom formations. But these factors are mediated by class conditions. Consequently, compared with middle-class youth who are outside these formations, working-class outsiders may become more familiar with and tolerant of fighting. However, being more exposed to violence does not necessarily lead to the extreme forms of violence (such as gang-fighting) sometimes found in stradom formations. These extremes have somewhat independent determinants that cannot be understood by merely comparing the amount of fighting or wrestling between individual youth.

In fact, gang fighting is especially rare during boyhood even among working-class youth; and there are vast differences between two young boys fighting according to specified rules (a fighting code) and the extremely dangerous forms of fighting that occur between delinquent groups in later years. Finally, it is important to recall that, despite the tolerance of a certain amount of violence at home for preadolescent working-class boys, people in all classes oppose the delinquent's use of deadly weapons. Adults are not generally tolerant of gang fighting, and the unrestricted use of violence among certain working-class delinquents is by no means favored by "centuries-old working-class traditions," as Miller claims—no matter how much individual fighting is accepted by working-class youth.

On the other hand, as a general rule, working-class streetcorner formations are more violent than the other stradom formations in the city as a whole. Once again, there are variations. Streetcorner stradom standards interact with the long-term effects of socioeconomic conditions on community life, and since the conditions that restrict extreme violence are more prevalent in middle-class communities, the overall level of violence among middle-class streetcorner youth is lower than among working-class streetcorner groups. However, the differential is not uniform. Within different communities, each on a higher socioeconomic level, the higher the level, the smaller the difference in violence between the stratified domains. Especially in affluent communities, bourgeois streetcorner boys are not much more violent than the socialite boys.

What are the characteristics of community relationships that affect the levels of violence among streetcorner domains? Extreme forms of violence are frequently concentrated within communities that lack stability and cohesion as a result of certain adverse socioeconomic conditions. These adverse conditions give free reign to the conditioning of violence. Perlman's account of the resettlement of the *favelados* into housing projects in Rio De Janeiro (discussed in Chapter 2) provides an example of how crime can increase because of the destruction of mutual-aid networks developed among families and friends. Variations in stability and cohesion affect communities in the United States as well. It has been found that working-class communities with specialized and direct links to the larger industrial economy are characterized by the highest levels of stability and internal cohesion. (These links include labor market conditions that support higher employment, higher wage levels, and income equality, especially among racial groups.) The presence of industrial jobs and the consequent presence of large numbers of manufacturing workers increases the residential stability of urban neighborhoods, while their absence has just the opposite effect (Yancey and Ericksen, 1979:259–60). It is the nonindustrial areas that are most vulnerable to abandonment and subsequent inflow by underemployed minorities and other highly marginal work forces (1979:258). However, economic crises affect all areas of the economy, including the industrial. When communities—industrial or nonindustrial—become unstable and lack cohesion, the possibilities for the conditioning of violence through direct experience or through modeling and self-reinforcement increase. When everyday community relationships do not actively restrict these forms of violence, the interpersonal relations established by violent parents, other adults, and peers provide the kinds of unrestrained social models that perpetuate and expand violence among children and adults.

The ideological supports for extreme forms of violence can also come from other kinds of community relationships. For instance, in some cases, the rationalizations that justify violence are dependent on the kinds of status rivalries that emerge in any given community. In certain communities, neighborhood "turfs" are the social space in which adolescents must prove that they can "stand up as a man." Frequently, however, these turfs are in impoverished communities where the streetcorner domains completely dominate status relationships. In fact, streetcorner youths may account for the only sizeable peer domain in the community, and the violent struggle for honor, under these conditions, revolves around the competition between streetcorner formations from the beginning of junior high school. Living in such a community, Carlos, a streetcorner boy, says: "In my territory that's the way they are now. That's the way we are. It seems to be the neighborhood that is the thing. You want to prove yourself to nobody but these people." "These people" are the other streetcorner youth who live in his neighborhood or in surrounding neighborhoods. Carlos and his friends, of course, do make comparisons with other types of youth, but these types are by no means status competitors. They are called Lames because they cannot defend themselves against violence at all, or Homos because they have no courage, or Brains or Study Dudes because they appear to be much more interested in school than in peer relationships. School, of course, has little or no attraction for many members of streetcorner formations who find greater respect or enjoyment from stradom relationships in their local communities. Johnny proudly admits that he prefers to be a Bad Dude "because there is more respect for the Bad Dudes than there is for the Study Dudes. 'Specially the girls, they say: 'Hey! I go for *him.*' It just seems to be that way."

There are also communities where the violent struggle for honor may engage a different constellation of types and values. In communities with a heterogeneous socioeconomic composition, streetcorner youth, in the eyes of most peers, have little honor and few possessions, and they are status inferiors, especially when compared to status groups from the other stratified domains. Most of these streetcorner youths can only dream about prestige through the adoption of conspicuous modes of consumption. A 15-year-old streetcorner boy poignantly reveals this wishful thinking: "Every time I see some guy cruising down the street . . . like I see Johnny's car [which is] real sharp looking . . . it makes me feel good. Like, why do people look and dress nice? Cars are the same thing. If you dress good, you feel good at the same time. If you get a ratty looking car you feel like hiding anytime a Cadillac pulls alongside of you. You got a nice car . . . and some Cadillac pulls alongside and you can say, 'I'm as good as he is'." The streetcorner youth living in this type of community grapples with this inferiority, in part, by emphasizing new rules by which the status game is played. This status maneuvering is structured by the rhetoric of egoism, but it is also organized around the youth's accommodation to the increasing violence characterizing his peer relationships. Under these circumstances, when making status judgements, the streetcorner boys compensate by elevating their own standards of virtuous behavior. Again, such compensation occurs because streetcorner youths *already* place great value on violence and on status relationships among stratified domains.[2] They engage in these compensatory maneuvers because they do care what peers in these domains say about them.

Rhetoric about Violence

During the first phase of stradom development, streetcorner boys in heterogeneous communities must deal with their own status. They collectively counter the deeply-felt negative judgements (directed toward them) by shifting the dimensions for evaluating personal worth. They contrast themselves, for example, with the Socs but emphasize their own honorific qualities. "An Ese is a guy who is not a snob," says Gus. "In Spanish, 'Ese' means Dittybop or Gigolo. To us we're the best group. To them [Socs] they're the best group. They have the education while we got the strength. That way it balances out. They make fun of you in class while we make fun of them in the street. It balances out that way."

"Look it," Gus adds, "a Soc, you know, looks down on an Ese. Because of his hair style and clothes. And an Ese doesn't have the money. So a Soc will look down on an Ese and an Ese will look down on a Soc. Look it . . . you kick a Soc's ass . . . you know . . . you kick him and you stomp him. You make him a big bloody mess. His buddies are gonna look at him and then look at you and say, 'Who's the best fighter?' They will say the Ese is the best fighter. They will look up to you as the best fighter. Even if they say you are a dirty fighter at least they say you won." Of course, this shift invokes standards of virtuous behavior that are not as highly validated by socialite stradom formations. The differences between the two types are widely recognized, and as Sally, a Low Soc girl, points out: "A Socialite is only interested in popularity. An Ese is one who thinks that they are tough and impresses others with this."

Although streetcorner youth have been romanticized, and theorists have accorded them laudable desires for equality (and indeed these boys adopt a democratic rhetoric when questioned by authoritative adults about why they fight), it is not a democratic ethic that really moves them.[3] If they possessed the power and wealth, they would use other means to usurp the Socs' prestige.

This possibility is indicated when streetcorner youth defensively shift the axis of comparison toward violent standards. With increasing emotion, for instance, the Socs are condemned while Whitey lauds his violent companions. "The Socs are afraid to put something in their hands," Whitey exclaims. "They do it . . . and if you have something [a weapon, too] . . . they'll just run! Some of these Socs have a bad [i.e., "tough"] reputation. But if you step up to them and say, 'I'll take on any number of you . . . I'll take on ten of you!' they have you outnumbered. They can kill you! There are so many of them that they can tear you to pieces! [But] I tell them, 'Who is gonna be the first one to hit the ground?' I tell them, 'Like, if I go down, I'm gonna take about three of you with me!' That gets them. And nobody steps out."

Melodramatically, Whitey emphasizes the virtue of courage in the face of impossible odds: "But if somebody badder than all of us

[Eses] walked up to us and said, 'I'll take on any three of you guys . . . I don't care who they are!' [Then] three of us will step up and there won't be no worry about who's gonna get it first. We'd all start swinging and we wouldn't stop until somebody gave. If we got mad enough and he said, 'I quit!', I don't think any of us would quit until there was blood or something."

Finally, Whitey righteously assures us that fidelity to the group absolutely demands this violent struggle for honor: "There is one thing our club puts straight, man. No one is gonna call our club Punk. I don't care how big he is or how old he is. The Soc that says to me, 'I think you club is Pimp, man!', you say to him, 'O.K., man, you step to the corner.' You try to fight for the club even if the guy knocks you down. You can quit, man, but at least you proved to your friends that you tried, man. If you didn't prove, *your ass is out*! That way you fight someone and he kills your ass. You still know yourself . . . and he knows as well . . . that he was wrong. These guys in the club aren't Punk. They are still willing to fight for what they thought was right."

Status maneuvering by streetcorner formations also gives their members an additional basis for making comparisons with the Socs. Jackie observes thoughtfully: "You can say that there are Ese climbers like there are Socialite climbers." Looking back to his junior-high-school days, a leader of a streetcorner gang recalls, "We all thought the same way about different things in junior high. We liked the crowds and thought the same thing about life. We wanted to get the best reputation . . . who can fight the best. In junior high the important thing was whether you were bad; if you were a conqueror or not a conqueror!"

Consequently, members of streetcorner formations are aware of the fact that they cannot win according to the rules established among other types of peer formations. It is not merely that the rules were not made for them. Streetcorner boys wryly comment that no one asked them for their opinion of what constitutes "fair play" in the first place. It is rather that they are not made for these rules. Some of them realize also that race, ethnicity, or relative poverty deprives them of attributes necessary for even making a good show. In their eyes, conformity to the general codes by which honor is assigned involves humiliation. Collectively maneuvering within the logic of their egoistic rhetorics and the ethos established by their stradom formations, these youth fashion their moral conceptions of the way things are from justifications for their preexisting patterns of behavior. "When a Soc fights," Bill declares, "he fights on his honor or something like that. When the Ese fights . . . he fights to win. When I fought that Nelson, the first thing he did was put up his fists like that. The first thing I did was start to kick him. The Soc doesn't expect you to kick him and it hurts like hell when you kick him in the balls. When you kick him you have four things on your side: two feet and two fists. So you're bound to win when he has only two things [his fists]. The thing is to win fair or win bad. One or the other is O.K. as long as you win."

When community conditions reinforce violence, the development of this kind of rhetoric heralds a change in the perception of the streetcorner youth's own behavior. In this development, the emphasis on the ability and desire to win, no matter the means, objectifies standards of courageous and honorable conduct. But the rhetoric also emphasizes the idealizations now being given lip service by streetcorner boys when they consider how to regulate their own responses to threat. In these idealizations, the willingness to fight according to the conventional rules of the game becomes interpreted as cowardice and inferiority, while the willingness to fight no matter the means or the odds signifies virtuous behavior. The standard of morality has been inverted; virtue and honor have been stood on their heads.

Statements that reveal just how dishonorable the Socs "really are" illustrate how these idealizations tacitly invert the rules of the game that normally enable people to assess the rightfulness of violent responses. For instance, Mousey exclaims: "A Soc knows that when he gets into a fight with and Ese he's gonna lose. He has to have some way to weasel out of it. He can always say, 'He fought dirty, that's why I lost.' Or 'I don't want to fight that guy; he fights dirty.'" Carlos says the same thing in fewer words: "I think a Soc is too chicken-shit to fight dirty."

Perry expresses a similar opinion: "My [junior-high-school] crowd don't stay around here [where the Eses hang out]. But once we had a war with them, throwing Coca Cola bottles with sand at them. I hit one of the girls in the head with a bottle and I walked up to the guy standing there and said: 'Are you gonna let me get away with that?' He didn't do a thing. That's how chicken-shit Socs are."

Some Age Factors and Violence

Toward the end of junior high school, the more thoughtful streetcorner boys recognize that "The Socs will grow up running the businesses, and we'll dig the ditches." However, for most, the attention is on the here and now. Moreover, this attention to the current situation is partly determined by the variation in class composition of the elementary-school districts that feed into the junior high schools. The older girls and boys in elementary school have gone through the status competition required to establish their positions in small streetcorner crowds or groups in the environs of the local elementary school. Junior high school, however, frequently represents the loosening of traditional distinctions among peers and the violent reworking of positional relations. "You're in the group that is in the neighborhood, you know. Everybody knows each other. Everybody knows how you live. When you go to junior high you're going to a place where four or five different schools are coming into one school. At that point I gotta prove that each punk isn't gonna push me," says Jimmy. Recalling his recent experiences in junior high school, George states: "Fighting was the thing. That seemed to be it. That's when you built your reputation." Peter agrees: "In grammar school you have a reputation. In junior high you gotta make your reputation."

However, certainly by senior high school at the latest in heterogeneous communities, streetcorner boys discover what their counterparts in impoverished communities already knew from the start. In heterogeneous communities, the streetcorner boy's elevation of his ability to use violence to achieve status and prevent degradation redirects his attention away from groups of socialites, or other types of formations, to status groups within the streetcorner domains. It becomes recognized that, in the violent struggle for honor, other streetcorner youth are the most qualified contestants. "There is only one Ese and that is the guy that can take anybody else," says Whitey. "Jim Rodriguez can't make a reputation by kicking a Soc's ass in. But if he says that he kicked another Ese's ass who is real bad . . . that makes Jim Rodriguez a bit badder."

Consequently, some of the independent determinants of violence are embedded in the nature of the community, the configurations of adolescent stradom formations, and the honorific codes subscribed to by certain adolescents.

NOTES

1. For instance, we have indicated elsewhere that the allocation of women to social production for use within the family is consequential for character formation (Schwendinger and Schwendinger, 1983b).

2. His violence is not originally generated by compensatory relationships, but compensation does influence the standards by which streetcorner boys evaluate their relations with other types of youth.
3. Note Cloward and Ohlin's (1960:118) stress on a delinquent's belief in the "democratic ideology of opportunity." The delinquent acts are seen as "compensation for the injustice he has suffered from officially supported norms."

IV

PHASIC DEVELOPMENTS AND DELINQUENT MODALITIES

14

Introduction

When we look at social types, we deal with delinquency-producing factors that vary on individual and group levels. Nevertheless there are parallels with regard to delinquency between types of individuals and types of groups. Individual intellectuals (and Brains) and the nonspecific derogatory types, for example, are the least delinquent youth in a peer society. The athletes and nonspecific neutral types fall in-between the least delinquent and the most delinquent types. Delinquent behavior, on an individual level, is concentrated among the socialite, intermediary, and streetcorner youth, and when these types are compared with each other, their levels of delinquency move upward, from the least delinquent socialites to the most delinquent streetcorner youth. When delinquency is analyzed on the level of the group, the major variation in delinquent conduct among peer groups, with the exception of differences in gender, is determined by their social type compositions. Consequently, these groups can also be assigned to a continuum that begins with little or no participation in delinquency by the least delinquent type of group and terminates in frequent engagement in a variety of acts by highly delinquent types of groups.[1] Paralleling the social type differences in individual level of delinquency, delinquent acts are committed more frequently by socialite, intermediary, and streetcorner groups. Among these groups, the incidence of delinquency moves upward from the domain of socialite groups through the intermediary types and peaks within the domain of streetcorner groups.[2]

A comparison between types of groups may be illustrated, in part, by Chambliss' (1973) study of the Saints and Roughnecks.[3] Even though he focused on individual groups rather than entire domains, the main point is still made. Chambliss' study is especially important because of the two-year time period devoted to the observation of two extreme types of stradom formations. The Saints have all the earmarks of a socialite formation, while the Roughnecks are streetcorner boys. Within the context of their high-school district, the Saints come from families with the highest socioeconomic status, and the Roughnecks have the lowest-status families. Family status seemed to count in school. The senior class selected ten seniors as "school wheels," and four of the ten were Saints. Seven of the eight Saints' members went to college, and the remaining boy became a used-car salesman. The Roughnecks, however, hung around a pool hall and were regarded with fear and contempt by community residents, who felt that the boys would end up in jail. These boys regarded school as a burden, and their grade averages were low. Two of the boys never finished high school, and one of them finally ended up in prison with a 30-year sentence for second-degree murder. Still another boy is serving a life sentence for first-degree murder. A fourth boy became a small-time gambler after working as a runner for a bookie. However, when two Roughnecks earned athletic scholarships to college, one of them did an immediate about-face: he adopted a demeanor similar to that of the Saints.

Thus, Chambliss observes, for instance, that the Saints were "eight promising young men—children of good, stable, white upper-middle-class families, active in school affairs, good precollege students—[who] were some of the most delinquent boys at Hannibal High School." The Roughnecks also attended Hannibal High, and their group was composed of "six lower-class boys." Despite the fact that the Saints' overall delinquency rate was about equal to that of the Roughnecks, *not one member* of the Saints group was officially arrested for any misdeed during the two years Chambliss observed the groups; the Roughnecks, however, were in constant trouble with the police.

The Saints were involved repeatedly in truancy, drinking, wild (and drunken) driving, vandalism, and petty theft. The Roughnecks duplicated this gamut of delinquent activities, but their thefts were estimated to be slightly higher, on the average, and they were more prone to violence. Although most of their fights occurred within the group, there were also rare instances when the group fought two blacks, a gang across town, and some boys from another school.[4] (On the other hand, while the Saints never fought, they endangered the lives of others with pranks such as removing street excavation signs that warned motorists of hazardous conditions.) On the whole, the Saints seemed to offend the law more frequently, but the Roughnecks engaged in more serious offenses.

Delinquent Modalities in General

When comparing groups, there are other important group qualities that help us understand the differences in types of delinquency. Certain distinct delinquent "modalities" are generated by age-related changes in the peer formations. During the long period of adolescence, the peer formations are altered, and various clusters of delinquent activities are engaged in. For example, during each phase of group development, factors associated with intra- and intergroup relationships determine the delinquent modalities that appear in succeeding phases. Let us first discuss such phases and then the delinquent modalities associated with them.

We were struck by three of these phases of stradom development because of their importance to delinquency. Briefly, the first phase, for all the stratified domains, is organized around the *consumption relations, invidious standards,* and *indifference* regulating the peer styles of life. The second phase centers around *ethnocentric standards* that shape conflict and competition between formations. The third includes peer relationships that sustain *illegal markets* and other forms of *economic criminality.* We do not assume that these phases are the only possible ones behind distinctive constellations of delinquent acts. (Others may be uncovered in peer formations by further research.) Moreover, we also observed departures from these developments: In some communities, for instance, the presence of numerous young adults engaging in criminal activity, right on the street, telescoped the temporal sequencing of the delinquent modalities. The more protracted developmental processes in other communities were shortened as younger adolescents were actively drawn into economic crimes by older teens and young adults. Finally, depending on community conditions, the modalities may appear earlier or later. Ethnocentric conflicts are not inevitable, and they may take a few years to develop in new communities. Even the numbers of youth in stradom formations are important in this context, because small numbers of streetcorner youth, for instance, may prevent the development of an ethnocentric modality. On the other hand, traditional conflicts over territorial interests are readily found in older communities, and if there is a large concentration of poor families in a community, illegal markets are more extensive than those found in highly affluent communities that may have only "minimarkets" restricted to narcotics or a handful of illegal goods such as stolen hi-fi equipment and automobile parts.

Particular Delinquent Modalities

The *generalized* modality, as stated, is highly dependent upon stradom consumption values and invidious relationships, which intensify an egotistical indifference to other people's welfare. It consists of a constellation of delinquent activities including petty thievery, vandalism, truancy, alcohol abuse, individual fighting, and other garden varieties of delinquent acts often referred to as "less serious" than others. The generalized modality also includes a variety of acts, such as "party crashing" or verbal abusiveness to peers and adults, that deviate from conventional rules of moral conduct; however, some of these latter acts, while irregular, are not unlawful. Although the age period for each developmental phase varies somewhat from community to community, the generalized delinquent modality can occur incipiently—in some communities as early as 8 or 9 years of age, when children belong to so-called play groups. However, the preteen years are much more important to this modality, because stradom formations emerge at this time on a much larger scale. The delinquent activities initiated during this first phase by invidious stradom relations and their consumption patterns persist throughout adolescence into young adulthood.

The *generalized* modality occurs on all class levels, but there is some variation in acts between the stradom formations at different periods in their life cycle. Alcohol abuse occurs early among all stradom formations. However, narcotics, at the time of our observations, were not used persistently until middle adolescence, and abuse was heavily (although not exclusively) concentrated within streetcorner formations. The availability of automobiles is also significant, because in the context of the stradom formations it expands the cluster of antisocial behavior that continues to be regulated by consumption values and invidious standards.

Ethnocentric concerns in the second phase, on the other hand, generally influence delinquent behavior significantly at around 14 years of age and decline rapidly at about 17 or 18.

The *ethnocentric* modality is activated by the development, usually around the end of junior high school, of competitive intergroup status structures. This modality includes, among other things, fighting between individuals and groups, vandalism motivated by group rivalries, harmful pledging and hazing practices, and placing graffiti everywhere on walls, stones, and bridges—proclaiming the superiority and power of a collective identity. This modality erupts on all social class levels, but its particular form and intensity varies greatly between stradom formations.

Toward the end of junior high school or at the beginning of senior high school these intergroup properties are generated by the emergence of distinctive clubs and crowds. One aspect of the struggle between these adolescent status groups is the establishment of a grammar of motives that "displaces" or "sublates" the normal expression of violence and subordinates it to such emergent status mechanisms as the honorific codes of individual groups. Of course, the preexisting standards for individual violence continue side-by-side with the newer motives.

This coexistence points to an important phenomenon characterizing the modalities in general. Not only do the developments in each prior stage overlap into the beginnings of the next, but the delinquent modalities can exist *simultaneously* and *interpenetrate* each other. For instance, fighting between individual youths persists throughout the entire adolescent period. Even in the ethnocentric phase, when violent encounters are also determined by the competitive relations between groups, the motivated character of individual fighting, on any given occasion, varies greatly. For this reason, self-report questionnaires cannot differentiate the modalities unless the motivated character of delinquent activities is identified.

The *illegal market modality* usually emerges alongside the others during the middle adolescent period. Along with the ethnocentric modality, it can overlay and interpenetrate the generalized modality. It includes the illegal markets that begin to take shape as thievery or personal services are offered for "sale" rather than "use value" alone. This modality is structured around, but is not wholly confined to, simple commodity exchange relationships, and hence it essentially involves economically oriented delinquent conduct, including robbery, larceny, gambling, and prostitution. In addition, this modality also supports "con games" and other irregular forms of victimization based on callousness and deceit.

This last phase is usually ushered in when youth are approximately 16 years old, and it terminates when illegal adolescent markets merge with adult markets somewhere around the end of adolescence and the beginning of young adulthood. Generally, the illegal market modality becomes concentrated in illegal market activities that engage older youth, who become suppliers and entrepreneurs during the middle adolescent years. However, markets can be activated much earlier among younger adolescents within communities characterized by acute economic deprivation. The forms and intensity of participation in irregular market relations also vary greatly between types of stradom formations. For example, during middle adolescence, among the socialites, thievery is still spontaneous in character, and even preplanned thefts are primarily for personal use. Socs engage in car theft for joy riding and theft of auto accessories for themselves and their friends. (In these acts, there may be no intention of making an illegal sale.)

On the other hand, although some socialites become involved in the demand side of the illegal market, there are exceptions conditioned by preexisting variations in delinquency among Soc formations. Some Soc formations develop a reputation for alcohol and drug use, incessant party-going, and wild escapades, and their groups sometimes become the "deviant poles" of extended networks formed by various Soc formations. The high-school performance of these Socs suffers because of this behavior, and they sometimes "skid" downward socially into the active side of the illegal market, where they engage in drug dealing or undergo rapid personality deterioration because of the frequent use of alcohol or drugs.

However, among the streetcorner formations, especially in poorer communities, distinctly different thieving patterns emerge and persist side by side with the preexisting delinquent modalities. Thievery, especially among subproletarian streetcorner youth, becomes increasingly transformed into serious financial enterprise; and the thievery that is consummated in an exchange for money gives rise to a market in illegal goods. Other kinds of delinquency, such as loan sharking, gambling, and prostitution, also become subordinated to market relationships as the general exchange of illegal goods and services for money begins to affect the final stages of streetcorner stradom developments.

Simultaneously, other pursuits of money through manipulation and extortion resonate with illegal exchange relations. These pursuits give rise to a variety of social types, such as the Dealer and the Hustler, who are equated with particular kinds of informal exploitative methods for sustaining their styles of life. When these other illegal forms emerge, the preexisting varieties of adolescent behavior disintegrate and are replaced by the social relationships that mark the transition to adulthood.

Thus, in sum, each of the delinquent modalities emerges at a different time in the life cycle of the stradom formations. The modalities are grounded in various kinds of social conditions or processes. When these conditions or processes pass away, the modalities either disappear rapidly or gradually lose their distinctive character as they merge with the illegal relationships characterizing adult life.

In the context of these developments, adolescents learn new vocabularies of motive and therefore new motives. (Their delinquent relationships are decidedly not driven by universal motives, as suggested by "opportunity structure" or psychoanalytic theories.) The vocabularies of motive (and the victimizations that are supported by these vocabularies) are dependent upon consumption standards, honorific codes, and human insensitivities that emerge among stradom formations. They are dependent upon the ethical standpoints that characterize these formations.

NOTES

1. The social, and especially ideological, processes that encourage delinquency make engagement in a variety of illegal acts more probable. These processes have been described in previous chapters. The involvement by delinquents in a variety of offenses is mentioned by Cohen (1955), Klein (1972), and Schwendinger (1963). This involvement is quite different from the expectations established by Cloward and Ohlin's concept of independent (criminal, conflict, and retreatist) subcultures.
2. These propositions refer to global comparisons between all stradom formations and nonstradom formations, as well as comparisons between entire domains of stratified formations.
3. Aside from our own work, we know of no other researcher who has simultaneously observed these different types of formations or who has made direct observations for such a long period of time.

4. The Roughnecks seem to be less frequently engaged in intergroup violence than groups we observed. But this might possibly be due to community characteristics that reduce the number of individuals in the streetcorner domain as well as the number of groups in this domain.

15

Small Groups and Status Conflicts

Delinquency usually begins among members of clique formations in the first phase of stradom development; nevertheless, as indicated, delinquent behavior itself is rarely a requirement for establishing adolescent subcultures. Group formations (having socialite or streetcorner styles of life that sustain delinquency) do not develop originally around delinquent goals. Consequently, our observations lead us to believe that theories attributing delinquent activities (or modalities) to the rise of "delinquent subcultures" are incorrect.

Furthermore, the descriptions provided by some authors of violent activities and psychologically disturbed gang leaders also deviate from our observations of delinquent groups. Violent intergroup conflict is usually regarded with trepidation by younger teens, who deliberately identify themselves with a particular group. Generally, only when threats from other groups actually arise do early group deliberations become concerned with defensive responses. On the other hand, within neighborhoods or "territories" already marked by a great deal of intergroup violence, the reputational goals of some groups may reflect concern with their fighting potentialities from the start. Consequently, it is important to mark the periods when types of delinquency occur because of intergroup conflicts and status rivalries. Intergroup violence generally occurs long after patterns of thievery and fighting on an individual, clique, or crowd basis have been established. The relationship between this violence and group structures must also be critically examined.

Group Activities

First, let us examine some of the less-well-"advertised" group activities. During our four years of participant observation, we attended numerous meetings of clubs that authorities would call "fighting gangs." We were even acquainted with an extremely delinquent club (composed partly of middle-class streetcorner youth) that kept minutes of their meetings. We examined the minutes covering a two-year period. The primary topics discussed by members of this streetcorner club differed very little from other clubs. They included plans for hayrides, hunting trips, baseball and football games, and competitions for the fastest and most superbly customized car. Members also argued about when to hold a party, meet at the beach, or hold a dance to raise money. There were periods in which delinquent events such as "gang wars" commanded everyone's attention a good deal of the time. However, in the normal course of events, the actual or potential delinquent activities discussed by these groups did not dominate their conversations.

Streetcorner youth clearly express nonviolent reasons for forming their groups, violent as these groups may become. They say: "We formed [the group] because we wanted to have parties and stuff like that." "We wanted to do things . . . to be known." "We wanted to have friends . . . to be in a club and enjoy ourselves." "We wanted to get the guys in a group and to get to know different people in other clubs." The members of the most violent group we observed always called themselves "a social and athletic club," and their retrospective accounts indicate that the original motives for forming their group had nothing to do with delinquent activities.

Another round of forming groups occurs in middle adolescence, which starts approximately around the end of junior high school or at the latest by the beginning of senior high. New groups are organized, and preexisting ones adopt a more defined public identity. (Some of these groups even formalize their group relationships. They may call themselves "clubs" and adopt such names as "Cavaliers," "Kings," "Majestics," "Debs," and "Mademoiselles.") The formation of such middle-adolescent groups involves a number of interlocking motives, and, certainly among the stradom formations, these motives encourage the cooperation that ensures parties, athletic contests, a place to go, and friends to be with in the context of a typically tedious and boring day-to-day existence. Stradom formations explore many possibilities for an active social life; however, contrary to televised soap operas about adolescent life, this life is not overflowing with interesting, exciting, or, for that matter, devastating events. Typically, a day in the life of the adolescent "hangs," and the adolescent "hangs" with it; he or she is suspended in a meaningless and often suffocating limbo. Countless hours are spent literally just "hanging around" and complaining about it. These youth can at least depend upon the company of their peers to provide some stimulation and enjoyment.

The middle-adolescent groups at least provide a degree of mutual support, prestigious companions, and a common identity. Such functions are revealed by the way good members are distinguished from bad. Phil, who is in the last grade of junior high, says that the good member puts the club first: "What makes the guy a good member? A bitchen guy puts the club first. No bull-shit! You can't rely on a bad member. He goes places without us. He's the kind of a guy that would rather go to the show with his mother and not come to the meeting." Carl emphasizes physical ability and coolness when he classifies a good member. Conformity is also important: "A bitchen guy can take care of himself. He's a cool head. Not a cheap guy. Acts like us. We don't ask any of the guys in the club to dress like us but everyone in the club does just the same." Bill mentions the importance of being a supportive member: "A good guy sticks up for the club; being there when we need him; helping us out." Consistent support from members also means supporting friendly clubs that will reciprocate by helping the club raise money.[1] Bill therefore concludes, "When we give a party, the other clubs help us out. When they give a party—we have to help them get some money in the treasury. If we help them out—there will be more guys coming to our party to help us out. We just got rid of a kid who wasn't going to other parties. He just didn't want to go. He was doing the club harm that way. If everybody just stayed in one group and didn't go to the parties—Man!—nobody would come to our parties."

In its formative stages, the 14- to 15-year-old streetcorner group gives social and athletic functions top priority. At the same time, the group members are sometimes forced to assess new developments and the need to maintain club prestige and integrity by fighting for them. Under intensely competitive intergroup conditions, these new clubs quickly develop a sense of the importance of their fighting ability in determining a club reputation. A desire to attain a "club rep" based on superiority in violent conflicts, in this formative period, is likely to be accompanied by anxiety and ambivalence. While members desire social and athletic activities, they may recognize the possibility of fights and wish to avoid them. Chico, for instance, was the president of a one-month-old club (composed of eleven 14- and 15-year-old members). He was concerned about forming an "alliance" with other clubs partly because it would help to further his group's social goals. He said, "I sometimes think it would be good to get all the clubs together. If we were in one big, good organization with all the clubs—it would be a good alliance and we could throw a party and everybody would have a successful club. Also, no outside clubs would mess with us because we would be strong. There would be no fights."

Chico adds: "We want to get together and go to the beaches and go to the park or something. We are not out to get a bad reputation. We are out to get a good reputation as being known . . . you know . . . and trying to be friendly with different clubs. But you gotta consider there's gonna be some Punks in some clubs. They may be in a bad mood and wise-off at the mouth and maybe you haul off and punch them in the mouth . . . and you have to punch-out with another club." Thus, the use of the alliance, not just for social events but also for mutual defense, is considered by Chico, but almost as an afterthought. As he points out, what else can one expect when there are always "some Punks in some clubs" who are ready to start trouble? Trouble may therefore come to you even when you are not seeking it.

In time, this young club president might come to value different alliances for other reasons. He may develop a personal stake in the reputation associated with the alliance and its membership. He may also become aware that his status within his own group and the cohesion of the group are elevated by conflicts with other groups (Short and Strodbeck, 1962).

Structures of Delinquent Groups

What is the structure of delinquent groups, once they are formed? Attempted typologies have produced a proliferation of classifications such as vertical group formation, kaleidoscopic group, cluster, crowd, solidified group, interest group, area group, klika (cliques), palship, mob, spontaneous gang, traditional gang, splinter clique, club, and near group (Thrasher, 1927:318–23; Richards, 1958, Moore, 1978; Yablonsky, 1959). This typology ranges from the vertical formation, which is a series of stable age-graded formations related by family and propinquity ties, to Yablonsky's "near group," the loosest assortment of peers imaginable because the core members are composed of emotionally disturbed boys.

Was the word "gang" in classical studies always associated with unstable and unstructured groups and emotionally disturbed members? The answer is negative. Instead of distinguishing gang formations on the basis of their instability or lack of cohesion, Thrasher (1927) emphasized the structural variations of such formations. And, although his usage of the word "gang" referred at times to nondelinquent as well as delinquent groups, he never based his observations of groups on the emotional states of their members. He wrote about palships, clubs, alliances, cliques, crowds, intimacies (two- or three-boy gangs), and publics (gangs split into one or more cliques or "parties"). He indicated that a gang may be incorporated into a larger structure such as a syndicate, a ring, or a republic.

The research we performed also indicates that delinquent offenses, such as fighting, thievery, narcotics use, rape, and vandalism, occur in a variety of group contexts. Our research convinces us that a comparative study of adolescent groups (including fraternities and sororities) will show that the differences in structure and stability can usually be explained by relationships other than the group's deviant status. On the other hand, it is true that delinquent streetcorner formations, in particular, are not structured like chapters of national youth-serving organizations or religious and fraternal orders. Most of the latter groups, because of adult influence and even adult guidance, have highly elaborated organizational patterns, with executive boards and standing committees. The lack of such structures among streetcorner clubs reflects the relative absence of repetitive, long-range, complex group tasks as well as of knowledgeable guidance by adults or emulation of adult organizational patterns. Usually, from our observations, the most complex task facing a streetcorner club involves an annual "band dance." For the most part, club goals can be achieved through periodic delegation of discrete "jobs" to members. Committees are sometimes created; however, these are usually not "standing committees" but task groups organized around short-term activities. Sometimes the development of repetitive tasks geared to a series of athletic events, such as basketball or football games with other groups, social affairs such as annual dances or picnics, and even fighting with other gangs, may force delegation of longer-term responsibilities to team captains or war counselors. But the streetcorner group rarely moves beyond this simple delegation of authority, which may be formalized to some extent.

At no time, however, can one equate the degree of structural complexity or clarity with the degree of group stability. To our knowledge, there is no empirical evidence indicating any direct relationship in this respect. There are, of course, many unstable group formations among working-class delinquents. On the other hand, it is extraordinary that the great number of highly stable working-class delinquent groups composed of boys who have literally grown up together from earliest childhood were overlooked by such theorists who believe that stable delinquent groups do not exist (Yablonsky, 1959). Surely, the status and roles among boys who have known each other for years must be crystallized in well-understood ways, whether or not their groups have highly developed formal characteristics.

An account by Juan, a member of the Midget Dukes, gives some idea of how long delinquent youth can be associated with each other. It also illustrates the vertical formation. The Midget Dukes lived in "Flats," a "territory" in Los Angeles composed largely of Mexican–American families. "The youngest guys who join up are about 12 and 13," explains Juan. "The Midget Dukes are mostly 14 to 16, but we got some guys up to 20 in there. The Midgets . . . they really got their eggs [testicles or 'balls'] to fight. One time they were going to knife a cop who slapped them around. Then there is the Vets. They are the older guys. A lot of Midgets have brothers in the Tiny Dukes and the Vets. *Most of us grew up together* in Flats."

If delinquent behavior can be supported by a variety of group structures, then a particular type of group cannot be taken as the causal locus for this behavior. The observation of loosely structured and unstable formations and even isolated delinquents provides the vanishing point on a continuum of groups with high to low degrees of structural complexity and stability. A variety of delinquent acts is distributed throughout this continuum, and no single type of group such as the "near-group" provides the important key to the understanding of delinquency.

We have suggested that, at the level of group relationships, stratified domains of groups should be seriously considered when making a causal analysis of the group processes sustaining delinquency. In the following chapters we point out that within the domains there are numerous types of group formations whose various phases of development initiate changes in delinquent behavior. The general changes in intergroup relationships occurring at the level of domain and interdomain relationships are also important. These changes stimulate intergroup violence because they generate status rivalries among streetcorner formations or between groups from different domains.

Having considered the effects of these competitive intergroup properties on violence, we have concluded that highly unstable group formations are far less important than stable group formations. The fact that unstable groups engage in violence does not detract from the greater theoretical importance of group or territorial names, insignia, jackets, officers, and all the formal trappings of stable group identities for structuring the ethnocentric attitudes and practices in the second phase of stradom development. Through these names and trappings, the more stable groups influence all the varied kinds of group formations within the local society of youth during the middle-adolescent years.

The Ethnocentric Milieu

In every part of town you can see names of teenage clubs painted in bright, splashy colors over highway tunnel walls, the sides of buildings, the pedestrian overpass bridges, the life-guard stations at the beach, and in places so high and so impossible to reach that it seems only a helicopter could have suspended the mad adolescent graffiti artist, who splattered the name of his group there in large luminescent letters. These sprawling signs acclaim the "LEGENDS," the "AMBASSADORS," the "ROYALS," the "HEAD HUNTERS," the "SINNERS," the "FABLES," the "SHAGGERS," the "MIDGET DUKES," the "DEMONAIRS," the "ROAD LORDS," the "ROAD MASTERS," the "KINGS OF THE ROAD," the "ESQUIRES," the "CORSAIRS," the "HUNS," and the "PROPHETS." There are also names that defy understanding without prior clues to the group's major interest: the "LOW-MEN" and the "LOW-RIDERS" are car clubs noted for "dropping" an automobile chassis until it is inches from the ground, and the "GALLOPING GOOSES" is composed of that genre of older motorcyclists who are often called "raunchy cycle-riders" (pronounced "sickle-riders").

The names of these groups seem to range widely in meaning; yet most settle around a few primary referents. These referents function as linguistic logos, informing the public about Glamorous, Popular, Powerful, Threatening, and Prestigeful groups. Like the institutional advertisements for IBM, XEROX, or RCA, which display corporate logos to the public, the club names adopted by youth advertise their own collective images to the local peer society. The named clubs, furthermore, announce their status with an array of formal accoutrements: insignia, titles, offices, club medallions, jackets, metal plaques for car windows, and the like.

The names and images herald a phase of adolescent living and style of life that are best described by the term "ethnocentric." At any given time, one undoubtedly finds the majority of youth within the stradom formations not belonging to named clubs. Most youth may belong to small or large cliques and crowds that have no named identity. Some are even fairly isolated on the fringes of group life. Nevertheless, these youth are influenced by the standards of ethnocentric groups, and they even expect members of named groups to display their identities like badges of honor.

Ethnocentric standards also stimulate interest in the current club or territorial "happenings"; and the incessant peer conversations about club events and group rivalries overshadow the talk about wars between nations, revolutions abroad, and the possible annihilation of the human race in a nuclear holocaust. In many communities there are youth who consider the interactions between named groups to be the most important events in the world, because these groups are the pace-setters for the middle-age peer society. On the other hand, this ethnocentricity is somewhat seasonal. The myths and rumors of group rivalry are intensified when the summer months draw near and streetcorner youth congregate in large groups on the streets, at the hot-dog stands or on the beaches. Varied comments fill the air: "Someone on the East Side told me that White Fence is going to march again!" "Last night one of the Lazy Gents got into a fight with two of the Embalmers! Heads are gonna be cracked open before that's finished with." "There were over a hundred Eses massed in Griffith Park! If the cops didn't break it up there would've been blood all over." "Man! If you think Hitler was bad, you should see the Huns operate!"

What accounts for these ethnocentric delinquent patterns during the middle-adolescent years? Sherif and Sherif (1953; 1956:280–331) have studied violence arising from competition between groups. The Sherifs conducted an experiment in intergroup conflict within a summer camp setting, pitting two nondelinquent groups (formed for the first time at the beginning of the experiment) against each other under competitive circumstances. As the competition heightened, intensive conflict emerged over a period of time and erupted into violence. The Sherifs then contrived a breakdown in the camp's water supply system, creating a crisis that justified cooperation between the groups to solve the emergency. Over time, the experience of cooperative relations while repairing the water supply system markedly reduced the intergroup hostility. At systematic intervals throughout the experiment the members of each group were asked to express their opinions about the members of other groups. The content of these opinions varied directly with the rise and fall in competitive relationships. As the competition heightened, the "out-group stereotypes" (which expressed the attitudes of the members of each group toward other groups) were increasingly charged with negative meanings. The members of the other groups were soon seen as untrustworthy, mean, and petty human beings. When the cooperation between the groups heightened, these negative attributions were replaced by positive ones.

How did the researchers control for other variables that might have caused these attitudinal shifts? Psychological tests had been given to the applicants for the summer camp, and only "well-adjusted, healthy, successful persons whose upbringing had not involved unusual frustrations and uncertainties were accepted" (1956:330). This selectivity allowed the experimenters to conclude that the negative attitudes (expressed by the campers during the competitive phase of the experiment) were not attributable to personality disturbances, hardships, or frustrations in individual life histories. Only well-adjusted adolescents with no unusual frustrations underwent the experimental conditions; yet, despite such favorable biographical characteristics, the experimental changes in intergroup relations first created hostile attitudes and violence; and later the experiment eliminated them.

The Sherifs' experiment is extremely important for understanding the violence among delinquent formations, because the study isolated highly competitive relationships between groups as an independent determinant of violence. Their study further indicated that changes in both intragroup structures and personal attitudes, often considered causes of violence, were themselves determined initially by the emergence of competitive relations between groups. An intergroup property, rather than the intrapsychic consequences of disturbed family experiences, therefore, was a prime causal influence.

On the other hand, the family and other "cultural" experiences were not discounted altogether in explaining the causes of group conflict. The researchers indicated how easy it was to get the groups to compete intensely in athletic games and other events. The Sherifs (1956:260) concluded: "the desire for competition and spontaneous derogation of the other group in specific respects can be traced to the cultural background of these boys, specifically socialization in a society in which competitive and aggressive behavior is at a premium." If this behavior was not at a premium, the Sherifs' experiment might not have succeeded.

Obviously, the experiment implicates cultural factors that influence all adolescents to some degree. But certain youth are influenced more than others; moreover, some youth are more embedded in highly competitive peer relationships than others. The three stradom formations, for example, are more highly competitive than nonstradom formations.

When named groups become organized, usually during the middle-adolescent years, these competitive relationships establish different conditions for violence. Prior to this period, physical violence usually ranges from fairly harmless wrestling and horseplay to the regular eruption of fighting between two or three male contestants. Fighting may be sparked on the street, on the beach, in movie houses, or wherever stradom youth congregate. Because of the prevalence of such fighting, an observer hears young adolescents repeatedly complain about the time they "bumped into the guy at the Taco Tia and his two friends held me while he gave me some lumps." Individual boys are frequently observed at the beach jumping up automatically, yelling, "Who the fuck is the wise guy?!" when someone accidentally kicks sand onto their towels. Their bodies are stiff and their fists are clenched for the impending violent conflict even before they can assess the reason for this apparent insult. Their warnings and epithets are addressed to all concerned, and they proclaim the inviolable self. "You fuck with me . . . you fuck with your life!" the boys bombastically declare.

This automatic posturing testifies to a state of readiness conditioned by the callous and internecine relationships that develop among some peers. Working class adults sometimes use the phrase "I grew up in the street" to signify such relationships. Given these internecine relations, social pressures make violence the only way to deal with these relationships honorably. Consequently, in public confrontations, once the posturing begins and threats are flung from one boy to another, the sudden gathering of peers reinforces the mandate to back up threats with violence. Either the boys "put their money where their mouth is," or they experience shame and public condemnation. The onlooking crowd members themselves jeer and taunt the boys to show their manly virtue, thereby heightening the tension between glaring combatants. Like Roman circuses, the crowds turn thumbs down to a peaceful resolution to the wounded feelings of hostile adolescents.

A Case in Point

With the increasing commitment of peers to named groups or territorial identities, streetcorner formations in some communities are propelled into very real violent conflict with other groups, sometimes within a few months. We observed one meeting of a large, newly formed club, the Corsairs, where a boy named Monk exclaimed to his friends: "Listen, we have to decide whether we are going to be all Ese or not . . . whether we are going to fight or not. A lot of clubs like the Roadmen are calling us Punks, and its a question of whether we choose them off [fight with them] or don't." In the discussion that erupted after this exclamation, some of the boys indicated their approval of individual fighting but not fighting between clubs. A few suggested that the club would become "Soc" and turn toward the "Soc" road; but everyone knew that they would appear like fools, and hardly any peers of consequence in their community would validate such a move. In the long discussion that followed, the members talked about how they could avoid involving *the club as a whole* in their individual conflicts with boys from other groups. It was generally felt that such conflicts should be restricted to a minimum of one or two club members. Interestingly, however, the club president and one of his lieutenants made a strong plea during the meeting for the responsibility of the members to protect each other when fights did break out. On the other hand, the leader also reflected the ambivalence that was being expressed, in general, about the consequences of providing mutual aid in violent encounters. At one moment, he would point out that any member who was attacked by "overwhelming numbers" should be able to rely on his club "buddies" for help. In the next moment, he would take the opposite position and suggest that the club be left out of "trouble," if possible. One could see the ambivalence of the entire group in the leader himself, in the vacillations that mirrored the conflict between the sense of fear and the sense of obligation to the group.

There were those in the club who declared, "If a club member stirs up a lot of trouble, we shoudn't help him at all." However, others indignantly pointed out that it is not easy to tell whether a member is to blame for starting a fight and, "besides, how can you let a buddy down?" Very basic obligations underlying group loyalties, mutual aid, and friendship were raised in the conversation. Yet even though the collective identity of this group seemed to hang in balance, the members decided to delay any settlement of the issue. Members were finally advised by the president to keep their relations with other clubs "as cool as possible" for the time being.

Immediately following this discussion, the boys talked about forming contacts with two other groups, the Highwaymen and the Gents, so that they could obtain "outside" help "just in case of a war." It became obvious that while the boys did not want to become involved in violent conflict with other groups, they were nevertheless being forced to consider such possibilities. They clearly perceived circumstances where they would have no choice in the matter, if they wanted to preserve their collective identity, honor, and dignity. Consideration of defensive arrangements with other groups was perceived as warranted by factors outside their immediate control. Furthermore, any agreement by one club to support another in a violent conflict also contained reciprocal obligations and risks. If a defense arrangement existed between the Highwaymen, the Gents, and the Corsairs, then the latter would be obligated to come to the aid of the other groups when they became involved in a struggle. These alliances, therefore, increased the possibility of becoming involved in violent conflicts with other groups. It also increased the scope of these conflicts, enormously.

Within the Corsairs' community, the possibility of violent provocation from other groups was heightened when at the beginning, for reasons of prestige, club jackets were puchased. (If and when the boys are able to obtain cars, the purchase of "car plaques," with their club name and logo etched in metal, also has similar consequences.) As their club membership was clearly identified in public, these boys were drawn into the status rivalries that characterize stradom formations within their own and adjacent communities. As this involvement occurred, their intragroup relationships were ordered by the ethnocentric phase of development.

A few months later, once the Corsairs had become more stable and had purchased jackets, one of the members gave this account of how far they had been propelled into ethnocentric relationships: "We were walking into this place," he said, "and a bunch of Mexican guys were standing out in front. The place was crowded. A few of the guys said 'those jackets of yours look 10%.' So one of our bigger guys went over and said, 'What did you say?' And one of those guys put out his cigarette and says, 'You heard me!' They got into a fight. A few more guys jumped in. There was a big mass roar. The next thing we hear that the Cobras of Santa Monica are after us. They are Mexicans. Then there was this thing at Rancho Park. We found out that we had chosen-off [challenged] the Legends. So there was a couple of Legends at Mar Vista. So we all were at Mar Vista and there was bloodshed. So we were talking afterward with a few of them and the boys had it arranged with the Legends to hold off fighting for awhile because we had to fight with the Cobras." This young club was now caught up in what an older, philosophical, delinquent boy called, "The Roaring Days."

Once triggered into violent combat, the early middle-adolescent groups often repressed their ambivalence, quickly becoming provocateurs "out to make a name for themselves." Of course, they usually chose their antagonists with care. A few months later, one of the Corsairs remarked, "The really tough guys don't give us any trouble. They don't say nothing. Its the punks that start wiseing off. Like the Diablos. The guys who are no bigger than we are; they're the punks that start wiseing off. But the hard guys; they don't say nothing. They just play it cool." The younger groups mostly fought amongst themselves. The older groups were not generally regarded as initiating threats, although entanglements sometimes occurred.

The older Studs are also present in the community. Often, like middle-age Babbitts scanning the town for excitement during convention time trying to relive their livelier days, they "cruise" around on special occasions like Halloween or New Year's Eve, "looking for a fight." A 15-year-old boy illustrates an encounter with older Studs. "My friends and me," he said, "got daggers, guns and everything. I had a German Luger and a thirty-two automatic. This was during New Year's Eve [because] some older guys, 18–19–20 [years old], threw eggs at the car I was in. We had just polished the car. So Harry got really mad and he pulled over to the side and honks the horn and the other car stops. So all of these guys get out of the car with clubs and one guy picked up one of these 'Stop Signs'. [He picked up a portable road sign and threatened to hurl it at Harry's car]. We couldn't do nothing. They threw us in the car and spit in our faces. All Harry could think of was to go home and get the gun. We did it and cruised around looking for the guys but we were stopped by the cops. We tried to throw the guns out of the car but they found them."

Faced with such humiliating possibilities, the streetcorner boy learns to discriminate between the groups within and beyond his local society to establish the identity of his most probable enemies. Knowing the identity of other groups also involves knowledge of their actual or potential strength and how far they will go when violence erupts. Any realistic appraisal, therefore, depends on the knowledge of a group's previous conflicts, group alliances, racial composition, and the locality from which the potential enemy might come, as well as their height, weight, and other signs of offensive or defensive capability. Even though a streetcorner boy is concerned about the absolutely fantastic tales and myths about other groups, he is acutely aware of the ethnocentric relationships engulfing him. He learns, therefore, about the geographical location of threatening groups and the types of candidates they select as their most probable victims.

"In [a junior high school in East Los Angeles], said a streetcorner boy, "there are mostly Eses. There are more gangs there because kids come from Clover, El Royo Soto, White Fence, and T.J. Matta. The colored guys in one bunch stick up for [the Mexican–American boys from] White Fence and El Royo Soto. They are good comrades. There are also wet-backs from Mexico in T.J. Matta. They think they can do things like other gangs. A lot of guys from Flats are in Jackson [another junior high school]. In [an East Los Angeles senior high-school] there are only a small bunch from Flats. Also a lot of guys don't fuck up because they want to get out of school."

Each school is "sized up" as the streetcorner boy becomes a repository of common knowledge about the conflicts and reciprocities that characterize group relationships around him. Particularly within communities that have high concentrations of streetcorner formations, this knowledge also adds to his current knowledge about the "natural order" of things.

NOTE

1. Larger networks of "friendly groups" partly develop because they provide mutual aid, goods, or money. The exchanges of goods or money involved "band dances," "gambling nights," raffles, and football or baseball games for beer or money. These events are hosted or organized by one or two clubs and supported by members of other clubs.

16

Maintaining Group Identities and Standards

Stradom formations seem to form easily enough, but maintaining groups after their formation requires a degree of resources and behavioral boundaries. To some extent groups supply their own structure and behavior control, but these are also imposed from outside. Group resources, especially, require contacts with outsiders who can supply them.

Stabilizing Stradom Relations

An accommodation sometimes develops between certain adults—for example, parents—who have more resources than adolescents and the three types of stradom formations. This accommodation may very well be forced upon the adults by the adolescents. On one occasion, we spoke with a mother who complained that her daughter's sorority often burned holes in the furniture because they smoked during their meetings at her house. However, she felt that the use of her home as a meeting place could not be prevented, because all the girls' homes were rotated. She also feared that if she prevented the meeting in her home, the girls would expel her daughter and "blackball her from ever reentering." The mother confided that even though she herself found the "sorority system" distasteful, she felt powerless to do anything about the club's irresponsibility. She simply tolerated the group to protect her daughter's interests.

Just as fraternities and sororities, within a populous domain, support and stabilize themselves by exploiting the resources of families, schools, and commercial institutions, the stabilization of the larger domains of streetcorner formations is also dependent upon certain characteristics of their own poorer communities. Streetcorner youth in these domains recognize that owners of hot-dog stands, ice-cream parlors, "drive-in" cafeterias, miniature golf courses, trampoline courts, and pool halls in their communities are often accommodating because they need customers. If financial pressures do not force an accommodation, then the threats of vandalism and theft might wring a cooperative attitude from the owners. This cooperation provides some of the formations with a steady place to "hang out," and it helps stabilize them, especially during colder weather.

Under certain conditions, such provident accommodations are difficult to find. This is especially true when streetcorner youth are a very small minority within the local society of peers. Moreover, this difficulty is most likely to occur within homogeneous middle-class and highly stable working-class communities. From our observations, many middle-class streetcorner formations must constantly recreate the conditions that stabilize their group identities and styles of life. On the other hand, if they are geographically mobile, middle-class streetcorner youth can travel to poorer communities, where the conditions are more favorable to hanging out. The consequences of this change of community can be considerable for their future delinquent careers. If streetcorner youth in middle-class communities have not organized formal groups earlier but have only "hung around with each other," contact with other streetcorner youth as role models might catalyze developments in their collective identity. The following description of a largely petit bourgeois stable working-class streetcorner group, whose members hung around a beach frequented primarily by working-class streetcorner groups, illustrates this conclusion and the importance of resources.

During the first summer they came to Wayside Beach, the group was composed primarily of junior-high students, but it also had a few high-school youth who urged the others to form a club. In addition, during this time, the members of the group interacted with the dominant group of older Dudes on the beach. The older boys were in a club of "Low Riders," and another older club that also frequented Wayside was noted for its toughness, violent history, and illegal market activities. Looking back at the end of the summer, Jerry and Scott, members of the younger group, recalled some of the older role models. One was a madcap Dude, "The Preacher," who used to produce gales of laughter in his parody of an evangelical preacher. He dramatically urged everyone to use marijuana and avoid alcohol, because the weed elevated humanity while booze "laid them low." (The fact that marijuana was illegal and alcohol legal added a touch of irony to his "preaching.") Almost a year after that summer, Preacher was shot and killed in an argument with another youth. Jerry also recalled how his friends, "Jackson and Bill and others, were protected by the older guys and that meant that they had the run of the beach. They wanted to impress the older guys and show them that they were one of the crowd. Scott said that his club in Chicago was called the Devils and we used the same name at Wayside because we thought it would impress everybody." When asked about the people they wanted to impress, this boy said: "Who do we want to impress? The teen-age public. At that time we wanted to have a bad reputation."

Under such conditions, where a number of streetcorner groups already existed, Jerry and Scott's group did not create the ethnocentric and delinquent attitudes that made them desire "a bad reputation." Nor did they have the fears and anxieties that often accompanied such attitudinal changes in communities with small concentrations of streetcorner types. Instead, they avidly emulated the older streetcorner youth who provided a reference group, and simultaneously they adopted the characteristics (e.g., a formal club identity) that usually emerge during the middle-adolescent years. As indicated, these self-reproducing relationships are more likely where there are higher concentrations of streetcorner groups and where, as a result, the youth "act older" earlier. Where high concentrations exist, streetcorner youth move through the phases of development in shorter periods of time, without some of the social-psychological dynamics that take place in other circumstances. Furthermore, the changes in their development are reinforced by stable traditions whose continuity is ensured by a steady supply of recruits. These youth simply take their new group names and wave them like banners to "impress others" with their fierce territorial or club loyalty. As one "generation" of boys succeeds another, they seem to slip in and out of the roles characterizing this phase of life as one slips in and out of a pair of boxing gloves, except that a lot of things happen when the gloves are on.

Club Member Roles and Reputations

In 1927, Thrasher (1927:336–41) reported the development of stable groups and the roles of some members, including the Funny Boy, Goat, Goofy Guy, Fighter, Sissy and Loud Mouth. Counterparts to these roles emerge in contemporary streetcorner groups, but they are sometimes called by different names such as Joker, Clown, Queer, and Big Mouth. Moreover, we noted during the ethnocentric phase that certain roles such as the Bad Stud also come into being on a larger scale than during the first phase.

The formation of ethnocentric groups ushers in other new roles in which the boys from different streetcorner groups relate to one another. Out-group members are defined as probable hostiles or unknown quantities who might become hostile. Such persons are further defined as "Strangers," and interaction with them is shaped by certain expectations. Monkey provides this illustration of how one should act with a Stranger compared with a friend: "If a friend says 'You're a pimp!' you feel that he's messing around with you. But if a Stranger went up to you and said that—you fire first! You figure he's looking for trouble. You don't ask explanations."

One of the most significant indicators of these estranged relationships is the "hard looks" repeatedly attributed to Strangers. An observer hears countless tales in which one boy "pins" or stares at another with a scornful eye or threatening demeanor. Rocky recalls, "We are at this drive-in [fast-food cafeteria] and these Socs were giving us hard looks. We stared at them and they chickened out." Mel proudly announces: "We are at this trampoline place and these Cats [other boys] were lined up against the fence. This guy turns around and starts giving me hard looks. I fired at him and they made their flight!" Rebel reports: "These guys were at the drive-in. This guy starts pinning me and I say to myself, 'What the fuck's the matter with him? Who does he think he is? Daddy Cool or something?!' I look him straight in the eyes and he starts talking to his buddies. I tell my guys about it and we lined up. He saw that we had an even number of guys as they. So he just turned and walked away." Some youth even report responding to "hard looks" when not accompanied by comrades. Apache Joe, for instance, carries a bottle opener, humorously called a "church key" because it opens beer bottles. He had scraped the wedge-shaped end of the opener on stone into a knife-edged point for use in close combat. Joe reports, "I see this Soc on the street and he's pinning me. I say what the hell are you looking at? He goes to the alley with me so that we can throw blows and I have this can opener in my pocket . . . and this

Soc is bigger than me. I fight with what I can fight. I fight to win so I have this church key in my hand. And this Soc sees it and he starts to back out. And we started talking and everything and I don't want to stab this Cat and get into trouble. We shook hands."

Like the crowning of kings, a victorious "pinning" is tantamount to a ceremonial confirmation of worth. Imaginary and real events blur in the kaleidoscope of ethnocentric rivalry and conflict. The world about these youth is filled, to some degree, by a fantastic ink blot dotted with staring eyes. How does one respond honorably to such conditions? What role should one take?

The Bad Stud, Bad Dude, or Bad Part is the role reciprocal of the Stranger. Playing the Bad Part also means that one will be treated as a Stranger in certain situations. How is one to act when this possibility presents itself? Sophisticated Eses answer with these comments: "No matter what the groups . . . high or low . . . a ruthless part, a hard part, or a deadly part, or a stern part . . . all fit the Bad Part." "When you are a stranger in a new situation, you sometimes play the Bad Part. You put on a stern face . . . or a hard face. You wait for an approach [on the part of the other] or try to think of a manner of approaching the other person." "You play the Bad Part sometimes because you do not know what will happen from any angle. The Bad Part is sometimes based on a fear and tension in regard to being burned [being hurt by others]."

Since the Bad Dude or Bad Part is a prestigeful adaptation in the ethnocentric phase, it is recognized that a boy sometimes plays the part because "he feels neglected and it gets him attention." Even though this employment of the part is not pivotal in ethnocentric developments, it is nevertheless important. Once differentiated and perceived honorifically, motives other than ethnocentric rivalry and conflict often drive its expression. Personal ideals, for example, emerge in this process; and some of the boys reason that even out-group members "play the Bad Part because they see something wrong about themselves. Playing the part eliminates this pressure of feeling wrong. You play the part to show the public [of Cool Dudes you are acquainted with] that there is nothing wrong about you." For some Dudes this process leads to the internalization of the Bad Part, and it is no longer played and discarded at will. They *become* the Bad Part and are eventually "known" everywhere as Bad Dudes or Bad Studs.

Mid-adolescent socialite formation members are more fearful of violence than streetcorner youth, and therefore they do not play the role of the Bad Dude. However, even though their conditions of life are more favorable, they exhibit equally intense group loyalties. The expression of their status rivalries is countered to a greater degree by the institutions in their community. Furthermore, reputation and prestige can come from other roles. In some communities, for instance, the Socs control the student organizations in their high schools, and the payoffs from this control are considerable. These advantages do not merely mean unique experiences, such as trips and contacts with prestigious youth in other schools, but also large and pleasant facilities in which to hold dances. Furthermore, their frequent control over the student council, cheer-leading squad, and student monitor system reflects their integration with prevailing systems of institutionalized power and enables them to establish an authoritative position in the eyes of other youth. On the other hand in other communities the number of Socs is small, or the socialites refuse to be sponsored by adults who impose restrictions on their conduct. Sometimes they are deliberately forced out of the school organization by administrators, because their groups have a negative effect on the academic environment. Also, administrators may only allow members of an officially sponsored group to run for student office.

Maintaining Soc reputations may be hampered by other constraints. We have said that adults often accommodate themselves to Soc formations, making adjustments resulting in mutually acceptable arrangements even regarding the use of homes for fraternity and sorority meetings. But the Socs are usually shrewd enough to recognize these as minor constraints, and they strive to maintain advantageous relationships that provide them with valuable family resources. If the socialites were to act "rambunctious" or burn cigarette holes in the furniture of all the houses they used—or especially the houses of the most prestigious families—they would incur the organized wrath of their parents. To maintain the accommodative relationships, these formations develop their own internal controls. They sanction the "wild" undisciplined member, the person who often "gets out of hand," giving his or her brothers and sisters a "bad name." The socialite club that systematically provokes violent reactions, even in the face of group rivalries, runs the risk of being branded a "Hoody Soc club," of acting more like "Beaners" [Mexican–Americans] than "Socs."

On the other hand, the necessity to invoke such sanctions repeatedly in order to keep individuals and clubs on the "respectable" side of the line, separating them from streetcorner groups, testifies to the competitive pressures on these groups. These pressures threaten to erupt at times into vandalism and violence. The male Soc's limits on such offenses are prescribed by time and space; but, as indicated, during the summer, when beach houses, mountain cottages, and motels are rented, wild and sometimes violent affairs occur, resulting in the destruction of property as well as personal injury. Likewise, the windows of houses belonging to rival groups may become targets for stones thrown by fraternities from adjacent communities. However, such incidents are considered with care, lest they get out-of-hand and endanger more important reputations within their own communities and career goals.

Consequently, as Brad observed, "We [the Socs] do not fight like the Eses, but each [Soc] group considers the other a rival." In this rivalry, painting club names on public or private property underscores a club's reputation. Dumping garbage at meeting places and other escapades (that poke fun at rival clubs) take the place of violent combat. Driving cars through popular intersections on a special holiday or weekend evening and flinging raw eggs into another car also serve to spark tales about mad fraternity stunts in a local society.

Of course, there are more acceptable means, such as annual "band dances" or football games for a barrel of beer between rival streetcorner groups, for advancing a Soc club's reputation. We observed one club that specialized in winning most of the officerships of the student organization in high school; another tried to corner the market on athletic stars. But perhaps the most important avenue through which reputations are made consists of sponsoring popular parties. High-school fraternities and sororities try to "line each other up" for invitations to a "club affair" or to conduct a joint party.

Often in the restless jockeying for the best parties alcohol is used in considerable quantity. Some groups gain a reputation for being "drunkards" by becoming repeatedly drunk and riotous at parties, even though many sororities downgrade such groups on their preferred fraternity lists. While drinking is frequently controlled by such conditions or by parental restrictions, the groups drink more freely at affairs away from home.

The ethnocentric phase is also accompanied by heightened sexual exploitation within all the stradom formations. The reputation of Soc boys, for example, can also be heightened by their sexual exploits. During this phase, cliques of socialite youth invite girls from streetcorner formations to small quiet parties. (They also frequent some of the parties given by streetcorner youth for similar reasons.) Enticed by the boy's money, prestige, and perhaps even celebrity status, the girls ignore the fact that they are considered "pigs" and "tramps" and become involved in sexual liaisons. Stories of wild escapades involving liquor and sexual intercourse with local "pigs" are circulated widely. One of these boys justified his behavior, simply observing: "We're gung-ho for sex right now!"

Group Standards and Behavior Maintenance

Psychoanalytically oriented scholars maintain that delinquent youth lead a normless existence; they have no standards; their group life is simply a projection of emotional disorders (Scott, 1956). Yablonsky (1959) further claims that delinquents are so disturbed they cannot develop an adequate consensus about group roles. They are even unable to achieve consensus on such simple matters as who is a member of their group. Violent gangs, according to Yablonsky, are especially incapable of evolving stable normative structures and other properties of group life.

We are aware of significant differences between streetcorner groups and other groups, but we disagree with Yablonski over the nature and causal meaning of such differences. With regard to consensus, role differentiation, normative stability, and other properties of small groups, we contend that delinquent groups are no different from other kinds of adolescent formations. With the exception of such roles as War Counselor and Bad Stud, role differentiation within delinquent groups is influenced by standards common to other adolescent groups. Such common standards are involved, for example, in establishing the leading members in crowd as well as club formations. Leadership roles in crowds fluctuate greatly; nevertheless, in time even these formations produce their own leading members. We are also convinced that almost every claim about the unusual nature of delinquent personalities, lack of consensus, normlessness, or "shared misunderstanding" can be invalidated by comparing delinquents with nondelinquents in similar types of groups (cliques, clubs, or crowds) existing for similar periods of time. Other variables, such as age, sex, and type of occasion, should also be controlled, especially if the analysis centers on crowd formations.

No studies have been set up with such variables as awareness of group membership specifically in mind. However, we might cite a study conducted in Melbourne, Australia, which, among other things, observed adolescent awareness of group membership (Dunphy, 1963). In this study, after comparing lists of members made by individuals in a number of beach crowds, the researcher found it impossible to determine the boundaries of the crowds. Disagreements about who belonged to each crowd were too great to make these lists useful for clearly differentiating crowd composition. What is important, in this case, is that the researcher was studying typical examples of "normal" adolescent behavior—not delinquent gangs. In light of this, some of Yablonsky's observations about lack of consensus may have been based on characteristics that delinquents and nondelinquents share. They, therefore, cannot be attributable to psychoanalytic causal variables.

Instead of centering attention on discrepant opinions or on misunderstandings among delinquents, we suggest there is much to be gained by studying the shared understandings by which collective relations are coordinated. Here, it is noteworthy that the kind of working consensus developed within groups varies greatly, depending upon the length of time members have been together. It also varies with the type of group structure and situation. In times of crisis—as in gang wars, for example—individual awareness of affiliates fluctuates widely. However, such awareness is paralleled among all kinds of individuals during riots, earthquakes, or other crisis situations.

Commonly shared standards are contained in the club members' descriptions of virtuous behavior. Members give their sage advice, at the drop of a hat, to aspirants who express their desires for clear and infallible guides to the good life. These comments, selected from recorded dialogues by Socs about desirable members, give some indication of club standards:

"A member of our fraternity has to be a bitchin' guy . . . not playing God. He shouldn't kiss-up . . . not too shy . . . and has to be able to go out and be fun with, and screw around with the guys."

"He has to date a lot unless he plays football and it's first string. He has to be cool. He has to be good for the club. A social asset who will be all right at parties. He won't get into the club if he goes to parties and sits on his ass."

"I don't want this guy. He's a wimpy guy. He's a baby. He's a bad athlete and he's ugly. We don't need ugly guys."

"He's the best athlete. He's ultimately cool. He can be the club runner. He runs the hundred pretty fast."

"He makes it with the ugly babes but what can you do? He's a good fighter and a good athlete. That's all right, too."

"He'll work for the club. He isn't a social climber."

"He makes it with the babes. He'll be good for the club. The club gets a reputation by throwing parties . . . throwing them with other girls' clubs. Some club brothers drink, others don't, but everybody has to pitch in and make the club party successful."

"Shared understandings" analysis can also lead to an exploration of the social mechanisms by which delinquent groups maintain common standards, particularly those defining acceptable and unacceptable behavior. Here we find behavior mechanisms that are also common to some nondelinquent groups, including gripe sessions, formal discussions about the worth of new members, exclusion practices, and scapegoating. In some groups these mechanisms take the form of rituals in which the sergeant-of-arms deals out "swats" to individuals who violate group norms. We have observed several groups using an "official" decoratively carved and painted wooden paddle for this purpose. Ritualistic mechanisms of this sort exist only among clubs, but it would be equally interesting to study the means by which crowd members maintain group standards, even though such means may not be formally instituted. Sanctioning a crowd member by "fooling around" aggressively or "ganging up" on him, either physically or through ridicule, is not unusual.

This chapter describes a few of the mechanisms for maintaining virtuous behavior among members of stradom clubs. The first mechanism is organized around the institution of pledging. (The pledging practice is most frequent among the socialite clubs but is usually absent in cliques and crowds.) The second mechanism involves the practice of "swatting" or fining members for errant behavior. The third mechanism is called the "round table." The round table consists of a discussion in which critical and self-critical assessments of individuals or the group are expressed by members. This kind of criticism need not be formally instituted, although we have found this to be the case with respect to a few socialite and streetcorner clubs.

Pledging Practices

Before one can fully grasp the ways in which pledging practices maintain standards of virtue, one must realize that pledging also has other functions. Pledging functions among the socialites maintain the system of group prestige, particularly in the eyes of non-club members. Indeed, the humiliating initiation experience inflicted by clubs on new members is as illustrative of competitive intergroup relations during the ethnocentric phase among socialite clubs as is gang warfare among streetcorner groups.

Not all clubs engage in pledging practices; nevertheless, where it exists, pledging is significant in setting the climate for socialite groups. Further, the significance of the pledging practice also lies in the degree to which it functions to enforce a deep conformity, not only among members who are already in clubs, but among all adolescent youth who are members of the main crowds and who aspire to club membership at one time or another. The pledging practice regulates the status passage to club membership.

Thus, pledging practices have a two-fold significance. One is to maintain club prestige in the fraternity and sorority system and its surrounding networks; the other is to confirm ritually the aspiring socialite's commitment to ethnocentric standards. This latter effect is supported by the other forms of social control, particularly the "blackball" and initiation ceremony. Chris, a socialite youth, said: "We formed this fraternity with some of the members. We are the only non-Jewish club in [the high school] because there are mostly Jewish guys there. We are not large because of this and *because of our initiation*. The first night of the initiation we give two rounds of swats with the paddle. The second night you drink this stuff. Not anything that will kill you . . . like a raw egg with a little pepper and everything. The third night you get Sloan's liniment on your testicles. That's pretty bad. And on the 'Hell night' we take the pledge to Hollywood and give him a round of swats in front of the show, or a swat on every corner." In Chris' view, only those who are committed enough to take the punishment are acceptable club material.

Streetcorner youth also have initiation ceremonies. Bo-Bo reported: "I belonged to a club in the Bronx before I came out here. It was the Aces. You had to write an A in your arm. They would cut an A with a razor to see if you could take it. That showed you were bad."[1]

The initiation practices vary widely. Some are similar to Chris and BoBo's, while others are not as extreme. We observed a Soc fraternity on the West Side apply their typical round of "swats," not with a paddle as above, but with the largest shoe available (usually provided by the husky sergeant-of-arms). The fraternity "brothers" gathered in the backyard, and after a running start cracked the sole of the shoe hard against the posterior of the boy who was "dying" to become a member.

An interesting feature of these spectacles is their public character. Most members mill about during these initiations and urge that the job be done with the greatest vigor. Often a few friends of the pledge attempt to influence the member administering the initiation to "take it easy." The socialite pledge chokes back his tears and his watery eyes are explained away by his club brothers.

The initiation procedures do vary, because some club members dislike inflicting humiliating experiences on the pledge. However, often we detected more "practical" considerations in the club's rationalization for "easing off" on initiation practices. Oscar told us: "We have only one contender for the initiation and that's the Top Hats. Most of the fraternities feel that they may not get enough members in if they have too hard an initiation. The way we feel . . . if they can't take the initiation we don't want them in the club. But the guys figure that right now we should go easy on the initiation in order to get a little larger and get some more guys in. After we get rolling we can go back to the older initiation."

Thus, the traditional initiation ceremony is sometimes waived informally or carried out with minimal humiliation for those who have considerable power for one reason or another. In the following participant observation notes, a streetcorner and a socialite group demonstrate this variation:

Jay and Joe Gonzales were widely known for their great physical strength. Hank, president of the Kings [a streetcorner club], treated them with kid gloves. They never received swats when they were admitted to the group. They hardly pay their dues; and while Hank complained, he did not press hard, as with the others.

Chuck, president of the Earls [a socialite fraternity], suggested that the club admit Johnson into the club. One member objected to this and pointed out that Johnson would "never stand still for being treated like a pledge." Charles angrily pointed out that Johnson was the top football player in the school and the club should be honored by his request to join them. He asked the club to admit Johnson without the usual initiation ceremonies and pledging period. This was placed in the form of a motion by one of the boys, and although some abstained no one voted against it.

On the other hand, sometimes groups regard the ceremony in

an uncompromising fashion (especially if a lower-status member is to be the target of abuse), and their arguments about adhering to principle verge on collective insanity:

At the meeting [of a streetcorner club], George pointed out that Pete was in critical condition at the hospital because of a fight. He suggested that the club make him a member and give him a car plaque and a jacket. However, Joe and Willie wanted to go by the "letter of the club constitution" and pointed out that there are no exceptions to be made; Pete should get his swats and hell night. Some of the members argued that Pete couldn't be given swats at the hospital. Considering his condition, they reasonably concluded that he might die from it. There was a fierce debate about the issue, and the conflict was finally resolved in a decision to make Pete a member and give him his swats and hell night six months from now.

While enduring the pledging rituals, recruits are simultaneously degraded and elevated to a new status. They are degraded because they represent the disparaged identity of an Outsider. They are elevated insofar as the ceremony of initiation, through ordeal, ritually uncovers their "real" "underlying" nature as "good club material." This ceremonial act marks the end of the ambivalent status of the novitiate and invests all the material and nonmaterial privileges of club identity on his person. His own status and honor now become wedded to the status of his group. In acquiring a vested interest, he also acquires standpoints that legitimate these interests. The powerless pledges testify to the superiority of those others who ceremoniously place them in painful and humiliating positions.

There are other characteristics of pledging practices to be noted. The delinquent "excesses" (bodily injury or even death) that sometimes occur during initiation and hazing ceremonies should not be theoretically minimized simply because they are rare, as compared to petty theft, for example. The social foundations for the serious injuries or mental abuses that do occur indicate that these hurts and humiliations are more than just situations that have gone "too far" or "gotten out of hand." These "excesses" are encouraged by the standpoints that consider degradation ceremonies vitally important for validating the superiority of membership. Consequently, it is not surprising that by 1984, 18 states had antihazing laws that prohibited hazing practices resulting in injuries. These laws specifically prohibited this kind of hazing directed at pledges, especially in the course of an initiation into organizations. In 1982, in the first case tried under the new New York State antihazing law, nine students and former students of a high school in an upper-middle-class surburban community were indicted for causing a pledge to suffer serious abdominal bleeding requiring surgery. The blows causing this bleeding were inflicted during a fraternity initiation ceremony. It has been estimated that 27 deaths have been caused by hazing between 1978 and 1984 (*New York Times*, April 9, 1984).

The public character of the initiation ceremony is heightened by its performance on the city streets (as in the reference to "hell night"), or in the backyards of members' houses with an audience of club members, pledges, and those who have not yet been accepted as pledges but who are required to "hang around" outside while meetings are in progress. The club's artificial creation of its own fawning in public is interesting in itself. We observed high-status groups holding meetings indoors, while courts of aspiring members waited outdoors. The clubs required aspirants to "be in with the crowd" for a limited period before deciding whether to make them pledges, but these aspirants were not allowed to attend meetings because they were not bona fide members. To show their interest and potential loyalties, they lingered aimlessly for hours outside meeting places. Their listless and abject appearance at these times testified to their powerlessness in determining membership and their low status in the domain of socialite formations.

The "blackball" ceremony consists of investing the power to veto a new club member with only one, two, or, at the most, three negative voters. In many clubs, one member alone can reject a club aspirant. This concentration of power to exclude aspirants, in the hands of any club member—even those possessing least honor in the group—converts club membership into a caste-like status. It guarantees that admission to club membership requires a deference to club members merely because they are members, independently of personal qualities. No matter how obnoxious he or she is or how poorly a club member is regarded by the teen public at large, he or she is fawned upon by those who aspire to make the passage into the club system.

The blackball, like outstretched fingers, extends the ideological influence of the club system into all parts of the socialite domain. To avoid the blackball, adolescents who want to join a club conform to the members' expectations of appropriate aspirant behavior, and, in validating the conceptions of good club material, they adopt attitudes that legitimate club standards. Some of those who have been blackballed or who have otherwise been rejected by clubs may hang around the edges of club life or form their own club and then strive to compete for status with the other clubs during the ethnocentric phase.

The blackball tradition has other effects as well. Typically, friendship groups accept outsiders into their inner circles for a great variety of reasons. But the blackball heightens the rating of those impersonal factors (e.g., wealth) or personal skills (e.g., athletic prowess) given greatest value within the entire fraternity system. The members of large fraternities often do not become acquainted with new members in equal degrees. There are always those who do not really know that the aspirant is a "nice" guy, although he may have a long-standing friendship with some of the fraternity brothers. Consequently, a premium is placed on those attributes that are useful to individual members or make the group popular. Good club material, for example, may involve an outstanding reputation in sports or the ability to establish advantageous relationships with the opposite sex.

The effective sanctions that club members use to support the ideal conceptions of good club material stimulate the fairly rapid development of those heterosexual, athletic, and, in general, "cool" characteristics deemed appropriate within the stradom formations. The term "cool" summed it up for the early 1960s. It encompassed ideal sets of virtues, irrespective of whether they encouraged morally questionable conduct. Sexual promiscuity, garbage fights, drinking, vandalism, joy riding, "spontaneous" thievery for personal or club use were not approved for all times and locations, but they were considered proper forms of behavior on certain occasions. They reflected on the individual and also the club; and they were weighed on the scale of reputational values. These relationships remain viable and can be found today among adolescents throughout the United States.

Maintaining Group Standpoints

"To me the Kings want to be on top and they don't care how they do it," Duane commented. "It's just their way of thinking." Duane, in so saying, reflects an awareness of the competition between groups occurring during the ethnocentric phase. As this competition increases in intensity, it produces internal ideological changes within groups in the various domains.

Central to these ideological changes are the abilities of leaders. Consequently, in developing their "way of thinking" about out-groups (or in the enforcement of practices such as the blackball and initiation ceremony), the relationship between leaders and followers should be considered. Except for the value of a Bad Stud for president, the following descriptions of the club president of a streetcorner group might also apply to socialite clubs. Thus, Mac speaks for many others when he says: "An ideal leader will devote a lot of time to his club. He is friendly with all the guys. He has to have knowledge of all the clubs. He's got to have the respect of all the guys and also control. If the guys respect you, they will listen to you. You don't have to be strong. But there is a period during the summer especially . . . because you go to the beach and you find all kinds of people down there . . . that if you have a Bad Stud as president of your club and some guy gives you shit at the beach . . . the president is gonna stick up for you. If he can take care of the guy, your club will get a good name. You're considered the greatest."

Jaime, a club leader, informed us that "During the summertime you've got to have a leader that can stick up for his club and club members. He doesn't have to be a Bad Stud but he has to be courageous. He's gotta have some courage. Some stand-up. Then you find in the wintertime . . . in school . . . you try to have a president who is active in some kind of school sport. He might be in the football team . . . or he'll have some kind of direct contact with some of the big shots around school . . . like the club presidents. I suppose you can say that he has to have a good personality. If he is well established with persons outside the club he gets a good name for himself. Like me. I was tight with the other clubs . . . and what I lack the other club members made up for."

Covering a different viewpoint, Bill, another president, was preoccupied with the influence and importance of girls. He said: "Outside of school you've got to have a popular leader because the girls . . . the gossip they make up . . . can ruin or make a club. If a girl says that the president of your club is a bastard, none of the girls will go out with the president or with the guys in the club. They won't attend your parties and they figure you are wise or something and only want to go out for a piece of ass."

Leaders can tell you about the attributes of fellow club members. According to Jaime: "A follower has to be tight with the president or with the officers of the club. Johnson . . . he's a follower.

He's got to be popular also with the girls. The main thing is that he has to be able to pick up ideas suggested by the president. He has to pick up ideas and be able to judge for himself in situations. If the president doesn't show up . . . he's got to be able to take over the place of the president. In that case he's an officer. He has to have support of the guys and make up his mind accurately and quickly. More or less like the leader does. The ordinary guys are just generally friendly with the club officers. He doesn't have to be popular with the girls. Like Gus, he's a low [status] club member. It usually doesn't pay for the low club member to hassle with the president who has the big pull. It's good to have a guy contradict you now and then because you don't get swell-headed. But you notice that I don't take shit from the guys. What about members of other clubs? They are Punks, Flips . . . but most of them are proud and loyal to their club."

Leaders of groups from various domains all reply that their club identity has considerable import—not only to themselves, but as they see themselves in the eyes of others in the community. Two leaders responded to a question about awareness of club identity among stradom members. The first leader replied: "If you go some place you are introduced as not just John Warton. But as John Warton of the club, Ambassadors the Esquires. . . ." The second leader remarked, "If a teenager asked me who I am, I would tell him 'I'm Chuck Ramirez, president of the Undertakers, former president of the Triple Alliance.' And I'd tell him what part of town I'm in. Of course, the guy might ask me what broads I know, or who I know. . . ."

Group standards are affected by both external and internal forces. The competition between groups affects the internal structure of the group. The more intense and salient in the lives of these youth the conflict becomes, the more authoritarian and rigidly insistent the group becomes about its code of honor. Internal relations become highly crystallized around the successful attainment of the group's primary aims. Neither parents nor any personal difficulties become readily acceptable as reasons for noninvolvement in group activities. Joe made the following relevant point at a meeting: "George's father won't let him go out at night and he tells him what to do. I think we ought to kick George out of the club because he won't be able to hang around with the guys regularly."

The clubs themselves increase their own control over each member's behavior through other kinds of ceremonies. In addition to the initiation ceremony and the "democratic" practice of voting for new members (with veto powers concentrated in few hands), we observed a ceremony known as the "round table" or the "round house." As mentioned, this practice consisted of a ritual of criticism and self-criticism. When the round table was instituted, meetings ended with each member, in rotation, expressing his opinion of himself, the club in general, or specific others. Most clubs did not use such formally instituted rituals to enhance group cooperation. However, both streetcorner groups and socialite fraternities were among those that did. The following comments, made by individual members at a meeting of a high-status fraternity in an upper-middle-class community, exemplify the round tables within the male stradom formations:

"This club is getting rank. We haven't had a decent dance in a long time."

"This is my first meeting since I'm a club member. I don't know how many minutes we wasted tonight."

"You guys are just fooling around during the meeting. If the president says that you should have a swat because you're acting out of line, you should take the swat without making all that noise about it."

"Listen Corey . . . I haven't seen you around with the guys since you have been pledging. You should be with the guys more often."

"I've got nothing to say except that Joe here is an ass-hole. How can a guy be screwed up with three broads at the same time? I don't know. Other than that, the club is cool and everything is tight."

"The meetings are easy and calm compared with the old ones. The president is rough but he is doing a good job."

"Only a few of us showed up at the activity we had last week. I don't know, but the club is really falling apart."

"Hey Carl, how about cleaning up my garage? You got your car parts all over the place and it looks like hell."

"Joe is an idiot. He had his fun with the girl. How about letting us have a little fun with her?"

"You act like a fool, trying to make an impression on people. But you don't make an impression. All you are is a stubby little ass-hole."

"I'm sorry I haven't been around with you guys. I've been working late. I will be quitting soon and I'll be at the beach regularly."

"I don't think Jack will ever graduate high school the way you are messing around. You'll never get out with me and your friends."

"Don't feel sorry about being in trouble at school, Jack. I was in school for 4 minutes and got kicked out . . . so you are not the only one."

"As soon as you got into the club, Don, you started turning out to be a prick. You better straighten out, because a lot of the guys are talking about you. They don't dig you. Talk with some of the guys and see what's wrong with you."

"I only missed three meetings since I've been in this club. I could go around with Virginia instead of being with the guys. But I don't when it's a club activity. It hurts me to see some of you guys staying away from the club activities."

"The club is doing a lot of things and I enjoy being in it. The club is tight and everything. You guys are about the swingingest thing that ever hit my life. However, the club president takes advantage of his position. He's a little too powerful."

"I am here against my mother's wishes. If I can attend meetings regularly, so can you. Homework or not. If I can come here with my Mom crying . . . you can get here also. The club comes first."

The round table elevates group norms, as a regulating influence, to a position of saliency. It moderates the competition for females, and it reinforces the priority of group meetings over other activities, the necessity for powerful leadership within specific limits, the obligation to give aid to club brothers, and the conformity to club standards. The club member runs the gamut of ceremonies from tentative acceptance to pledging to initiation; and in some clubs the member is never free of ritual as long as he remains in the group.

Better to Be in Than out

Continual observation reveals systematic attacks on the integrity and honor of one member or another. Yet one cannot grasp the reason for continued loyalty to these friendship groups, particularly in streetcorner clubs, in the face of treachery and disillusionment, without understanding that the friendships that exist are more acceptable than being abandoned in a hostile world largely composed of strangers. Because of the conflict between groups, relevant strangers or out-group peers are often generalized as "weird" and degraded souls or "operators." Sometimes the anarchic conflicts among streetcorner groups immensely intensify this generalized definition of strangers. In light of this, close "compadres" in the club must be "trusted" (within common-sense limits, of course), even though it is realized early in the game that a friend can be two kinds of people: a Nice Guy in one way and a Punk in another. On all levels, group relations provide mutual aid. Also, some stable, predictable types of reciprocities emerge, which are helpful in moderating interpersonal competition within groups. Such support from friends is important in the face of numerous personal arguments and disappointments.

For example, during a meeting of the Lords, Clark indicated that he had had an argument with Johnson. Jimmy brought up the matter and said to Clark: "Maybe you would like to talk about it? The guys are with you, Clark." Clark said that he didn't want to talk about it since he was the one that was "burned." But he did say that Johnson had promised to sell him his car but sold it to a non-club member for five dollars more than Clark had offered him. Clark stated: "I'm just gonna ask Johnson one question and if he gives me a certain answer, I'm gonna punch it out with him. Because that would show that he is a punk!" The others in the club nodded their assent and promised to stand behind him.

At the height of the ethnocentric phase, members repeatedly insist on their group's superiority. Sean, a socialite, spoke up: "In a way my club is superior to the other clubs. We are closer than they are. Of course, I wouldn't really know because I've never seen all these groups. I suppose all clubs say that about themselves." Willie, a streetcorner boy, proclaims: "People look up to me because I belong to a popular club." Being a Lord or a King, an Ambassador or an Esquire, means "respect from all the others in the school." The value of club membership can also be rationalized in terms of self-preservation and other benefits. In reflecting on club importance, Greg, an Ese, said: "In my case people are trying to get down on me. It's natural because I'm colored. But they don't try to fool around with me when they know the club I'm in. They are scared of our reputation, and you can get away with murder."

And Ronald, a Soc, observed: "It's hard to say why I belong to the Esquires. It has so many advantages."

Streetcorner youth adopt the role of the Con, Clown, and Flunky to cope with power relations within their friendship groups. However, the cleverness of a Con, the humor of a Clown, or the servility of a Flunky is often useless for dealing with rivals outside one's group and territory. Security and predictability are always greatest when one is "home" among friends; and even after the ethnocentric phase, when the boys are nearing 20 years of age and have left their group rivalries behind, one observes the lasting effects of this period. Jack once remarked when we were driving through his old "stamping grounds": "You know, every time I drive home at night, I suddenly feel relaxed when I cross this street and enter West Adams territory. Ain't that stupid for a guy my age to feel like that? It's like coming home to my own country after I've been away."

NOTE

1. Years later, Quicker (1983) also found similar practices among Mexican–American gangs.

17

Social Type Conversions

Social type identities occasionally change, and several types of conversions are possible. At the beginning of the ethnocentric phase and during its development, some youth break away from streetcorner formations. Although most join intermediary networks, some become Athletes, because athletics represents a widely acceptable channel of social mobility. Also, athletic status frequently confers immunity from stradom norms prescribing deviant behavior. Nevertheless, making the change is not free of ambivalence.

The kinds of pressures involved in breaking away from streetcorner relationships through involvement in athletic activities can be illustrated by Fred, who was on the brink of making this change. One night we noticed that Fred looked different. His hair was cropped halfway between Soc and Ese styles. None of the major leaders, Willie, George, or Johnny, were present, and the conversation may have been freer because of this. Answering our inquiry about the change in hair style, Fred said that he was trying out for the school football team and had to play the part. He felt that his chances were better if he "looked Soc." Further observations indicated that he was under great strain. Although his decision to "look and act like a Soc" was acceptable to his streetcorner friends so long as athletic goals were involved, he was being careful to express his identity as an Ese in front of the others. He repeatedly uttered the old cliches about the Socs having no guts, about their not standing up to a fight but backing down, etc., as if he had to demonstrate publicly his continued loyalty to his friends and their codes of honor, even though he was trying out for the team and was, therefore, "forced" to act differently than he "really" was. At one point, Fred also said that a number of peers changed from Ese to Soc (at 16 or 17 years of age). In actuality, this so-called change from "Ese to Soc" usually involved shifts into intermediary or athletic formations. Fred's decision triggered a certain amount of status anxiety among the others. A number of teens at the hangout that night saw themselves in an inferior status compared to the socialites; underneath it all there might have been their own desire to move out of their streetcorner crowd in an acceptable and honorable manner. Other boys and girls at the hangout that evening pointed out that no one went the other way—from Soc to Ese. This judgement was not completely accurate, but the likelihood of movement in that direction was certainly small.

In communities where there are populous socialite networks, the movement of streetcorner youth into the intermediary stradoms (usually into small cliques on the fringes of these formations) can be recognized by the Socs and Low Socs because the streetcorner youth change styles of life as well as associations. This movement is interpreted by the socialites from their own point of view. One socialite from an upper-middle-class high school said, "the Eses seem to be turning into Socs, because they are outnumbered. Because most people appreciate you for being a Soc. You are supposed to be a big man on the campus. If you are rejected like the Eses are, they want to become noticed too. So they change."

Although Fred had recognized that shifts away from streetcorner groups were occurring among his age-mates, a prior exodus had already taken place during the transition from junior to senior high. Several factors seem to account for shifting allegiances. When streetcorner youth enter senior high school, at the beginning of the ethnocentric phase, the rapid events that force them into intergroup conflicts bring about reprisals from police, parents, and school personnel. The police, in particular, in their "inventories" of local gangs, sometimes pay special attention to information about new formations and either restrict the frequency of delinquent acts or the conditons under which these acts take place. With the emergence of more serious violations—systematic theft, intergroup violence, narcotics use—youth in all stradom formations are increasingly made aware of the role of the police and have considered the possibility of being caught. Furthermore, contact with police and other authorities supports parental pressures on youth to discontinue associating with delinquent friends.

Obviously, not all parental and police pressures are effective. Both parents may be employed, and control over their adolescent children may be weakened at this late date. Other parents are not respected by their children, and parental pleas are interpreted as demands involving their own selfish ends. However, we have observed cases in which parents effectively restricted their son's leisure hours and associations with delinquent friends. In one case, the father and brothers effectively enforced a complete severance between a boy and his delinquent associates in a high-delinquency area. Such success, however, requires exceptional family resources, which are sometimes brought to bear only when parents are informed that a son or daughter has been apprehended by police for breaking the law.

For example, one summer we watched the formation of a streetcorner group consisting of 28 members. During the coming fall they became increasingly involved in intergroup violence, and at this time almost one-third of the members dropped out. While isolated, at first, in small cliques composed of old friends, some of the boys who had dropped out sought to become members of relatively nondelinquent intermediary groups. When we asked the reasons for dropping out, we were candidly told that the old club "was getting into all sorts of trouble. It was getting worse all the time." The boys also reported constant pressure and arguments with parents as a major reason for quitting the old club.

A growing awareness of longer-term consequences may also influence changes. Some streetcorner youth become aware that most members of the older streetcorner groups either drop out or are pushed out of high school. They realize that a similar fate may be in store for them if delinquent relationships continue to determine their lives. Furthermore, other, more fortuitous conditions may effect a change. For example, if the members of a group live in an area that cross-cuts more than one high-school district, they will find themselves separated from each other as friends are forced into different high schools. This separation reshuffles friendships in high school and presents significant opportunities for making the break-away without losing face.

In the following comments, the break-away process is recognized and interpreted by a boy who remained in a streetcorner crowd. Observing that some of his friends moved to Sorrento beach (a favorite hangout at that time for Low-Soc groups) he said with sadness: "The junior high kids migrated to Sorrento like birds. It seems that the guys are taking the Soc side more than the levi and khaki's side. We are dying out. We're a dying race. I suppose that when an Ese grows up and gets married he doesn't want his kids to be like us. Everything goes bad for us."

The streetcorner youth left behind are not merely those under the least control by parents and school. They also include the leaders, who have internalized the norms and values of their formations to the fullest and have attained positional advantages unmatched by their intimate friends. Such factors, as well as the habits, attitudes, and fears of reconstructing their friendship relations, bind them closer to their formations. They stay with their remaining friends, leading them through the halcyon days into the final years of adolescence.

A Group That Changed Communities

As indicated, adolescents sometimes change allegiances because of factors somewhat outside their control. The reasons for these changes may involve the dynamic interaction of stradom, ethnic, socioeconomic, and delinquent relationships. We illustrate the effects of such an interaction with an unusual case of a group that switched identities. In this account, a streetcorner group was withdrawn from stradom conflicts in a fairly impoverished working-class community when some of the parents moved to a socioeconomically heterogeneous community with a sizeable proportion of working-class families, but skewed in favor of skilled blue-collar, entrepreneurial, sales, managerial, and professional families.

In the early days of its formation, the group had not been a streetcorner group at all. Although a number of the boys had previously been close friends, the group itself had been formed within a local community center in a working-class neighborhood. In the early years of junior high, model building and athletic activities were important group interests. Until high school, only one member had a record of arrest, and virtually all the others were nondelinquent. Some eventually went on to college.

Various factors distinguished this community-center group from the neighborhood streetcorner groups. The latter met outside any agency (although some of their membes participated in athletic programs) and were primarily or entirely composed of Mexican and Mexican–American youth. The community-center group included a mixture of Jewish and Mexican–American boys. In addition, one member of the club was an Apache Indian and another was Afro–American. The socioeconomic status of the families of this group also set it apart from the streetcorner groups. The heads of these families had generally found more stable employment and higher-status jobs. Toward the end of junior high, the style of life exhibited by the center group also differed from that of the streetcorner groups. Their style of life generally represented mainline working-class rather than subproletarian patterns. On occasion, the group's style of dress and behavior was also indicative of incipient Soc characteristics.

However, by the end of junior high, the members of the group took the title "Kings" for their club name. Also, at this time, other groups in the community began to force the group into a defensive fighting posture in certain situations. For example, the unusual ethnic, racial, and religious composition of the group became a pretext for harrassment by members of streetcorner groups, who objected to intermixing of this sort. In addition, the Kings found themselves challenged by one particular streetcorner group when they accepted Leon, a club member's brother, who had previously belonged to the other group. Leon had left the streetcorner group but in doing so refused to submit to the "gang-up" (a beating by all club members) traditionally inflicted on members who left voluntarily. The Kings supported Leon's refusal and thereby earned the enmity of the entire streetcorner group.

On the whole, the conflicts between the Kings and other groups were sporadic and infrequent. However, intergroup conflicts began to erupt in an intramural basketball competition sponsored by a variety of community social agencies. The Kings' team fought fiercely for the winning title but found themselves in a number of ugly incidents with opposing teams that included boys in the antagonistic streetcorner groups. The normative boundaries between the streetcorner conflicts and the intramural competition began to break down during the heat of the games. Fights with the Kings broke out regularly during and after the basketball events.

Although the number of violent incidents increased, for various reasons the Kings still did not adopt an aggressive policy toward other groups. At the time, most of the members rejected the violent style of life among streetcorner groups. In addition, they were aware that an aggressive policy would ultimately fail, because their group was smaller than most of the streetcorner groups. Furthermore, the Kings did not belong to any of the intergroup protective alliances in the community. On the other hand, the membership of the Kings did decide to stand their ground if attacked, and they operated as a defensive group that dealt with violence as it appeared.

The group underwent various internal changes during the period it was under attack. Several members, who were more or less "outsiders," left the group in order to avoid further personal conflict. A few of the boys (who would attend college in the future) also left because of increasing pressure to maintain high scholastic averages. Since some of these boys had been in the leadership, the remaining members were forced to restructure their group relationships. New leaders emerged, but in the context of the increasing violence, these leaders were chosen partly for their personal strength and potential for commanding a defensive fighting club.

In a short time, the changes in the group's composition and structure initiated a new period in its life. During this period, the remaining boys became more positively oriented to the ethos represented by local streetcorner relations, even though the group was clearly on the outermost boundaries of a network formed by these predominantly Mexican and Mexican–American streetcorner groups. Subsequently, a substantial number of new boys became part of the group. The rapid increase in size emboldened the members, and they decided to acquire club jackets. In spite of the great possibility that this would further provoke every streetcorner group in the area, they purchased jackets embroidered with *The Kings of East L.A.* in large letters. Steve, a member of the Kings, commented: "I knew that they were going to get into fights. They were walking around in black pants and jackets, like they were big and bad. I'm the only club member who never did buy a jacket. I told them I didn't have the money and I started playing basketball in school and staying away for a long time."

This new phase of the group's development was suddenly aborted. After additional provocations by other gangs, in an act of desperation, the parents of approximately half the boys in the Kings, especially the Anglo boys, moved to the previously mentioned heterogeneous community one after another. Here they hoped to put an end to the increasing danger involving their sons. The club itself, however, did not dissolve in the face of this change. The half of the group still living in the original community was primarily made up of Mexican–American members. These members were able to marshal two or three cars to travel to the new community, where they rejoined their friends almost every evening. A club hangout, a combination miniature golf course and refreshment stand, was selected in the new community.

Unfortunately, the streetcorner clubs in the *new* neighborhood began to focus their attention on the Kings when they became well established at the new hangout. The Kings soon found that they had literally moved from the frying pan into the fire. Rachel, one of their girl friends, described this period: "When they first came out here, the Kings in their own minds didn't want to be considered East L.A. bums. They wanted to be respected and wanted to be Soc, but on the East Side they couldn't be. They were sort of Socs on the East Side. They came here, in their opinion, to better themselves. But when the boys came here . . . although they wanted to be goodie-goodies . . . other clubs who were Ese went up to them and said, 'You're from the East Side. You're supposed to be bad. Why don't you prove it to us.' Again they were defending themselves." Rachel continued, "They were pushed into this division of being bad and near the top in the neighborhood. The West Side Socs considered them Eses from the East Side. They thought that they were starting all these fights. The Kings couldn't back out of them when these guys were picking on them."

The situation confronting the boys was more complex than is suggested by Rachel, because, according to the members, they were "pulled" as well as "pushed" into their new status as a fighting gang. Our observations of the boys indicate an immediate awareness of the advantages accrued from their new-found reputation as a "rough" gang from the East Side. Perhaps one of the most important advantages was their attractiveness to the streetcorner girls in the area. The girls were fascinated by the "best of all worlds" offered by these boys, who related to them like Socs and yet dealt with all neighboring groups like Eses. In fact, the term "Soc-Vato" was actually used to characterize the unusual identity acquired by these youth at the time. (Vato in this context is equated with Ese, because both words are derived from Ese Vato.)

As indicated, ambiguities in stradom identity had also existed when the group had lived on the East Side. Moreover, this ambiguity had been maintained by the marginal status of the group vis-a-vis the streetcorner groups in *that* community. However, any ambiguity in identity carried over to the West Side began to vanish once the group members had assessed the possibilities of action within their *new* social environment. In the new community, the Kings made no claim to being a socialite club, because such a claim would be altogether lacking in credibility. Irrespective of the fact that a few of the boys did wear clothes that were nicknamed "ivy leagues" at the time, the age and model of their cars and their limited spending money very clearly distinguished them from the socialite groups in the new community. These latter groups were exclusively drawn from white families. Moreover these families were largely middle-class. The Kings were now at the bottom of their community's socioeconomic status ladder.

In the first months, the Kings were in conflict about the name of their club. Should they continue calling themselves "The Kings of *East* L.A." or change to "The Kings of *West* L.A."? Obviously the latter name was more appropriate, considering that the group was now located on the west side of town. But the realistic appraisal of their status as a streetcorner club in the neighborhood and their desire to exploit the advantages of their new position finally crystallized in a group decision to retain their name, "The Kings of East L.A." This decision accomplished two aims. It maintained the unusual attractiveness of the group for the girls in the area. It also enabled the boys to capitalize on the reputation that East Side clubs had among both the hostile streetcorner and the haughty socialite groups in the new community. Other youth in the community gave them wide berth, deferred to them, or regarded them as powerful antagonists. In certain respects, the Kings found themselves regarded as superior beings. They were perceived as a virile and powerful gang.

However, this peaceful situation also changed. Driven on by the considerable advantages to a club with the top reputation among stradom formations, the Kings again found themselves in one conflict after another with local streetcorner formations. Most of these conflicts ended in short, swift skirmishes, usually involving the most aggressive cliques in the group. Despite this, the club as a whole gained a reputation for being a formidable enemy. Although most of the stories surrounding the development of this reputation far exceeded the actual events, some of them were accurate. One violent incident, for example, involved a member of another club who received an almost fatal brain concussion. This concussion was inflicted when someone from an opposing gang was beaten by three members of the Kings. In the beating, he was trapped between Bob, Chuck, and Dan, who had a garrison belt wrapped around his fist. Dan recounts the events: "Bob sidestepped him and caught him and hit him in the mouth. And when he hit him . . . Chuck was on the side . . . Chuck caught him and held him while Bob hit him. And the cops didn't know this, but Bob had a nice trailer hitch bolt in his hand and I had a belt in my hand . . . and Bob hit him and he spun out of Chuck's hand and Chuck hit him. And he came to me and I [Dan] hit him and he fell down. On the way down, I hit him with the belt in his head and Chuck said, 'Goddam, you sure are ugly!' . . . and stomped on his head."

The Kings had become an aggressive fighting gang. Their reputation was actively maintained for over two years. The aggressive activity then declined with the final major conflict, lasting several months, between the Kings and another group. This conflict was terminated when the police actively sought opportunities to intercept and arrest gang members from either side who were involved in "hit-and-run" attacks. A community newspaper account of one such police interception reads:

> NAB YOUTHS READY FOR GANG FIGHT
>
> Eight cars [filled with] police officers swooped down last night on a gang of juveniles getting ready to fight and arrested 20 of them on a variety of charges.
>
> Detectives said there was a fight at a doughnut shop . . . [on] Thursday night in which one youth was cut. Police received a tip that there was going to be a gang fight in retaliation last night.
>
> After the 20 youths were loaded into the police cars, police gathered up baseball bats, bowling pins, lead pipes with beer can openers taped on the end, string black jacks, barbecue forks and taped-up chains.
>
> Most of the suspects were booked for curfew violations, but a few were also charged with suspicion of possession of deadly weapons.
>
> "I just hope we saved somebody's life tonight," one of the detectives remarked.

The increasingly violent activity was not the only change for the Kings. Other significant changes occurred as well. Rachel continued: "I went with them because of what I had heard about the Kings. I expected . . . God only knows what . . . but they were entirely different. When I met them, all of them were going to school . . . and all were getting good grades. Some of them had cars. They dressed neat. They were not hoodlums as I expected. They got the reputation because most of them came from the East Side and were supposed to be bad. But they came here . . . in my eyes to better themselves."

"When I first met them they didn't drink so much . . . and most of them never got drunk. *Now* they drink more and get sloppy drunk. The girls that hang with them now are . . . completely changed. They are sloppier and from their actions they are tramps.

They put on anything that makes them look sexier. They still have a crowd of followers but they are entirely *new*. I haven't been around for a while but I went to a party just a little while ago and it hit me that they have changed."

It is possible that the Kings might have evolved into an aggressive group in their original (working-class) community; but it is highly unlikely that any claim to status dependent upon violence would have been anything but a short-lived disaster in that context. It is our belief that the major factor in the actual development of the group's highly aggressive fighting stance was its unambiguous transition to a streetcorner position within the new community. This transition placed the group members more squarely within a network of ethnocentric streetcorner relationships. It is ironic that over a relatively short period the Kings became firmly embedded in the general pattern of life among the streetcorner formations in the new locality, even though some of their parents had in fact moved them to that community in order to keep them "out of trouble."

The change in this group's status relationships and the concomitant change in membership attitudes and behavior testify to the difference in conditions and effects of socialite and streetcorner life. The marginal status temporarily held by the group and typified by the title "Soc-Vato" is suggestive of similarities in the standpoints of socialite and streetcorner groups. It also suggests the importance of structural determinants on the lives of youth within the stratified domains of groups.

18

Vehicle Codes and Peer Formations

In California, adolescents devote considerable time to automobiles. By the age of 16, they count the days until they get their licenses and are allowed to drive family cars. Thousands also acquire funds to buy their own motor vehicles, and early studies indicate that teen-age drivers reported spending 20% of their buying power on cars (Los Angeles Chamber of Commerce, 1967). Their cars symbolize independence, status, and power. Cars are used for commuting to school and work; for cruising, street dragging, drinking, and sex (Bauman, 1978; Goldberg, 1969). Yet, Higgins and Albrecht (1982:39) observe, "Since the symbolic value and use of the automobile is so central to American adolescent life styles, it seems surprising that juvenile use of cars has not received more sociological attention."

A similar judgement can be made about the importance of automobiles to criminology. Law enforcement officers, in most states, find that the automobile brings them into daily conflict with adolescents because many 15- to 18-year-olds come to the attention of the law, either directly or indirectly, in connection with motor vehicles. The incidents creating this attention are diverse and include such things as speeding, joyriding, stealing gasoline, street dragging (racing), transporting marijuana, and even damaging front lawns by driving over them (McFarland and Moore, 1961:180). In fact, even though general theories of delinquency have little or nothing to say about vehicle violations, disobeying vehicle codes may be the most common offense among older adolescents.

On the other hand, theories specifically devoted to "deviant" uses of the automobile do exist, but they strike a very familiar theoretical chord. One participant observation study, by Myerhoff and Myerhoff (1964), described the centrality of the automobile to an apparently socialite or intemediary stradom formation. They indicated that most members of the crowd had access to late-model sports cars, and thus to mobile parlors, club houses, dining rooms, and bedrooms. The car was "the setting and symbol of much adolescent deviant and nondeviant sociability and sexuality." Yet, even though the "bull sessions," "drinking bouts," and "necking parties" that took place in cars were typical for working-class as well as middle-class stradom formations, the Myerhoffs explained these relationships on the basis of freudian propositions about the sexual ambivalence of middle-class boys.

Other psychoanalytically oriented researchers attribute the deviant use of automobiles by adolescents to "emotional conflict and insecurity," "sexual anxiety," "psychopathic maladjustment," "oral–sadistic fantasies," "megalomania" and "hostile, acting-out tendencies." Automobiles are "phallic symbols," and "extreme need for recognition" leads to reckless driving, and a "need for escape" may be manifested in excessive speeds. Even in "the simplest cases," Gibbens (1958:262) declares, "joy-riding is of the common 'proving type' in which an overprotected lad from a 'good' home commits an offense to prove his masculinity. . . . the daring act represents a bid for independence, and the car provides a feeling of power in which he feels so lacking. . . . "

Some researchers avoid such facile generalizations, attributing the high incidence of vehicle violations and accidents to factors correlated with driving experience. Yet many adolescents continue to violate the law once they have gained experience; moreover, adolescents generally do extremely well when tested for those physiological abilities that influence safety and propriety in automobile driving. In this respect, ". . . reaction times are shortest, night vision and glare resistance are best, and the ability to learn coordinated skills is highest in the late teens and early twenties." Accordingly, "evidence that accident rates among young drivers are disproportionately high presents the paradox that the driver is most susceptible to accidents at the time of his greatest potential operating skill" (McFarland and Moore, 1961:181).

Violations and Styles of Life

Recognizing that automobiles are integrated into preexisting adolescent relationships is an alternative way to understand the high rate of vehicle violations and accidents. In cities such as Los Angeles, where public transportation is both limited and expensive and where the automobile is considered almost as essential as a roof over your head, many streetcorner youth have cars. Violent conflicts occur between streetcorner groups even though they are prohibited by law; but vehicle violations come into play when automobiles are utilized in such conflicts. For example, intergroup violence that involves throwing rocks or other missiles from cars and discharging firearms at vehicles or their occupants are considered felonies by the California Vehicle Code. Here, gang wars between youth who drive between territories miles apart occur because the automobile enlarges the geographic space in which groups contend for status. Moreover, the automobile compounds the offenses connected with illegal market developments and ethnocentric relationships. Not only does automobile misuse (speeding, drunken driving, etc.) generate new violations, but it can be used to carry illegal goods such as narcotics and weapons, and to transport culprits away from the scene of the crime.

Adolescent styles of life, including conformity to minor fads, also contribute to a higher incidence of vehicle violations and accidents. For instance, faddish styles at one point included sunglasses with very wide temples or opaque side pieces. While these features were attractive to some adolescents, they had an adverse effect on driving; therefore, vehicle codes prohibited the use of glasses with temple widths that interfered with lateral vision. Such codes, however, were often disregarded when style was considered more important. In a conversation with a socialite wearing glasses with very wide temples, we asked whether she knew that they might restrict driving vision. She replied that she was not only aware of the legal restriction but removed her glasses while applying for a license because she was afraid the clerk might compel her to get new frames. She added, however, that immediately after getting the license, she stepped into the car, put on her sunglasses, and drove away.

The violations based on life styles are produced by very understandable social relationships. Wearing stylish accessories provides pleasure and heightened self-esteem. Reasons for the use of automobiles as "mobile bedrooms" are equally evident. However, the motivated character of sexual intercourse in automobiles is hardly different because it takes place in automobiles rather than in houses or barns or out-of-doors. The car can simply be a more convenient and private setting for sexual liaisons; and those types of youth who engage more frequently in intercourse will do so wherever it is convenient.

Joyriding (temporarily stealing a car to take a ride) is also connected with certain adolescent patterns. The recurrent interest in wild car escapades is prevalent among streetcorner youth, including, incidentally, nondrivers. Socialites may engage in a greater amount of joyriding, while streetcorner youth may steal rides on the backs of trucks, street cars, and subway trains. But in this context, any differences in the motives behind their theft of motorized transportation are not usually due to sexual hangups, the means of transportation, or the seriousness attributed by officials to such thievery; rather, they are due to stradom norms and values whose meanings are expressed in the conversations that initiate the escapades. Sometimes these conversations demonstrate that an escapade is stimulated by an adolescent's desire to "prove himself." But such desires usually originate in group standards (especially sexist standards that define masculine behavior) and not in latent homosexual tendencies.

Finally, the incidence of driving under the influence of alcohol or narcotics is high among teens. However, the consumption of alcohol or narcotics by the adolescents we observed did not represent new conduct that started when they reached driving age. Adolescent drivers whose styles of life had previously included frequent consumption of alcohol or narcotics continued to consume them in automobiles when they learned to drive.

These and other considerations suggest that the incidence of vehicle violations and accidents is correlated with the adolescent social type developments described in previous chapters. Some published research on vehicle violations may be relevant in this context. For instance, in a review of such research, McFarland and Moore (1961:184–88) found that frequent offenders were characterized by higher school truancy and "drop-out" rates. They note that studies also found "a group, ranging up to about one-third of all youthful offenders, who are repeatedly being apprehended for vehicle violations." These offenders also have contact with a variety of judicial and public service agencies for other kinds of violations. Personality test findings are also interesting. These youth have considerable "disregard of the social mores and more defiance of authority" than others. They are more likely to manifest an "urge to do something harmful or shocking" or a "desire to frighten other individuals for the fun of it." They exhibit "a tendency to become readily impatient with people" or a "tendency to become suspicious of overfriendly people." Can these adolescents be members of stradom formations?

The possibility that these frequent violators are disproportionately represented by socialite, intermediary, and especially streetcorner youth is indicated by further studies. Reminiscent of Coleman's belief in the apparent opposition between athletics and academic pursuits, some studies support the allegation that "among boys especially, the desire to get a driver's license and to own a car is probably the most powerful anti-intellectual force that our schools meet" (McFarland and Moore, 1961:175). It is also reported that automobile ownership encourages poor school performance. One study indicated, for instance, that the drop-out rate was about four times higher, absenteeism was almost twice as great, the grade-point average was less, and more courses were failed among frequent drivers than among nondrivers. With regard to repeated offenders, further studies show "that four-fifths of these drivers were working below the level of their ability in school, two-thirds were discipline problems in school, three-fourths had poor relations with teachers, and half were considered to be aggressive" (1961:88). And, last but not least, Higgins and Albrecht's (1982:29) study concluded: "Contrary to previous research, auto theft is not a 'pure' delinquency specialty. Auto thieves and traffic offenders were likely to be involved in other delinquent activities as well. Further, gang members were more likely to be auto misusers than youth who did not belong to a gang."

Reflecting upon these relationships, we have concluded that the correlations between traffic violations and either school performance, delinquent behavior, "antisocial" attitudes, or narcotics and alcohol consumption are symptomatic of the styles of life and ethical attitudes we have discussed in previous chapters. Consequently, our evaluation of these studies suggests that even though vehicle violations and accidents are much more evenly distributed among the adolescent population than is robbery or assault, for instance, problem behavior with vehicles is still overrepresented among members of the stradom formations in areas where autos are driven regularly by older adolescents. Members of the three stradom formations can therefore be expected to be involved in more violations and accidents than other types of youth.

Car Clubs

It seems clear that there is mutual interaction between adolescent styles of life and automobile use. The adoption of the automobile impacts on stradom life styles because it provides a focus for the development of aesthetic tastes, specialized knowledge, and social activity. More importantly, the car is central to the development of stradom formations called "car clubs" or "car crowds," even though these groups are frequently composed of friendships that predate adolescent automobile use.

Thus, toward the end of high school, there emerge a number of groups identified by their ownership and use of cars. The members of some clubs can afford sports vehicles, even expensive foreign models such as Porsches, and they may equip their cars with "all the factory extras," including specially designed power equipment. Most clubs, however, must remain content with inexpensive stock cars. Consequently, the entire claim to being a distinctive car club is frequently warranted only by the fact that most members own cars. Even though these clubs sport metal plaques with etched logos or club names in rear windows, they are similar, in most other respects, to social clubs not identified with automobile use.

Some members of car clubs and crowds make up for the lack of money for sports cars by making minor automobile modifications, such as installing a stick shift or a higher-power motor, themselves. Others make more distinctive modifications to the automobile suspension. The "low-riding" streetcorner clubs, for instance, lower the chassis until the space between the bottom of the car frame and the ground is approximately the size of a standard package of cigarettes. Other clubs raise the back suspension and lower the front, creating the "Diego rake" or just a "rake." If this modification is not appealing, they conspicuously elevate the entire chassis. These "high riders" sometimes have a center of gravity so high, they are unsafe at normal cruising speeds. Sometimes adolescents elevate the back of the car to accommodate wide racing tires, called "slicks," on the axle. They install "Hollywood mufflers" so that the entire car emits a mighty roar whenever it is accelerated. They decorate the body with fantastic striping or flame-like flourishes or scalloping. They buy chrome-plated spotlights or wire racing-car wheels. They remove all the chrome-plated trim on the exterior of the car including the grill, and "leaden" in the cracks. ("Shaving in" a car in this way creates an illusion of a smooth, one-piece fiberglass or metallic body.) They spray the entire automobile with brilliant purple, yellow, or bronze paint flecked with millions of tiny particles of shiny aluminum. Only their imaginations limit their creative improvisations.

Adolescents sometimes spend their last penny to obtain a "tuck and roll," magnificently colored leather upholstery, below the border in Tijuana, where highly skilled Mexican workers perform wonders on the interiors of cars. These same youth often paint a unique name on the side of the car, such as Daffy-Duck, Apache Wagon, Lover Boy, Cherry Buster, the Invader, Los Vatos, Cowboy, or Voodoo Wagon. These names usually signify a sexually potent attractive male, the game-fighting Dude, or courageous, insane defiance of the conventional world. Automobiles are sometimes fetishized, and then one hears streetcorner youth say: "the guys sometimes make heroes out of their cars." Some adolescents brag, "this old car can do everything but tie your shoelaces. It's a boss car!"

Hot Rodders

Hot Rod clubs emerge especially in suburban areas, or in central cities where public transportation is very restricted and the automobile is the most widespread means of transportation. Contrasted with the members of other car clubs, who usually represent just another stradom formation, the Hot Rodder is a distinct social type. Moreover, most Hot Rodders seem to have been preoccupied with automobiles earlier, when they were members of various kinds of stradom formations.

Ostensibly, when the Hot Rod tradition first started at the end of the 1930s, it centered on the creation of the fastest car, the most efficient engine, and the most advanced mechanical innovations. The development of these cars was a direct result of the experience, knowledge, and time expended upon them by their builders, who were primarily young adults and adults. In these early years, the builders designed their own cars, did their own "head work" and "crank work," redesigned and built new frontal areas to lower wind resistance, or altered the chassis to give the car stability at high speeds. They became familiar with power-to-weight ratios and generally mastered the principles governing the car as a complex machine.

The widespread development of adolescent interests in hot rodding during the postwar period laid the foundations for a new market for the auto manufacturers and parts industry. When Detroit introduced their high-powered, overhead-valve V-8 models, the adolescent was able to purchase a powerful engine over the counter and have a mechanic install it in an older, lighter body such as a Ford coupe. Because of this, faster cars became available, not only to individuals able to construct and design a custom racing car, but to adolescents who had the wealth to lavish on them. The availability of automobile parts had a similar history. Small spare-parts manufacturing companies, known as "speed houses," often managed by older Hot Rodders who manufactured products of their own design, now profitably produced special cams, superchargers, and the like. The changes during the decades after the Second World War have been summed up by Mort Sahl: "When I grew up in California, you built your own car—a hot rod—and it was evidence of your personality. Now you can buy a sports car as a short cut to character. People ask you who you are and you show them your car." The rapid development of cars for "show" rather than "go" paralleled this process. A show car represented the customizing of interior and exterior features of the auto for its "looks."

Like the pure Athlete or Surfer, the Hot Rod's special interest, and the standards governing its attainment, became an important basis for organizing peer relationships. For those who belonged to Hot Rod clubs and spent all their spare time working on their cars or racing them, their identity as Hot Rodders was the primary identity positioning them meaningfully in the social distribution of peer identities.

When we asked Hot Rodders to describe other kinds of youth who used cars, they described groups that were similar to socialite and streetcorner formations. They mentioned the "sports car" and "Cadillac clubs" composed of "snobs" who were distinguished primarily by their fashionable tastes and possession of money. These latter youth were held in contempt because they didn't know "what's going on under the hood."[1] Finally, there were the "Shot Rodders" or "Outlaws," who were regarded contemptuously because "their cars look squirreley." These particular youth reportedly gave a "bad name" to hot rodding because they drove unsafely and modified their cars without regard to driving safety. The Shot Rodders and Outlaws were generally described as being poorer than other car buffs, and the Hot Rodders identified them with streetcorner groups and styles of life. This analysis suggested that Hot Rodders could not be associated with typical vehicle-violating teens and young adults.

A study of outstanding Hot Rodders reports that these individuals were not involved in many accidents (McFarland and Moore, 1961:174–75; Neavles and Winokur, 1957). Their superior ability in operating a car was said to account for this low accident rate. From our own observations of adolescent car enthusiasts, it is clear that these youth do have to be differentiated to understand their incidence of vehicle violations and accidents. One summer we observed and travelled with an upper-middle-class Hot Rod car club called "The Rails," whose 11 members were sufficiently wealthy to possess their own individual hot rod cars as well as a "club car." These senior-class high-school boys had invested thousands of dollars (as well as their personal time and energy) in the construction of a racing car, which was never used for street dragging although the personal cars were employed in this fashion. The car was regularly towed to official drag strips and entered into competitions there. The members had belonged to formations in all parts of the peer society, but most were previously in stradom formations. In fact, two of them had belonged to a middle-class streetcorner crowd prior to their adoption of the Hot Rod identity.

The members of the club had ambivalent feelings toward vehicle codes. There was a strong practical tendency among them to disparage racing under hazardous conditions. This applied especially to street or highway drag races. Nevertheless, it was apparent that their zest for racing made it difficult to turn down a challenge. Further, although perhaps increasing age and length of membership in the group would have revealed an increasing interest in "professional" drag-strip racing as opposed to street dragging, the latter type of racing was much more frequent, even though it provided enormous potential for serious code violations and accidents.

Street dragging represented potential hazards to Hot Rodders as well as unwitting motorists on the highways being used for races. Dead-end streets and passing motorists unavoidably created highly dangerous situations. This was reflected in the sage advice provided by one of the Hot Rod club members, Carl: "Don't let anybody else pick the road you're gonna race on. One of our boys raced a guy on this road and he beat him. But near the end, the other guy [the competitor] shut down [his motor speed] real fast. We suddenly realized that the road was a dead-end road! We were able to go around in a circle but wrecked a good set of tires."

Sometimes, the appearance of the police escalates the danger. The informal racing meets held by adolescents and young adults provide examples. Carl observed, "A few hazards occur at the meets. It is not the races themselves, but what happens when the police come. The cars tear-off in all directions. Like when we were out at the A & W [a fast-food drive-in whose location was near the place where races were frequently held; consequently, A & W identified the locale]. There was a fog and the cops came. I had to turn my lights on. And off down the street I go . . . I was doing about 110 [miles per hour] and nobody else turns on their lights . . . and all of a sudden there is this car in front of me. I almost hit him."

Frank, also a member of the Hot Rod club, recalled, on another occasion, "We raced next to the International Airport . . . on a private road and we got in about 5 or 6 races before we stopped. We thought we saw a cop [patrol car]. We had at least 300 people at that race [and many became alarmed and prepared to leave]. Airport guards were looking through their little houses wondering what was happening. Everybody uncorked their cars and you got loud rumbles. It looked and sounded like a race track out there. You should'a seen the cars tear off in all directions at the end."

In part, the frequency of street racing can be attributed to the lack of inexpensive drag strips. Most strips near Los Angeles are either privately or municipally owned and charge high racing fees for Hot Rodders. On the whole, the citizenry are not interested in supporting drag strips, and Hot Rodders say, "even the police will say that since the citizens around here will not build a strip, the kids have to race somewhere." Consequently, the Hot Rodders would move their racing from place to place to avoid the police. "We went to race the Hustlers in Englewood and had one good race," Jim, another Hot Rodder, observed. "Then we went back to get some of the big machines and brought them with us. But the police raided the lot. They lined us against the wall. There was, as I heard it, 143 of us there. So far, outside of the L.A. river days [when racing would occur on the Los Angeles river bottom's concrete bed] that was one of the best meets around here. The cops told us to kindly leave their city. We got out of there and raced somewhere else. But it was a lot of fun racing there. We did "blow out" [beat] every machine they [the Hustlers] had."

There is both humor and pride in the stories these youth tell of the races and encounters they have had. For instance, Jim related: "We had this car, the Ruptured Duck. A pretty good car. An old Chevy with a 238 in it, bore 301. Well, everybody knew about it and didn't want to race it. So one night I went to Bob's [a drive-in restaurant in the San Fernando Valley, a favorite hangout for Hot Rodders] and everyone knows about our club there. We were ying-yanging [talking] back and forth and a guy says, 'You want to race?' He asks what club I was in. I told him. He asks if I was the guy with the yellow '40 [a yellow 1940 Chevy coupe with a high-powered engine]. *Everyone* knew about the yellow '40. Then, Raymond drives up in his Ford and this guy looks at the Ford and asks 'What's it running?' Raymond says, '348,' The guy looks at him and says, 'What is it?' Raymond says, '380 with a three speed.' The guy says 'That don't sound so hot. My car will beat that.' Raymond says, 'Daddy-O, that Ford *ain't* the car you're gonna race!'"

With regard to other types of youth, these Hot Rodders complained bitterly. "It's the younger guys, many of them Socs who race just to show off. They get their daddy's car, and race other guys on the street and often get themselves killed and give us a bad name." The streetcorner boy was recognized as the most dangerous violator of all. Persistent streetcorner practices, such as driving while drunk, were reproached by club members and, in fact, might result in expulsion from the club. Their identity as bona-fide Hot Rods overrode other interests and habits, some of which remained from prior adolescent identities. From their standpoint, the automobile was a machine to be controlled by a highly capable driver who required efficiency, speed, and safety to win the race. Practices conflicting with these aims were usually condemned. Consequently, sentiments toward the types of violations and accidents committed by Hot Rodders varied somewhat from the sentiments held by other adolescent social types, especially streetcorner types, who drove frequently under the influence of alcohol and narcotics.

NOTE

1. It is interesting to note that similar references to streetcorner youth were also made by those interested in motorcycles. The counterpart to the Hot Rodders might be the boys who drove "limey bikes" (or bikes produced by Japanese companies) and raced with them. These youth were forever tinkering with

their machines. Then there were the Hog Riders who modified their powerful American-built Harley-Davidson motorcycles with a particular assortment of chrome-plated parts, such as "sissy bars" and futuristically shaped tail pipes. Some Hog Riders cut through the motorcycle frame to lower the height of the motor and called their bikes "chopped Hogs." These youth were especially condemned as Outlaws by highly conventional motorcycle riders of all ages, who preferred "fully dressed" Harley Davidsons with chrome and leather accessories and windshields. These concerns of the conventional riders were similar to the reactions of the American Surfing Association members to rowdy Surfers, Gremmies, and Hodads, who were said to be "ruining the beaches" for bona-fide Surfers.

19

Social Context of Streetcorner Marijuana Use

When we were engaged in participant observation, narcotics use spread like wildfire, especially among streetcorner boys during the middle and final years of adolescence. Drug use largely consisted of smoking marijuana and "dropping" a variety of stimulants, tranquilizers, and other psychoactive pills. At the time of our observations, persistent marijuana use by individuals began at about 15 to 17 years of age on the average, but some junior-high-school students temporarily adopted and then discontinued its use until their senior-high-school years. Finally, the streetcorner groups in this age range were the earliest and heaviest consumers of narcotics, although small groups of other types of users also existed. Drug use was heavily concentrated among boys and not girls. Older adolescent streetcorner girls preferred pills, although they increased their marijuana consumption in young adulthood.

We will devote this chapter to marijuana consumption among streetcorner boys. At the time of the study, marijuana use was very severely repressed by police. Despite the repression and, in part, because of it, marijuana use had an enormous impact on group life. This repression, however, had virtually no effect on the availability of marijuana, even though it created security problems for consumers. In Southern California marijuana was readily available and inexpensive most of the time, because it was supplied by numerous dealers who drove across the border into Mexico and back again. U.S. Customs had virtually no control over the massive narcotics traffic between Mexico and the United States. Even adolescent drug dealers commuted to Tijuana to replenish their supplies of marijuana and pills.

The experience of marijuana consumption seemed to vary depending on the individual. While consuming marijuana in a comfortable and secure setting, these boys dreamt of materialistic goals or nostalgically relived their past. Sonny was high on marijuana when he reported, "My favorite dream is having a black Buick, with low white tires, black and white interior. You dig? Appeltons bossed down real nice [car spotlights that shine brightly]." Others who just smoked a joint in a friend's house sat quietly combing their hair until it was "just about right" while they continued to dream about themselves. Friends of a boy who was an immigrant from Poland remarked, "You know Henry goes on a weird trip every now and then and talks all about his old friends from Warsaw." Henry's "trip" on marijuana reflected a nostalgic longing to relive his life in Warsaw.

There were also many who recognized that marijuana slowed their physiological coordination and dulled their mental abilities; nevertheless, they reported using the drug because it helped them "have a good time." Nate's remarks provide a good illustration: "I once went to a party and I was tired and I lit up a righteous joint and it made me feel like I wanted to dance and it makes me feel that I can have a better time and when the guys make wisecracks I don't care about it. It doesn't make me feel that I can dance better but it puts me more into it. It makes me crack-up and have a good time."

The effects on personal appearance, self-esteem, and mental abilities might also be considered important. "Look at the Kings when they go around," said an older streetcorner youth. "They are more or less shabby [because most of them do not use marijuana]. The Low Riders are dressed better because they get high. When you are down you don't care about nothing but when you are high you dress better and care about things." Despite the negative effects of marijuana on coordination, learning, and response time, some consumers were convinced that the drug made them more sensitive and discriminating about music and encouraged them to care more about their dress and appearance. They felt they could think more rapidly and effectively because of it and they could solve problems heretofore beyond their grasp. "If I started getting higher when I was in 5th or 6th grade, I could have been through college right now," said one youth in response to our inquiries into the effects of the drug. Another also emphasized its "mind-expansion" effects: "You know how the computer works on a naval gun. It's the same thing. Your mind works like a machine when you're high." Still another made the same point: "The talk went around for a long time that that Dude . . . what was his name? Albert Einstein! There was talk that that Dude, Einstein, got high. I can believe it. Now I won't say he did or I won't say he didn't. But I can say this: For what he could figure out and for the way his mind worked, I can say that he possibly could have been high [on marijuana]."

Thus, generally, the interpretation of marijuana's effects depended upon personal interests, outlooks, and concerns. For most streetcorner youth, marijuana was an escape from their drab everyday lives. It enabled them to enter a delightful subjective and social world. Often almost an entire group became involved in marijuana use. This virtually total adoption of the drug indicates the possibility that a variety of motives and personalities were being served by marijuana consumption rather than any specific kind of immaturity, frustration, or emotional disturbance. When the older adolescent consumers were relaxed and free from fear of apprehension, they created, in fantasy, what they wanted most out of themselves and others. At the same time, most of them were able to drop whatever they were doing and attentively scan their environment at the slightest suspicion of detection.

Marijuana Consumption and Life Style

Especially in its early stages, marijuana consumption never seemed confined to the individual consumer or to the sensations of using marijuana alone. The relations between the consumer and the environmental stimulations (including, above all, the stimulations that were planfully organized by the consumer or that were dependent upon interpersonal relations) seemed to be quite significant for "turning on" and maintaining marijuana use. The most significant relations were interpersonal. We found that, in the beginning, the drug was usually consumed in a group context consisting at least of a small clique of two or three boys. For several years, even when the boys reported "lighting up alone," they added that most of the time they "went to see a friend" shortly after. We also noted cases in which marijuana consumption took place in groups of as many as 15 to 20 persons. Most of the time, the consumers belonged to groups within the same social type domain. However, small crowds of consumers were sometimes composed of members who belonged to different types of groups and who met together at a hangout just to engage in marijuana consumption.

The styles of life of these members were determined by their other associations, and we did not observe a distinct "style of life" that could be identified with marijuana use alone. The term "retreatist" or "narcotics subculture" did not seem at all appropriate for understanding the changes in stradom developments. The adoption of marijuana and/or pills certainly influenced the everyday life of some of the groups we observed, but it did not alter their streetcorner identities.

Marijuana consumption seemed to fit well into a streetcorner style of life, although it was only one of a host of drugs and stimulants used to differing degrees. Alcohol consumption appeared among streetcorner youth early in adolescence, and experimentation with glue sniffing, tranquilizers, stimulants, and many other drugs also began at least by the middle adolescent years. For these youth, enmeshed as they were in anarchic social conditions, drugs or alcohol were generally regarded favorably despite the violence, accidents, and illness sometimes accompanying their use. Even the police, under certain conditions, were hardly considered a deterrent, and their status as moral authorities was insignificant. Also, it seemed that the absence of conflicting vital interests was important for the adoption of drugs. Without these interests—including jobs or long-term occupational goals—each event was greeted with an eye toward immediate sensual gratification, and marijuana consumption easily fulfilled this aim. It also required virtually no skills, no expense beyond its immediate cost, and no other resources than a fairly secure location. Under these conditions the cost of marijuana and police pressure often seemed to be the only factors restricting its dissemination. When police pressure was especially severe and the price of "grass" skyrocketed, the consumption decreased, and peer groups shifted to other drugs. Pills of various types were desirable substitutes, especially because their use was a misdemeanor and not a felony. (Marijuana possession of any sort was a felony at the time.) We even observed the limited use of heroin as a substitute for marijuana when it was scarce.

Marijuana Diffusion within Groups

Despite the easy availability of marijuana, not all streetcorner youth used it. Those who refrained became aware, however, "all of a sudden that a whole group of friends goes on a kick." A marijuana consumer reported: "All of a sudden narcotics appeared, and it encircled me right away. Fighters were lighting up! Burglars were lighting up! Everybody was lighting up!" Sometimes the diffusion process was simply defined as something that "just happens." "You just fall into it."

Among streetcorner groups, once marijuana was available, its consumption or avoidance depended, at least in part, upon the attitudes of leaders who had considerable control over their members. In some cases, leaders discouraged consumption because it undermined control of the group or threatened their own criminal enterprises. The calculations behind such a policy can be seen in this candid and confidential account by a leader of the Kings, toward the end of the club's existence: "The club that goes to using pot cannot be controlled. If you try to get something done, the members say 'Hang it up! We want to blow pot!' If you've got some [illegal market] scheme going, the chances are that your friends will be picked up by the Heat [police] for blowing pot and the Heat will find out all about you."

How do such leaders prevent marijuana use? Interestingly, members of the Kings never expressed the belief that abstinence was due to fear of violence from their club leader or expulsion from the club. Nor, when justifying his opposition to marijuana in front of club members, did this leader ever admit that he was concerned about losing his domination of the group. Instead, he, and the membership in turn, publicly deplored the effects of narcotics on personal health, powers of thinking, and "morality." Ironically, this public line of attack was even adopted by a clique of members who were actually consuming marijuana secretly. Equally ironic is that the sober commentaries on the evils of marijuana did not deter the members of the club from becoming completely "wasted" from alcohol—that is, "stone drunk" at every opportunity.

However, compared to alcohol, marijuana use was frequently considered a preferred mode of "getting high." Even when youth stopped this use because of fear, many protested "marijuana [use] is still better than getting drunk." One boy observed, "Liquor makes you smell and makes you like a pig. I hate it. Pot gives you the same feeling [but] you feel better and you are never out of your mind like when you are wasted [from alcohol]." Another confessed, "I dropped it after Tony and Jack and all the boys got busted. But, it's a good kick if you don't get busted."

While exploring the rationalizations for noninvolvement in marijuana consumption, we found abstinence justified by fear of police, anticipation of workaday status, and the possibility of "staying clean" in the conventional world. Such practical concerns included the hope of entering the armed forces, which was impossible with a narcotics record. The fear of police was certainly real enough, and it was widely (but erroneously) believed that over 50% of the people in California jails at the time were narcotics offenders. Yet, despite the extraordinary police concentration on narcotic offenses, the use of pills and marijuana was spreading among adolescents. This spread, moreover, was not being reversed by legislation, which had become so harsh that many judges were reticent about invoking anything but the minimum stipulated penalties. Older adolescents believed that a conviction on the charge of armed robbery was sometimes preferable to a narcotics conviction.

Abstinence from marijuana use also depended on peer relationships. Frequently, as indicated, the relationships between streetcorner youth themselves (especially the relations with leaders) were underneath the manipulation of rhetoric that defined marijuana use as an ethnocentric, security, or moral issue. Yet wherever peer interests were not in conflict with using it and whenever it was felt that legal risks were minimal, then marijuana smoking could be, and was, engaged in by youth as young as 12 and 13 years of age.

If we turn to the consumers themselves, then the process of recruitment to marijuana use can be accurately identified after a period of observation. The role of leaders, in this context, can be positive as well as negative. Leaders greatly influenced the diffusion of marijuana within their groups. In the Violators and Low Riders, most of the club consumed marijuana after the leading cliques encouraged its use. As mentioned, in the Kings, however, the leader was a Hustler who dealt in marijuana for a while but adamantly refused to let his group use it. Only a minority consumed "weed," even though it had diffused rapidly among the other clubs in their area.

After observing the first two groups over several years, it was ascertained that a leader, Jose, became a consumer through the influence of his cousin's family. This family sustained themselves through the illegal marijuana trade and introduced Jose to the drug when he was about 15 years old. Bob, or "The Dude," as he was called, was a couple of years older than Jose but one of his best friends. He was also introduced to the drug through the influence of the same family. Although both boys lived together under the same roof for a while, they belonged to two different clubs. The groups were friendly to each other and operated in the same area; but one group was composed of older boys than the other. For a long time, Dude was the president of the Low Riders, and Jose filled this office in the Violators.

The diffusion of marijuana moved from high-status to low-status members, from close friends of leaders to peripheral club members. For instance, a lieutenant of the Low Riders, Mole, was introduced to marijuana by Reverend and Wally, two highly respected older delinquents. In addition, Pete, a lieutenant of the Violators, had smoked marijuana when he was only 13 years old. He was part of a Japanese–American and Mexican–American streetcorner crowd at the time, and the drug was reportedly smoked by most members of this group. Pete dropped marijuana for several years, until he became friends with Jose and started it again. These boys "blew Pot" sporadically for about 8 months, and then Jose and Pete "turned on" Dave, Carl, and Oscar, all members of the Violators. These latter boys were close to friends of Pete and Jose prior to their introduction to the weed. During this time, moreover, Dude and Jose introduced marijuana to Jester (an officer in the Low Riders). Also, Dude and Mole turned on another high-status member called Dozie, while Mole converted his close friend, Sailor. Then the diffusion process temporarily slowed down. Shortly thereafter, police pressure decreased the supply, and for a few months marijuana sessions were restricted to groups of two and three boys who were already familiar with the drug and who were carefully hoarding their personal supply.

However, with the renewal of the drug's availability, a few members of the Low Riders, under Dozie's instigation, turned on Jackson and Murray. After this, Gonzo, Hank, Moose, and Daffy (four other members) followed in quick order. One of these boys, Daffy, was extremely disturbed emotionally by the initial drug experience and refused to attend further sessions. He left the group shortly thereafter. His reaction was rationalized and analyzed by Dude in the following way: "There are guys that try it and don't go for it. But, usually, man, the guys who don't go for it . . . it's because of the bust [police arrest] behind it. They go for the pills because they are a misdemeanor. And pills are legal to get. Look at all the girls getting pills. They're getting it because their parents have prescriptions for the stuff." Dude added righteously, "Outside of the fact that they can get busted for it [marijuana], they should never put it down because it's enjoyable. Daffy did it and said he didn't go for it. He said, 'I might as well quit the club,' and he did. At least he got the satisfaction of knowing what it's like." (Dude's explanation makes Daffy's retreat seem simple and rational; however, it is likely that more complicate psychodynamics were behind Daffy's drastic rupture with his old friends.)

Marijuana consumption also spread throughout the remaining Violators, with the exception of a few members who dropped out of the club after a crisis caused by the arrest of three members. These boys were intercepted by the police in the act of making a connection for the purchase of the drug. (More on the effect of this arrest on the group as a whole later.) Shortly after his arrest, his isolation from the boys, and his visits to a probation officer who apparently had social-work training, one boy adopted a psychoanalytic vocabulary and redefined his own reasons for being "turned on." He told us that he had originally agreed to smoke "pot" when "three of us went for a ride and I was turned on. I did it because I didn't like myself very much . . . and [didn't want to] face up to things. It's an experience you share with somebody . . . it's an unhealthy experience." Prior to this period, however, we had detected no shame at all in this boy's responses to marijuana consumption. In fact, his prior conduct had been very much like that of the others, who generally acted as if they were involved in an exciting and irresponsible activity without a care in the world. Two months after his probation had begun, he again engaged in a marijuana session with a few friends. This time, however, regular consumption did not follow, because he was very fearful of being detected. Also, interestingly, the interpretation of his conduct was now free of references to self-esteem or "mental health"; it merely emphasized his fear of being apprehended. He said, "I got turned on and it wasn't half as big a kick as I thought it would be. I just decided that I didn't need it. I worried about it [being arrested] while I was on. I just wanted to see if it was all I thought it was. I said, 'The hell with it! Why should I get messed up the rest of my life.'" Because of his other interests, he had too much to lose.

While this boy faced the experience of drug use after his arrest with considerable trepidation and fear, the others in the Violators went in a different direction. The group of boys who had been using marijuana prior to the arrest continued to consume it regularly, except for one boy who abstained from use just before he entered the armed forces.

Changes in Group Relationships

The use or nonuse of marijuana sometimes resulted in club members breaking away from their friends or even in the breakup of a group. Some members who held out from using marijuana were finally forced to leave the company of their old friends. This process was filled with much sadness. In their groups, the formation of cliques of "pot" users had resulted in secret caucusing behind the scenes and the manipulation of club rules to favor those who were sympathetic to the narcotic. One example of such manipulations consisted of the expulsion of a lower-status member from a club called the Bishops. This member recognized that the primary reason for his exclusion had nothing to do with the pretext manufactured by the other members; he had refused to "light up" with some of the boys a few weeks earlier, and this refusal was the basis of his expulsion. The group was rapidly being reorganized, and marijuana use had become the distinguishing characteristic that divided the in-group from out-group members.

Another example of change can be drawn from the Violators. In this group, the vice-president at first tried to prevent the spread of the drug. "I heard about the boys blowing pot," he said, "but they knew that I was against it. So they didn't let me know [about the spread of marijuana]. Right after George got busted we passed a law. Anybody blowing pot was supposed to be automatically thrown out of the club. But nothing was done about it." In order not to show their hand, the large clique of marijuana consumers concealed their practice from the other members and actually voted for the expulsion rule. This clique included almost all the other officers in the club, and they made sure that the rule was not implemented. As most of the group became realigned by the consumption of marijuana, the vice-president, who continued to abstain from use, became increasingly estranged from the president, who was a long-standing friend. He finally left the group. The vice-president was the only boy in the club who eventually attended college, and he held fast to his academic goal, foregoing all the dangerous acts that might possibly interfere with his plans. At the time, the president confided, "If I wasn't straight [a marijuana consumer], Murray would probably be my best friend. He is real righteous. He wants to be somebody. He studies hard. I can trust him. I know I can. But I only talk with him about a few things. When I'm cruising down the street with him, I can't say, 'Hey, man, I'd like to get loaded!' "

The previously mentioned arrest and conviction of the three Violators drastically changed the group and, in fact, marked the beginning of the end of the group as a formal club entity. Furthermore, these events also affected their buddies, the Low Riders. While almost every one of the Low Riders used marijuana systematically, in time the arrests resulted in clearly defined lines between consumers and nonconsumers. Fear and ideological commitments were intensified by the conflict over marijuana consumption. Not only were the nonconsumers more convinced than ever about the danger and immorality of the drug, but the consumers were highly reticent about recruiting these members into the secrets of their drug practice. This reticence was based partly on the suspicion that one of the boys who had been arrested might have turned police informant at the time. From then on, the consumers became very cautious.

Social Effects of Use

In looking at the diffusion of marijuana among streetcorner formations based on the groups we studied, certain features stand out. First, the motives accounting for the initial rise of drug use vary among group members. For example, it was obvious to the less prestigeful members that the group was being splintered because of the exclusiveness of marijuana use within tight cliques. The established prestige enjoyed by some of the clique members posed a special threat to the nonconsumers, and their initiation to the use of the weed was at least partly due to an interest in remaining a member of the group. Second, the anticipation of the pleasurable experiences, in this case, was far less important than the desire to maintain old friendships, especially when such friendships were hard to find.

The frequency of using the drug also varied. Some of the boys who used marijuana "fell hard" for the drug. "Falling hard" means that these boys were "loaded" day in and day out after they were initially "turned on." Most restricted its use to occasions when they were in the company of only a few friends. The persistent use of marijuana also varied considerably depending on its social context. For at least a year after the rapid spread of marijuana use among the members of the Violators and Low Riders, the boys spent a great deal of their time and money "getting loaded," talking about the relative merits of marijuana and other types of narcotics, finding new sources of the drug, and elaborating a prestige order predicated partly on knowledge about and access to the drug. One important topic was finding the right setting. Because listening to music was an important component of pot smoking, considerable effort also went into locating and accepting "good" music. The friend with a fine record collection was regarded favorably, and there were invidious distinctions about musical tastes. Top-grade marijuana, good music, and personal prestige were woven into standards dividing the Pot Heads from the Squares.

Over the course of time, a status order emerged among marijuana consumers. The Pot Head who dealt directly with his own Connection had greater prestige than the one who must buy his weed through another Head who functioned as an intermediary because he had connections. There was sharp discussion over the quality of marijuana, and discriminating tastes could recognize the variance between differently aged marijuana. Competition arose over the ability to obtain marijuana that had been cured in heroin or other opiates as opposed to green or well-cured marijuana.

Fantasizing under the influence of marijuana was called "going on a trip," and "in tripping-off" the boy was immersed in a situation where emotional experiences were heightened. While the collective use of marijuana was usually accompanied by continuous chatter and sympathetic gestures, pranks were occasionally played on suggestible users while they were tripping off. For instance, one boy whispered to another: "It's wonderful to be on an airplane breezing through the sky at 200 miles an hour." After further suggestions prolonged this trip, the boy rapidly ended it by describing a plane plummeting to earth in a flaming crash. This rude end snapped the boy who had been tripping-off back to reality filled with panic and fear. To prevent old but playful friends from "fucking with his mind," such a boy tried, whenever possible, to remain on guard against such practical jokes.

Deliberately destroying the sense of peace with the world or euphoria is known as "bum kicking" a person. Taking a friend on an enjoyable trip and then nastily crashing the plane is considered a "bum kick." Although such playful activity was tolerated, especially if it emanated from higher-status friends, the boys declared that they did not want to light up with a guy who "bum kicks" them all the time. One said, "A bum is a little person and if a bum kicks you, he's a dog. That's why they say 'bum kick'." The boys clearly preferred friends they could have fun and "goof" with.

In addition to smoking with friends, marijuana consumers preferred listening to music. In fact, music was the invariable background to the marijuana session when it was held indoors or in a car. Some of their musical tastes stemmed from the unusual effects marijuana had on the figure-ground configurations that structured their perceptual field. With little effort, the drug user claimed to hear or even see certain musical sounds in complete isolation from other sounds, like a drum beat that is totally independent of the innumerable orchestral sounds surrounding the drum. Compositions that emphasized sharp, staccato rhythms with highly contrasting tonal effects lent themselves to this perception. One boy said, "You're hearing some music. Well I'm sitting back loaded and I'm hearing the drum. But you hear everything. I can put everything aside and only listen to the drum. The rest of the instruments will be just silent to me. Then suddenly I'll just switch my ear to the piano, and I'll only hear the piano." Another boy agreed: "I like Latin rhythms. I can feel them. I can see them. One thing I can't understand about weed is how the sound of one instrument goes into your mind and stays there."

The ability to completely lose oneself in the various stimuli seemed to have added importance for understanding reactions to marijuana. The boys indicated that when they were high, they could exclude personal troubles and negative self-attitudes. After a while, some boys said that they were even capable of "getting high" without the drug. Tony reported that he would go home and put a record on the player and lie on the living-room floor. Then, by concentrating on the sounds, he would "get high." The crucial barrier that had to be surmounted to achieve this effort was "not thinking about myself." "You do it naturally," he said, "but if you concentrate on yourself you won't do it. But you can relax to a point where you listen to the music and you can concentrate on it so that after a while you don't even know about the time . . . and there is nothing but me and these sounds floating in space."

The collective use of marijuana took place in a variety of settings. It was consumed in apartments, houses, and in cars cruising down the street—their occupants laughing at the people and things along the way. Large group sessions sometimes occurred on deserted beaches or even in the Planetarium where, under the influence of the drug, a consumer sometimes gripped the arms of his seat tightly in fear of the sensation of hurtling through space. All considered the trip to the Planetarium a "boss kick," because the drug actually made the boys lose contact with reality and merge in a fantasy with the projection of moving stars.

The large city park was another favorite spot. On one occasion, a club arrived at the park to play a football game with an equally delinquent group. The club parked their cars in a lot above the field where their opponents were practicing and then sauntered down the hill to the playing area. The president of the club addressed the players who were practicing and said: "We put all the cars around in a circle . . . and blew pot and had a ball. We could look down and see all of you. We goofed around while you guys cut each other's throats like you always do." These remarks were insulting, but they were said with a smile because even the response to strangers and enemies is changed somewhat by the drug. Amos remarked, "When you meet a stranger when he's not high you don't even talk to him. When you are both high, you try to get to know him and find the common things and then goof with him."

Every situation in these varying settings was examined by the user for its weird, funny, and unique features; consequently, we found them playing on words, making up rhymes, and "cracking up" when they tried to tell each other about the funny incidents that occurred during the day. They mentioned that they could not remember how much time they spent on various things, or the names of cookies, or whether two and two equaled four; but, the adverse effect of marijuana on the ability to remember was converted into further provocations for laughter.

We have mentioned the degree to which marijuana consumption enhanced group solidarity. The following accounts illustrate this effect. Henry reported, "You feel a lot closer with the guys because you can goof with them. You appreciate it more with two guys. It's a real strong thing." Banjo observed, "It's a happiness. A real strong happiness. And the more you seem to give, the more the happiness impresses on the next one [the friend who is consuming the drug on the same occasion]. And the boys, at the same time, realize this." The depth of feeling about the difference between smoking marijuana alone or with friends is firmly stated by a third user. Oscar said, "I hate to be alone when I blow pot. I always want to be with somebody I can talk with and goof and be friendly with and trip off together with. I blew pot once by myself and I tripped off and it's lousy. All you can do is listen to the music."

Heightened rapport partly explained the positive effects of marijuana consumption on group solidarity. Normally, when not under the influence of the drug, these boys eschewed the expression of tender feelings; however, the drug seemed to loosen the inhibitions conditioned by their masculine ideals and by the instrumental attitudes that regard compassion and sympathy as effeminate or easily manipulated traits. Under the influence of marijuana, the boys knew that they could usually count on sensitive responses, and the marijuana sessions, particularly in their early phases, were considered to be outside the instrumental standards reinforced by the growth of illegal market activities. The first time we ever saw a leader openly sob when remembering a personal calamity was during a marijuana session. Under these conditions, such an act was not shameful.

Usually, when the group consumed marijuana, the air was filled with giggling and smiling faces. At times, members lapsed into silence, tripping off on the music or their own fantasies. Sometimes they sat for a while, combed their hair, and watched television in silence; then conversations would be resumed, and their sympathetic gesturing was in evidence once again. We found the transformation that occurred in this context amazing. "Tough guys," who frequently treated each other callously and who had even less regard for others were transformed into little kids, who rubbed their stomachs and gestured freely, all the while giggling hilariously. The smallest joke or faux pas was an occasion for unrestrained hilarity.

Since the interpersonal context is so important, the theoretical understanding of why streetcorner youth used marijuana has to consider both the group context of its use and its relationship to the needs of individuals. We concluded that marijuana use was maintained because it served multiple functions. Use of "grass" affected the solidarity of younger groups. The new marijuana recruit perceived the solidarity that prevailed among the cliques of consumers, but this closeness was first perceived from the point of view of an outsider, with a wall dividing nonusers from old friends who were consumers—a wall symbolized by guarded references and innuendo as well as exclusion practices. The beginning user sometimes felt caught in a cross-fire between a feeling of guilt, concern about parental reactions, fear of police, or the desire to recapture the closeness of old friendships. It is in this context that we can understand the response of youths who were questioned by us before they had actually "converted" to marijuana use. Barry, caught in this situation, was beset by enormous anxiety and said: "Pills are [legally] safer than marijuana, and I don't want anything to do with it [marijuana]. I just don't see it. I felt hurt when the guys first started messing with it. Like Dude says that he's been doing it for years. I don't know. All I know is the group of guys started and [during that time] we used to meet up at Angie's drive-in restaurant. I used to feel so bad because I had to cut out [leave them] at 12:00. [Previously] we used to meet and go somewhere, have a couple of cans of beer or something but then they switched to that [marijuana] and then we'd meet at Angie's and they would all go out to light up at 12:00 o'clock and I would have to make it [leave and go] home. It hurt! It actually hurt. But inside I said to myself,

"I'm not going to mess with it." Barry finally asked his friends to turn him on to marijuana, but they mockingly refused to do it at that time. He wrongly interpreted their response as "helping" him to stay away from the drug and recalled shortly: "At first it was 'No!' because I was chicken shit [not cooperating with the guys]. Then it got to the point that I said 'No!' so many times and turned them down that just last week, when I said 'Turn me on,' they just laughed. They're helping me. [But] I want to be with the guys. Inside I say it's something I can be proud of . . . showing them that I'm not as strong as them health-wise or fighting it, but in *will power*. The only reason they start taking it is to be one of the boys. That's the only reason you smoke or drink." These remarks were made in confidence a few weeks before this boy began to use marijuana. On the day he finally put "will power" aside and "fell hard for weed," everyone in the local crowd who was not present at the occasion heard the news. Another Doubting Thomas had fallen, and a new convert had arrived.

Yet the righteous consumer regarded such conversions to be "incontestable proof" of marijuana's virtues; consequently, by implication, the conversion had nothing to do with peer pressure. In defense of marijuana, the consumer declared; "People knock weed because they don't know what it is really like." One boy recalled, "Carl always used to be with the Gents and knocked weed. He said 'It's not worth it because you're getting high and you're gonna be busted.' Until one of the guys said, 'You can't talk about it until you know about it. Then Carl tried it and now he knows about it and feels the same way about it. Now that he knows what it's like, he can't contradict it; he knows what's happening."

Each conversion becomes its own final testimony of the correctness of those who like weed. And the details of each conversion are told and retold in the same intense and almost stylized manner:

"See! What did I tell you? Now he can't say it's lousy or a bum kick!"

"You can go through all the medical books and find out all about it. But I don't know man, only until you try it you won't know. You felt it. You didn't read it."

"It's the human feeling you get. You know it's real. You *really* know."

"It's weird but it's true. It's like the guy who paints the masterpiece. You know you did it. It's a satisfaction. [You can then say:] I did it man. I know what it's like!"

Streetcorner marijuana consumers were aware that millions of tranquilizers are taken daily throughout the United States, and they reckoned that if marijuana wasn't illegal the entire population would "light up a weed" sooner than they would "light up a Lucky." In addition, they firmly believed that they were in complete control of their habits, and some users exclaimed: "If it were ever legalized . . . I would get high just as soon as not get high." Yet such legal concerns were contradicted by the fact that once they had adopted marijuana, the streetcorner youth we observed frequently took advantage of every opportunity to get high.

On the other hand, the effects of marijuana, especially in group contexts, profoundly contradicted the fantastic myths promulgated by the federal narcotics bureau and law-and-order movements that defined every marijuana user as a dope fiend. This contradiction between myth and reality was undoubtedly one of the major reasons why the young people repeatedly defended marijuana consumption, appealing to peers to "try it and see for youself."

But the presence of the law itself was not a myth. The necessity to conduct oneself as normally as possible to avoid suspicion when walking or driving down the street became an important issue. The users learned to "maintain" themselves—that is, to act as if they weren't "loaded." At this time they reported: "The fight is being high and maintaining yourself so that you can go through society in a normal way." These concerns were obviously due to the conflict between continuing marijuana use and the increasingly hostile social environment.

As these youth became young adults, the pressures increased enormously. During their early twenties, there were the constant fear of police, actual arrests, lack of skills and inadequate work habits, a lack of job opportunities, and consistent failure to adapt to the demands of employment. These kinds of factors contributed to the destruction of the stable ties that had been reconstituted around the use of marijuana. The concern over "making it" in everyday life permeated the fantasies of marijuana consumers, and they increasingly used the drug to adapt to failure itself. Whenever they were feeling "low," they dropped some tranquilizers or lit up a joint. Some walked through life's experiences in a perpetual narcotic fog, immune to the harshness of life about them. These young people were always "high," and it was said of one in jest, "He would trip off if he came down instead of being high for a day."

Most streetcorner youth, however, adjusted to the use of marijuana in a less dependent fashion. Their self-control under the influence of the drug was, if anything, greater than their control while using alcohol. Marijuana usually moderated interpersonal conflicts and reduced violent predispositions. It enabled them to escape temporarily from the serious consequences of delinquency, school failure, and lack of job skills. When they were "high," the stark contrast between the collective use of marijuana and the harshness of their drug-free existence was pathetic.

20

Adolescent Illegal Markets

Some adolescents in junior high school start to engage in illegal markets when they buy narcotics or consume other illegal commodities and services. However, while there are exceptions, teen-age involvement in the "active side" of the market as suppliers or middlemen usually begins later, in middle or late adolescence. Consequently, adolescent illegal market activity, where it does emerge, is especially noticeable during the high-school years, when some of the older youth turn to economic crimes fairly regularly. Once again, the main actors—sellers and buyers—belong to stradom formations.

However, the social organization of economic crimes pivots around a distinctive ensemble of social types that exists in most urban communities. For instance, the Chicago study by Ellis and Newman (1971:305–6) found two types in addition to the Ivy Leaguer and Gowster, the Hustler and Mackman, that engaged in dope dealing, extortion, conning, thievery, and the manipulation of women. The Hustler was called a "classic middle man" who adopted dress styles that blended with the social climate and surroundings. Hustlers were reported to be smart, skilled and sensitive to street life, taking advantage of every situation, and engaging in diverse ways of obtaining money, goods, or services illegally. Such abilities contrasted with those of the Mackman, who aspired to the role of the Hustler but did not possess the finesse and maturity to fulfill his aspirations. The Mackman was also different because of his preference for the fashionable "walking suit" with loud shirts and suede shoes and for a preoccupation with controlling women for economic gain. A third type associated with economic crime was called Continental because he wore fashionable European-styled suits. According to Ellis and Newman, the Continentals attended school fairly regularly, although they considered it a place for "squares." Their parents were a source of money, but, in the event that they were not, the Continentals preferred gainful employment to stealing. On the other hand, if jobs were not available, they resorted to "whupping a game" or "pushing pot." Also, to meet their needs, the Continentals were especially known for their ability to manipulate and control women.

When Ellis and Newman's (1971) study was made, similar social types with illegal market roles appeared in a variety of other regional and socioeconomic settings. The Chicago Continental, for instance, had his southwestern counterpart—a study by Horton (1967) reported that "a really sharp Los Angeles street Negro would be 'conked to the bone' (have processed hair) and 'togged out' in 'continentals'." Horton's research concentrated on economic crimes by members of a streetcorner crowd. The crowd consisting of males, 18 to 25 years of age, who lived in a tiny segregated enclave of black families located outside Venice, California, at quite a distance from the central Los Angeles ghetto communities. The "local dudes" and "cool people" who belonged to the crowd numbered about 45 and represented "the hard core of the street culture." Horton (1967:6) says: "They called their black 'turf' 'Ghost-town,' home of the 'Ghost-men,' their former gang. Whatever the origin of the word, Ghost-town was certainly the home of socially 'invisible' men." The members of the streetcorner crowd had backgrounds common to highly impoverished ghetto youth. Though some were still of high-school age, they had "dropped out" or been "kicked out" of school. The vast majority of the other older members had also not finished school; and, though they were proficient in their "street tongue," most were not able to read or write standard English. Of the 17 who provided Horton with figures, half reported that they had made less than $1,400 during the previous year. The rest claimed incomes of between $2,000 and $4,000 annually. Half were living with and were partially dependent on their parents. "The financial strain," Horton adds, "was intensified by the fact that although fifteen out of the seventeen were single, eight had one or more children living in the area." Two-thirds of these adolescents and young men had either full-time or part-time employment in unskilled and low-paid jobs. The overall pattern reported was one of sporadic and unsatisfactory work, followed by a period of unemployment compensation and petty hustling in the form of gambling, conning, stealing, and selling dope, whenever necessary.

Horton (1967:11) points out that older Ghost-town adolescents used the laudatory phrase "Cool Cat" or "Cool People" as a social type to characterize some of their crowd. Individuals were called cool simply because they were liked by their peers. However, especially when they were idealized, Cool People in Ghost-town also signified the Dudes who could get you anything you wanted; furthermore, a Cool Cat was "big with the women," had "a low-riding car" and was greatly admired by the people who "know what's happening." Some of the Cats "processed" their hair and had a distinctive walk and manner of speech. They avoided the "tacky" clothing associated with the Lames, who were sloppy in their appearance and wore baggy pants and shirts in colors that did not match.

As indicated, Horton's study concentrated on economic crime. Among the older members of the Ghost-town set, changes in economic circumstances affected their attitudes toward illegal market activities. Horton (1967:6) found that more unemployed members of the set felt that the street provided better economic opportunities, while the part-time Hustlers, who were employed at regular jobs, were likely to disagree, saying: "A dude could make it better on the job than on the street." Horton accurately observed that the difference in attitude between the employed and the unemployed Dudes was not due to moral ambivalence about hustling and thievery. These adolescents and young adults were simply afraid of losing whatever security was provided by their jobs, believing that illegal activities would eventually get them "busted" and imprisoned.

Relatively Autonomous Contexts of Market Relations

While Horton conducted his research, we were also studying the socioeconomic and racial differences between Ghost-town's street-corner crowd and similar crowds in other communities. We can therefore further describe the context within which this illegal market operated. Our study suggested that such markets were affected by the socioeconomic compositions of peer networks. To explain this effect, let us examine the Cool People in Ghost-town in relation to their peer universe. First, their economic status remained severely depressed even though some Ghost-town youth increased their discretionary income through legitimate employment and thievery. Also, since their community possessed only a bare minimum in recreational facilities (a small, filthy baseball field without a single Parks and Recreation Department staff member or custodian), their deprived status strongly restricted the social type developments formed by black youth in other communities. For example, even the high-school students never used the term Athlete to label any members of their groups; nor did they use other terms such as Shiddity, Surfer, Brain, or Intellectual. Furthermore, Ghost-Town families were so poor that there were no socialite counterparts to the Ivy Leaguers found by Ellis and Newman in Chicago. Interestingly, black socialites, who wore Ivy Leagues but were called Shiditties, were found in the high school attended by Ghost Town adolescents. These Shiditties came primarily from steadily employed working-class families living in a public housing project a distance from Ghost-town.[1] Moreover, although the Shiddities sometimes associated with white and Mexican–American youth, they did not associate with youth from Ghost-town. In fact, the latter complained, "The Shiddity Bloods [from the housing project] think they are better than us."[2]

Similar socioeconomic relationships depressed the illegal market in Ghost Town. The members of the old Ghost-men gang lived in a community that was so small and impoverished, it only supported extremely petty forms of hustling. Although the hustlers dreamed of "the good life" by pimping, this particular hustle was almost unknown. Exploiting women was, however, common. For instance, the Dudes would "play the woman game" by threatening or conning their "women" into providing money from welfare checks (Horton, 1967:7).

Yet despite the prolonged engagement of adolescents and young adults in illegal market activities as a result of underemployment, there is no simple connection between economic deprivation and illegal markets, and connections between stradom formation youth in illegal markets and socioeconomic relationships are more complex than meets the eye. Illegal markets are neither ghetto-specific nor restricted to the most impoverished peer formations in the city. In impoverished neighborhoods, these markets may appear simply due to poverty. Yet, in the communities surrounding Ghost-town, illegal markets flourished among white youth even though their socioeconomic status and discretionary income was higher in comparison to the Cool People of

Ghost-town. Even though the status of many of these youth was lower than that of other white youth in their community, too many of their families were above the poverty line and too few of their parents were being supported by public welfare for poverty to be the only answer. Furthermore, their "delinquent careers" were strongly influenced by their social status, which was established from early adolescence by their poor performance in school and their adoption of a streetcorner style of life. Although the socioeconomic status of their families of origin was important, this variable did not affect their active engagement as suppliers and sellers in illegal markets independently of several facets of adolescent life such as school experience, social status, and the effects of adolescent stradom formations themselves.

In Chapter 7 we emphasized the relative autonomy of the stradom formations and indicated that the formations mediated the relationships between socioeconomic factors and delinquency. The illegal markets shared the relatively autonomous characteristics of the stradom formations, even though the markets emerged in later adolescence. In addition, for some youth the illegal markets shaped the transition from adolescence to adulthood. Especially during the initial period of this transition, some of these markets had characteristics that stamped them indelibly as adolescent relationships.

An Illegal Adolescent Market Flow Diagram

The markets that cater primarily to American adolescents become fairly independent of adult markets when supply-and-demand crowds are largely composed of adolescents. Moreover, when the thieves, "middle-men," and customers are primarily adolescents, their preexisting social connections also affect their market activities. If these social connections are embedded in highly structured peer networks, then their influence on market developments will be stronger. Figure 20.1 is an example of such a highly structured influence. It represents an illegal market flow diagram based on exchanges between four long-standing streetcorner youth clubs that operated in Los Angeles communities not too far from Ghost-town. It illustrates the connections between preexisting streetcorner developments and market structures. The data for this diagram were obtained in 1960 by participant observation and were

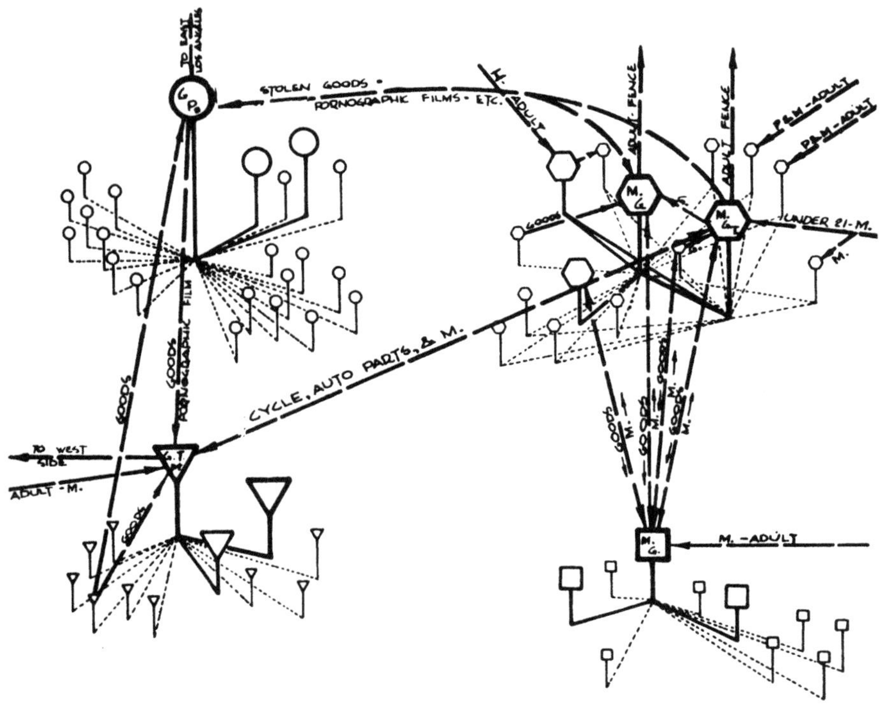

FIGURE 20.1 An adolescent illegal-market flowchart

verified by the major leader of each club. Six of the seven "connections"—or social links—integrating the intergroup flow of goods in this market were leaders of major groups in the complex. Their active social relationships, which were based on social status, enabled them to function successfully as "middlemen" within the market as a whole.

Each group is identified by a specific set of geometric shapes: circles, hexagons, squares, or triangles. Variation in an individual member's peer status is indicated by the size of the geometric shape: the largest shape signifies a major leader, the intermediate indicates secondary leadership status, and the smallest represents the remaining members of the group. This rough trichotomy of individual statuses was constructed from sociometric choices and field observations.

Symbols inside the circles, hexagons, squares, or triangles indicate types of commodities that have been handled by adolescent "connections" and "dealers" over a two-year period. Connections with *T* symbols engage in systematic thievery as well as dealing in hot goods and services. The symbol *M* is used for marijuana, *H* for heroin, *P* for pills, *Po* for pornographic literature and films, *G* or *Goods* for stolen goods, *Under 21* for an older adolescent marijuana dealer, *Cycle* for motorcycle parts (stolen), and *Adult* for adult pusher or fence. (Generally, young entrepreneurs handle any type of goods or services as long as they are profitable and the risks are tolerable. In the group designated by the circles in Figure 20.1, for example, the major leader was an entrepreneur who had sold marijuana for a short time just prior to the period represented in the chart; his chief illegal activities, at the time we observed him, were selling stolen goods and pornographic literature and films. Thus, although he had previously engaged in narcotics traffic, at the time the diagram was made he regarded the sale of narcotics to be very dangerous and refused to handle them.)

The inter-group complex represented in Figure 20.1 actually consisted of approximately 160 boys and girls between 16 and 19 years of age. However, only the four major male groups, who were the primary nodes of this complex, are indicated in the chart. The female clique formations were lacking in solidarity because of the jealousies and priorities given to heterosexual relationships, which were strongly dominated by the males. Also, the females were not organized into clubs, although there was one abortive attempt to organize a club, which was abandoned after their boyfriends strongly opposed the idea.

The racial composition of the market in Figure 20.1 was predominantly white and thus quite different from the market centering around the Ghost-town streetcorner crowd. The socioeconomic statuses of the groups in this market were much more heterogeneous and less depressed than statuses of the groups in the Ghost-town market. Furthermore, and very important, the entire "inter-crowd complex" comprising the major nodes in the market network did not consist of groups originally emerging in the same community. Although these groups interacted with each other and shared some of the same haunts when the figure was made, they arose from communities with different socioeconomic compositions. Consequently, even though all were or had been streetcorner youth in junior or senior high school and were capable of engaging in semiskilled labor at best, their ascribed socioeconomic statuses were much more variable by comparison with Ghost Town. Most of the club members in this market were from working-class families, including skilled workers; and a small minority were from petit bourgeois families. It is notable that while all the middlemen were streetcorner youth, the families of two out of the four most important middlemen were petit bourgeois.

Adult and Adolescent "Informal Sectors"

Illegal markets involve a variety of informal sector relationships supported by adolescent status groups.[3] They also have a number of distinguishing features. For example, unlike some adult enterprises, adolescent markets are usually outside the capitalist mode of production, and they contribute little, if anything, to capital accumulation. By contrast, adult markets do accumulate capital when they produce and distribute bootleg whiskey, illegal narcotics, "kiddie pornography," pirated records, or counterfeit copies of stylish clothing, purses, perfumes, watches, medicinal drugs, electronic appliances, and other commodities, which are sometimes manufactured by illegitimate corporations at home or abroad. When adolescent markets circulate such commodities, they, too, become part of the illegal accumulation process. But most of the commodities in their markets are stolen and, as such, have not been produced by illegal organizations. The exchange of these commodities merely transfers part of the existing supply of money into the hands of criminals, and it does not increase the overall supply of capital.

Illegal adolescent markets can also be distinguished in other ways. Despite the similarities between adolescent and adult robbers, burglars, prostitutes, and hustlers, adolescent market activities operate at a very low degree of organization and never achieve the organizational levels that can be found among some members of the adult markets. Furthermore, apart from certain elementary tendencies and restrictions that characterize their price-making market relationships, members of adolescent markets are not regulated by economic laws that affect the competitive or monopoly sectors of the economy. Consequently, the relationships instituted by these sectors have extremely limited heuristic value for understanding adolescent forms of economic criminality.[4]

Finally, in advanced capitalist countries such as the United States, both large and small corporations engage in supportive economic arrangements with individual criminals or criminal organizations, but usually only small entrepreneurs support adolescents who participate in illegal market activities. Examples of such support include "junk" or "auto scrap" dealers who buy stolen appliances and automobile parts and "audio shops" that buy stolen stereophonic equipment and musical recordings.

On the other hand, such relatively independent adolescent markets may not be as evident in less economically developed capitalist countries. Such a possibility is implied by Lin's (1958) study of Chinese delinquent peer formations, the *Liu-mang* and the *Tai-pau*, in Taiwan. Briefly described, the *Liu-mang* were tough delinquents who adopted traditional lower-class styles and engaged in violence or economic crime for their families or themselves. They had little or no education, and they resided in the old sections of cities and small towns because they were mostly from poor "lower-middle" or "lower-class" families.[5]

The *Tai-pau*, on the other hand, adopted western clothing styles and came from "middle-" or "upper-class" families. They were mostly found in high school, although some of them were unsuccessful students.

> Movies, billiards, ping-pong, cards, eating or smoking in cafe-restaurants, and some sports in the parks are their favorite activities. When the means for this expenditure are exhausted or when a junior member is compelled to please his group leader in terms of money or goods, improper ways of getting money—lying, stealing, black-mailing, or occasionally robbing—are the outcome. (Lin, 1958:246)

Unlike the *Tai-pau*, the *Liu-mang* were identified with the traditional culture and illegal markets. Lin (1958:247) states, "The relationship of *Liu-mang* . . . to the community is rooted in the traditional pattern of life and their group structure is intimately interwoven with that of the community. Their respect for and cooperation in community affairs at festivals has a strengthening effect on this tie." Lin does not analyze the variations in ages among *Liu-mang* formations, but he suggests that their leaders, who must be young adults or older and who are called "professionals" because of their criminal status, have a strong voice in communal affairs through connections with temples and elders. These "professionals" maintained a strong grip on the economic affairs of the area by using their subordinate *Liu-mang* as agents, particularly in prostitution, gambling, and trading with stolen goods, black-marketing, and narcotics peddling. This control is undoubtedly supported by extremely corrupt political officials.

Unfortunately, Lin also does not indicate the age at which the *Liu-mang* regularly adopt more serious economic crimes or when they actually join the illegal market labor force. Since they are expected to seek employment at an earlier age than their North

American counterparts, it would not be surprising if ties between older delinquents and criminal organizations headed by adults were established at an earlier age. For the same reason, these ties may be more extensive in Taiwan than in the United States. Also, in the United States, the influence of corrupt political officials on adult markets that influence adolescents are more restricted. Moreover, the greater prolongation of adolescent dependency relations sustains the illegal markets that operate largely within peer societies.

Further Market Characteristics

After observing market relationships, in 1960, we concluded that they were particularly important because they promoted the transition of some delinquents to so-called "criminal careers." In the process of acquiring and transferring illegal goods and services and organizing other supply-and-demand relationships within the markets, divisions of labor arose among delinquents. When stabilized, divisions of labor encouraged the development of roles such as those of burglar, prostitute, narcotics connection, and fence. Although there was a considerable amount of experimentation in role-taking among adolescents and while many never actually "specialized" in only one role, the recognition of such role-taking was indispensible to understanding the etiology of the criminal roles adopted in young adulthood.

On the other hand, adolescents did not engage in illegal markets for the purpose of learning a career. Adolescent engagement was stimulated by a desire for discretionary buying power that could support desirable consumption standards, especially among stradom formations. The need for such support was markedly evident among subproletarian youth; in fact, the emergence of market relationships consolidated the marginalization processes begun earlier in the life cycle of the streetcorner stradom formations. For impoverished youth, the illegal markets have far greater significance for everyday life than they have for other youth, and therefore poor youth are likely to be more active participants in market activities.

However, the need for supporting desirable consumption standards illegally is also evident among other youthful types. For instance, while illegal markets are less significant for maintaining everyday life among bourgeois youth, they provide goods and services that parents will not or cannot provide. Moreover, for some forms of consumption, such as narcotics use, the markets are absolutely necessary, regardless of the consumer's class situation. Consequently, streetcorner youth are by no means the only members of the markets, even though they may be disproportionately counted among the "Heists", "Dealers," and "Hustlers" who organize the distribution of goods and services. The demand crowds are much more variable in their class and social type composition.

Other characteristics of adolescent markets are also important. The etiology of adolescent Dealers and Hustlers, for instance, is based not just on the relations brought about by the illegal character of dope production, processing, and distribution, but also on the demand for narcotics. The demand crowds established by narcotics consumers are basic preconditions for the career of the Dealer. The same demand considerations hold for prostitutes, burglars, pornographers, and car thieves. Without paying customers, these thieving entrepreneurs might turn to other ways of making a living. The customers of these businessmen and women come from other types of stradom formations and, although they are less representative, some even come from fairly conforming adolescent groupings such as Intellectuals and Brains.

The determining power of the demand crowds is illustrated by the futility of trying to repress illegal markets when the conditions that preserve the markets still dominate everyday life. Although the extensiveness and level of complexity of the illegal markets are sensitive to police operations, the elementary forms of these markets are fairly impervious under these conditions. As a rule, the attempt to disintegrate a market by arresting and incarcerating some of its members eventuates simply in the reformation of illegal activities to meet the continuing demand.

We observed the disintegration and reformation of such markets during our four years of participant observation with delinquent groups and during three years when the field operations were conducted by our large research project. During these years, we observed that the demand crowds in the illegal markets were always available, even though the suppliers were occasionally destabilized by official sanctions. However, since the demand generally guaranteed the creation of new suppliers, the frequency of sanctions imposed by officials had virtually no long-term effects on the existence of the markets themselves.

By way of illustration, we observed a large network of small crowds that frequented a particular group of taverns and other recreational areas during the week. This crowd usually had one or two suppliers of narcotics (or other illegal commodities) who were in jail or prison at any given time. However, with regard to narcotics dealers, four individuals informally rotated among themselves the narcotics sales to most members in the network, depending on who was actually not incarcerated at the moment. When federal or local police occasionally concentrated on arresting people for narcotics, the network would dissolve temporarily into smaller formations and then reorganize around alternative recreational spots. Meanwhile one or two of the usual suppliers would regenerate new lines of supply to meet the demand. Consequently, the fluctuations in sanctions only affected the turnover rate of suppliers, because there were always new and enterprising businessmen ready to fill the "opportunities" created when the previous supplies were temporarily out of commission.

Alternative Theories of Economic Delinquency

There are several competing explanations for the systematic emergence of economic crimes among adolescents and the transition to criminal careers. Sutherland's "differential association" theory is among these explanations, but our observations have demonstrated that most of his ideas were inadequate. For example, he proposed that delinquents become criminals by learning criminal attitudes and skills through personal contact with law-violating adults.[6] Yet we found that while adult relationships influenced illegal adolescent markets, they were not a significant influence during the *formative* delinquent stages. In fact, the growing influence of adults was primarily due to system-wide effects; it was a reflection of the degree to which adolescent and adult marketplaces became economically integrated with each other over time. Consequently, the personal "adoption" of individual delinquents by adult criminals was the exception rather than the rule; and the major points of integration between the age groups were largely based on the complementary flow of illegal goods and services between the two types of markets. Much more important for understanding the delinquent transition to systematic criminal behavior were the practical effects of the exchange relations established by the markets. The market itself was the key to understanding delinquent careers rather than the socialization of adolescents by contact with and emulation of criminal adults. (More on this topic later in the chapter.)

Sutherland also insisted that criminal activity requires the learning of developed skills and a technical body of knowledge. While this may be true for highly "professional" criminal pursuits, our observations convinced us that the skills and attitudes necessary for most crimes committed by adolescents were so rudimentary that illiterate and unskilled youth had no difficulty acquiring them. Furthermore, most of these skills were simple adaptations learned and developed in legitimate pursuits as opposed to illegal relationships. The young car thieves and auto-parts thieves, for instance, used skills and knowledge acquired while learning to drive and repair automobiles belonging to themselves or relatives. Also, much of what we saw convinced us that a goodly number of "tricks of the trade" (used to commit offenses) were innovations by adolescents. Moreover, some of the knowledge shared among older adolescents was largely gained through concrete experiences in illegal enterprises with peers.[7]

The second competing explanation, Cloward and Ohlin's "opportunity structure theory," combined Sutherland's propositions with those advanced by Merton. Cloward and Ohlin proposed that delinquency is caused by frustrated occupational striving. They suggested that adolescent "criminal subcultures" emerge whenever "differential opportunities," created by adult criminal organizations, operate within a community. Reportedly, the criminals within these organizations provide adolescents with successful professional "role models" and job opportunities in "the rackets." Cloward and Ohlin conceded that thievery does occur in communities with no "rackets"; but they also claimed that without "differential opportunities" such youth were likely to become petty "outcasts" of the criminal world rather than "high-status" syndicated criminals.

We quickly rejected Cloward and Ohlin's theory, for several reasons. First, we concluded from our observations that if an adolescent identifies with and learns from criminals who specialize in a particular type of crime, it is because that youth has *already acquired* the values encouraging delinquent behavior and hence his emulation of criminal role models. Such values would probably be acquired after years of involvement with peers in various types of delinquent behavior. Second (as indicated with regard to Sutherland's propositions), the emulation that may occur in later adolescence is based on pragmatic experience in market relationships rather than on other factors such as frequency of contact with adult criminals or frustrating social mobility experiences, as proposed by Cloward and Ohlin.

Third, we "spot-checked" the basic proposition behind Cloward and Ohlin's theory, when we interviewed highly delinquent junior-high-school adolescents about their occupational aspirations.[8] The interview process assumed that although Cloward and Ohlin posited three "subcultures," their theory starts with the formation of a delinquent "criminal subculture." (That "subculture" theoretically represents the first likely adaptation to frustrated mobility striving.) We reasoned that since delinquency rates begin to soar during the junior-high-school age range, boys of that age would exhibit the frustration central to Cloward and Ohlin's theory.[9] If they did not exhibit a sense of frustration about occupational goals, then the most significant mechanism in the theory was factually in error.

We knew delinquent junior-high-school boys because of our previous contact with their groups, and we rapidly discovered during the interviews that they were sublimely indifferent rather than anxious about their occupational futures. Although these young adolescents were in the early phases of their delinquent development, most of them expressed the reasonable opinion that they were too young to make any serious decisions about their occupational careers. Moreover, this opinion correlated with our concurrent research into studies of how adolescents make occupational choices. We found that most young adolescents—not just young delinquents—do not seriously consider the matter of occupational careers before high school. And impoverished youth may not even think about such matters seriously until they actually leave school.[10] Since the interview responses were significantly devoid of the interest and anxiety that should have accompanied seriously frustrated mobility striving, we abandoned this line of investigation. It seemed pointless to continue if we were not gaining knowledge that advanced our understanding of delinquency.

Further, if any delinquent modality were analogous to Cloward and Ohlin's "criminal subculture" (reputedly oriented toward economic offenses), it would be the adolescent illegal market modality. Yet Cloward and Ohlin's belief that these economically oriented offences emerged first among the subcultures was obviously mistaken. As a rule, this modality did not emerge as a significant factor until later in the adolescent life cycle, once the other modalities had been established among stradom formations. Further, our extensive contacts with delinquents and young criminals revealed that the individualistic "entrepreneurs" and "workers" in the illegal adolescent markets (who became the so-called lower-status "outcasts" in Cloward and Ohlin's theory) provided the *basic* "labor force" for these markets. Not only were they the backbone of adolescent market relationships; but some of these individualistic young criminals even defined the young adults who were runners for syndicated bookmakers, for instance, as flunkies rather than "high-status" young men.

There was simply no evidence that emulation or anticipation of job opportunities with criminal organizations had anything to do with systematic engagement in economic offenses by most adolescents. In fact, we observed that such organizations bypassed adolescents and recruited young adults who had reached 20 years of age and more. The local heads of these organizations made their selections on the basis of rational criteria, and their general feeling was that adolescents were too risky and inexperienced.

A young entrepreneur who had been approached by a bookie to work for an illegal organization commented on the unsuitability of adolescents for employment in criminal organizations. He said, "The rackets never ask the little people to work for them. They would be crazy. They'd lose their shirts. The little people are still wild. They don't have to work for a living and they don't know how to do it regularly." (The "little people," in this context, are the delinquents in their middle-adolescent years.) This young entrepreneur had reached 20 years of age and had been selected by the bookie after undergoing the discipline of hustling in the illegal adolescent marketplace. Also, his reputation as a hustler, with "connections" to young adults, was important because the bookmaker knew that his social connections would produce additional clients.

Because of such factors it would appear that the delinquent careers of those hired by criminal organizations are already established before their entrance into the organizations. These employees have undergone the discipline demanded by the illegal commodity "production-and-exchange" relationships. No longer are they interested in fighting with a gang or leaving school or work to go on wild escapades with peers. As the young entrepreneur observed, "In this way, it is business. You have to think about things. You can't just jump out of a car and steal a tire if you need the bread. When you are married you need the money regularly. You can be this [have a regular income] in the syndicate. But they won't take most guys. They feel you out. They have you pick up some money [i.e., as a "runner"] here and there to do them a favor at first. See how cool you are and even if you have enough friends to start your own book. If you can start your own book you are snapped up right away."

The reluctance to hire adolescents applies to girls as well as boys. Regarding prostitution, for instance, the young entrepreneur noted; "The Pimps that are attached to syndicates don't use young girls [under 18]. They are too dangerous. If they are caught they [the adult criminal organization] are in for a lot of trouble. Most of the young broads that are selling their ass are doing it all by themselves. They ain't part of a syndicate. The syndicates won't touch them."

These observations were verified by a young prostitute who was hired by a syndicated house at age 17. She informed us that she had lied about her age to get the job. She noted that she was the youngest prostitute in the house and was even afraid to tell the other women her real age for fear that word would leak out and she would lose her job.

Among the boys, illegal economic activities were largely conducted in very small cliques. Also, the easy access to narcotics from the Los Angeles area (at the time, marijuana, pills, and other psychoactive drugs were primarily imported from Tijuana, Mexico) resulted in the proliferation of independent one-man distributive operations. Because of the nearness of Mexican border towns, narcotics were often picked up in Tijuana or Ensenada by adolescents who functioned as "self-employed" businessmen. Their relationship with larger narcotics organizations was similar to dealings between wholesalers and independent retailers in the legal economy. The adolescents who purchased their narcotics from strangers a hundred or so miles away from Los Angeles, like retailers in business for themselves, certainly could not be assigned a subordinate status as "workers" or "labor force" within any criminal organization or labor market.

The major sociological flaw in Cloward and Ohlin's theory is that their concept of "differential opportunity structures" is based on a *labor-market* analogy. Their theory essentially hypothesizes, as a starting point, the impact of corporate criminal institutions on adolescents. This seems plausible for the following reason: in economic relations formally instituted by capital, the development of occupational careers is conventionalized to some degree by labor-market mechanisms or by socialization processes that orient adolescents to particular occupations in legitimate labor markets. Consequently, whatever heuristic value this analogy has depends on whether the predominant mechanisms leading to "criminal careers" are similar to those in the legitimate labor market. However, in actuality the labor-market analogy is inappropriate, and the mechanisms are not similar. Rather than corporate organization of career lines, most transitions to systematic criminal behavior are organized around highly individualistic and informal economic relationships. In fact, some criminal careers are distinctly petit bourgeois enterprises created by independent older adolescents who "hustle" stolen goods or promote "capers" by working with one or two other delinquents.

Still other theoretical explanations, such as labeling theory (Lemert, 1951), should be considered. In this theoretical approach, the social stigma applied to an adolescent by teachers or police reportedly encourages "career" delinquency. But the habitual activities we observed within the illegal adolescent markets had little to do with such "social reactions to deviancy." As indicated previously, these activities were inherent products of the unfolding illegal market and of its structural and ideological properties (e.g., its instrumental ethic and division of labor). Thus, it was the interrelationship between the market and its suppliers, not the response to official labels, that held the key to understanding delinquent transitions to criminal careers in young adulthood. Also, behind these market relationships were the macroscopic economic and political conditions that stimulated delinquent behavior prior to the formation of the illegal markets. Finally, once the market had emerged, these conditions influenced the degree to which the active workers became dependent on economic crime or, on the other hand, could break away because of such alternative options as *decent* job opportunities.

In our field work, we found no evidence for the symbolic power attributed to official labeling processes by labeling theorists. If the delinquents we observed were really sensitive to official attitudes, we would have expected serious personality problems, such as deep anxiety about their immoral behavior and social worth. Certainly youth, especially in streetcorner groups, can be found with such problems. But most of the habitual delinquents we observed did not have them; fear of apprehension was more important to their decision making because they had already developed their own collective standpoints. Consequently, as early as 1963 we pointed out that labelling theorists have concentrated on the wrong labelling processes to understand why some adolescents were habitually delinquent. The labels that delinquents themselves create are far more important in this context than official labels. Policemen, for instance, were derogated and called Fuzz and Heat and other names by streetcorner youth because they were considered annoying and dangerous; they were given obscene names like "ass-hole," which hardly suggested that official ethical standards were taken seriously. There was ample evidence that delinquents constructed their self-images and concepts of virtue from their own standards of conduct and belief systems, not from symbolic processes involving official "labels."

Social disorganization theories were a final alternative to our view of delinquency. But we have contended that illegal market activities are not necessarily produced by socially disorganized conditions, even though they are correlated and interact with these conditions once they come into existence in economically marginal communities. This point is illustrated in the discussion of prostitution in San Juan, where both social disorganization and prostitution are outcomes of larger economic relationships. The inadequacy of this approach is further validated by Perlman's study, which indicates that social disorganization theorists have been far from the mark when analyzing communities of the poor in developing nations. Certainly, capitalist developments frequently destroy communal resources that not only organize adolescent life but minimize delinquency in local communities; but while "socially disorganized" communal relationships become important contributing factors, the primary determinant of the expansion in delinquent relationships under these disorganized conditions is not the mere lack of social controls; rather it is the laws of capitalist development, the articulation between capitalist modes of production and noncapitalist units of production and exchange, the repression of political movements that oppose the unchecked sway of capitalist developments, the individualistic ethic of capitalism, and the changes in the life cycles of peer formations.

When evaluating the crude assumptions behind social disorganization theory, it should also be kept in mind that illegal activities are not monopolized by people in "socially disorganized" communities. Illegal activities are habitually adopted by corporate executives and government officials, who belong to the powerful, stable, and highly organized institutions in our society. Moreover, the heads of criminal organizations form social estates or networks, which are far more dependent upon the well-organized circles that control American society than they are on the "disorganized" populations of economically marginal persons who also support organized crime.

Social disorganization theories conveniently ignore the theoretical implications of these class variations in criminal behavior. They also ignore the fact that the lives of criminals from varied class backgrounds, economic relationships, and styles of life are governed by a degree of "organization" that is similar to most other members of their particular class. Some of the mainstream families in Ulf Hannerz' study, for instance, derived their income from well-established illegal businesses based on bootlegging and the numbers game. "Except for these illegal means of income, [these] households seem to lead mainstreamer lives. Their houses are well kept, the families keep largely to themselves although they are friendly with their neighbors and well liked by most people, and they sometimes voice concern with the improvement of the neighborhood," reports Hannerz (1969:57).

The social disorganization theories cannot even deal adequately with the types of adult crime that are almost the same as adolescent illegal market activities. Here we refer to the individualistic criminal enterprises occurring on all class levels. Thus "classy" drug dealers and call girls maintain their bourgeois styles of life independently by selling goods or services to affluent clients. In some respects, these individualistic enterprises are no different from those of streetcorner pimps and pushers, local porno hustlers, and a variety of fences who operate as independent agents within the loosely integrated popular markets for illegal goods and services.

NOTES

1. In another segregated black community in the hills to the west and south of Ghost-town we found formations of black socialites called Shiddities who dressed just like the Ivy Leaguers, although from 1966 onward Shiddity fashions were just beginning to change toward "natural" hair styles and the "mod" or "high-English" style of dress. This black community was largely composed of middle-class families who had achieved considerable affluence compared to most black families in Los Angeles. In the 1970s, we also observed the use of this same metaphor for relatively affluent black socialites in the San Francisco Bay Area.
2. The relationships differentiating the Ghost-town Bloods from the Shiddity Bloods in the public housing project primarily reflect the intraclass developments that separate subproletarian families from relatively more secure working-class families. Also, the development of racially segregated stradom formations is more sensitive to the socioeconomic composition of families from segregated populations alone. These relationships are discussed in Chapter 6.
3. Many informal sector activities engaged in by adolescents are legal. To obtain

cash, youth will sell personal possessions and occasionally hire themselves out to people in the neighborhood or acquaintances who want their lawns mowed, furniture moved, or snow shoveled from driveways and store fronts.

4. For this reason, Schellings' (1967) suggestions for analyzing economic crimes are not useful for analyzing adolescent illegal markets or many other illegal informal sector relationships.
5. Similar relationships also occur in the United States, but to a lesser degree. Moreover, in some cases such third-world age-graded market relationships may be adopted here among certain nationality groups because of immigration as well as local conditions. For instance, in San Francisco Chinatown during the early 1970s, older adolescents and young adults who had *immigrated* from Hong Kong and Taiwan were hired as "Look-See Boys" by tongs sponsoring illegal gambling. However, these youth soon organized themselves into an extortion gang and became independent. They terrorized the shopkeepers and other people in their community and ultimately murdered 15 youths and adults. Some of these murders were a result of hysterical attempts at preventing others from betraying their leaders to the police.
6. Modern researchers often use Sutherland's "differential association" hypotheses to justify propositions assuming that delinquency primarily takes place in groups and that peer influence is important for understanding it. However, these ideas have been around for centuries, and they are by no means at the heart of his hypotheses, which converge on the diffusion of criminality through socialization experiences based on the relations between potential delinquents and adults or adolescents who are carriers of "definitions" that encourage violation of the law. Further, even if his perspective is extended to include the symbolic identification via "reference groups" or the emulation of idealized criminal types, as Glaser (1956) suggests, it would prove fairly useless because it focuses on ideological relationships that are patently conducive to the violation of the law. On the whole, the theoretically important ideological relationships establish a state of readiness for victimization, and they cannot be discovered by focusing on immediately apprehensible motives, rationalizations, or "differentially organized" groups etc., that obviously encourage illegal activities.
7. This generalization even applies to such varied activities as burglary and "conning."
8. "Spot checks" based on small samples were made throughout the course of our participant observation, to test ideas about delinquent relationships. In this case we interviewed 31 boys before terminating the spot check.
9. Empirical research into the validity of Cloward and Ohlin's theory generally concentrates on senior-high-school youth. However, that concentration is unjustified, because the rise in delinquent rates and the development of "gang" behavior begins earlier. We therefore chose the junior-high-school boys because of their greater theoretical importance.
10. Today, after Short and Strodbeck's (1965) research has disconfirmed the existence of the independent "delinquent subcultures" posited by Cloward and Ohlin, the further reliance on this opportunity structure theory seems even more pointless.

21

Adolescent Entrepreneurs and Illegal Markets

Let us recall some of the information about why adolescent markets exist and how they develop. These markets emerge within preexisting interactional frameworks composed of networks of cliques, crowds, and clubs. If the frameworks are highly organized, then their higher-status members are likely to become enterprising "middlemen" because of their preexisting social connections. Also, although adolescent markets generally disappear as youth become young adults, an increasing demand for discretionary purchasing power in later adolescence makes illegal as well as legal economic options important. If the legal options are restricted to subemployment, menial, humiliating jobs, and other adverse economic conditions, then the attraction of illegal markets remains strong into adulthood.

On another level, the expansion or contraction of these illegal markets is also determined by the *articulation* (coexistence and interaction) between the capitalist mode of production and other modes of production. Capitalist governments and economies vary considerably. Welfare policies or supportive noncapitalist relationships that absorb the shocks of capital accumulation processes can be maintained or destroyed rapidly, depending upon economic and political conditions. If supportive relationships based on informal systems of reciprocity, archaic forms of production (such as barter, petty trading, and cottage industry) or informal labor activities are allowed to flourish, petit bourgeois as well as working-class families fall back on them when faced with economic adversity. Consequently, whether or not capital accumulation processes produce high rates of streetcorner crime and delinquency depends a great deal on how these processes influence supportive economic relationships. Where capitalism extensively recomposes class relationships and does not provide alternative resources for economically marginal families, illegal adolescent markets are likely to flourish.

But these larger political and economic relationships are invisible to the adolescents who are immersed in market relationships. On the level of everyday reality, the market itself appears to emerge virtually spontaneously, without any macroscopic economic and political determinants. Delinquent forms of conduct present themselves phenomenally as spontaneous choices freely exercised by individuals. Even though severe economic, political, and ideological constraints are often operating behind the scenes, the profound changes in the lives of youth just seem to take place because they are going by the rules of the game. On this level, furthermore, the transition processes that lead to individual delinquent careers are often guided by the relationships between preexisting streetcorner developments and the market structures. Some of the changes in personal identities of youth following delinquent careers are described later in this chapter.

Styles of Life and Need for Ready Cash

As they move into young adulthood, some youthful suppliers obtain enough money to completely support themselves and their styles of life. For instance, we observed one enterprising older adolescent who tried innumerable ways of making money, including dealing in pornographic films and stolen guns, jewelry, liquor, cameras, and appliances. When he became a young adult, he added the profits of loan sharking to his gains from hustling other illegal goods. Finally, in his early twenties, he purchased a small photography shop for processing pornographic material and invested in a run-down motel to service prostitutes and their customers.

However, the great majority of adolescents supplying the illegal markets never accumulate the surplus for lending money, setting up shop, or buying property. Their offenses do not cover their basic cost of living, and they rely heavily on parents, relatives, and friends to satisfy such vital needs as food, clothing, and shelter. Also, the personal consumption patterns supported by their offenses are not geared to reproducing gainful employment, because most are only employed occasionally and are not actively preparing for better-paying steady jobs. To a large extent, they spend the money gained through the market on such items as fashionable clothing, going to the movies, and buying phonograph records. In addition, they usually sleep late and conduct their economic activities and social interactions during the afternoon and night; their rhythm of social activities is certainly not set by the eligibility principles and time clocks that bind personal consumption to capital accumulation.[1] Their social and economic relationships are geared to the reproduction of their customary styles of life rather than their roles as "economic agents" expending labor power to generate capital for commodity production. On the other hand, this reproduction of consumption relations is not completely outside the capital accumulation process. (For example, the purchase of narcotics ties these adolescents to accumulation via the crime syndicates controlling portions of narcotics traffic.) Commodity production is so generalized that even farm families must purchase the necessities of life from commodity markets. To maintain their style of life, these delinquents also have to exchange their goods and services for cash. They become part-time entrepreneurs in order to achieve their lifestyle goals.

The commodification of daily life also hastens their need for ready cash. Having fun usually means paying for entertainment. These youth are emphatically oriented toward commercialized leisure-time interests and they even participate in their popular ethnic cultures primarily as spectators. Although they enjoy creative activities—dancing at parties, writing graffiti on exterior walls, or customizing their cars—they rarely if ever participate in groups or programs oriented to drama, dance, music, crafts, photography, or other art forms. Groups of this kind exist, but they serve a very small segment of the adolescent population. And while these illegal market suppliers are usually not self-motivated to participate, neither are there significant government (or private) investments in cultural programs that would genuinely challenge and elevate their interests to higher levels.

Given these economic, political, and cultural restrictions, as indicated, the adolescent market seems to emerge almost spontaneously as the amoral consciousness of its active members takes advantage of the demand for illegal goods and services. These delinquents *actively* create their own "opportunity structures." Moreover, because there is no conventional or unconventional organization of opportunities to aid their enterprise, these illegal marketeers make up their own "occupational" terms. They participate in their enterprises as "Hustlers," "Operators" and "Dealers." These metaphors can be applied to all their illegal market activities. A hustler or an operator might engage in thievery or pimping. In fact, such general terms and their application to diverse situations and social relationships is not surprising. Similar legitimate terms such as "small businessman" and "commissioned salesman" are no less general and apply to self-made, petit bourgeois entrepreneurial roles.

Among the youth we studied, broad categories were also adopted to signify the structure of their daily activities and milieu relationships. Their milieu was classified by metaphors such as "set" and "scene," which tacitly reflected the episodic character of everyday life. Their individual biographies were filled with spontaneous events, and the history of their peer relationships seemed completely circumstantial. Both ideology and reality fragmented their comprehension of recurrent situations and any regularities in personal or group behavior. The adolescent illegal markets also contributed to this fragmentation of consciousness. As we explain in the next section, this market activity, especially among streetcorner groups, undermined solidary relationships. Furthermore, the markets themselves were ephemeral structures, arising for a short time and then vanishing. After a short duration they were often replaced entirely by adult illegal markets.

Market Activities

There are additional characteristics of these adolescent market activities in addition to unique terminology and ephemerality. The items available for sale or trade are also unique. For the short duration of their existence, youthful tastes regulate the flow of goods and services in the markets. While adults may have had similar tastes, the following comments, by Dude, an adolescent entrepreneur, indicate that the demand crowds within the markets are chiefly composed of peers. Responding to our questions about the market, Dude said, "The demand is custom cars and things like that. That satisfies. The demand is hub caps, spotlights and shit like that. Anything that looks like custom work for cars. Anything that has to do with that. It [automobile accessories] goes up by stages. By age, basically. Most of the stuff stays in the younger [adolescent] group. Maybe a little of the stuff goes up [to adults] . . . mainly tires." The ages of the consumers also affected the items found in the market. "When the guys get to 18 [years of age], they look for different things," Dude added. "Their entertainment changes and they want clothes. They steal suits and things like that. Or they may start to want speed in cars and they will steal engines or drop [disconnect and steal] transmissions."

As youth grow older, the motivated character of illegal economic activities changes. At first, cash value is not paramount. During early adolescence, as indicated, objects are stolen largely because they satisfy the personal needs of the thieves or their immediate friends. In time, the act of theft itself acquires added value, because it validates such personal qualities as rugged courage or cleverness. Nevertheless, such acts of thievery are still not directly motivated by cash values. Among older youth, however, the use values of goods and services generally become subordinated to monetary exchange. Cash becomes king. For one thing, the growing awareness of a ready market for less expensive bargain goods draws everyone's attention to illegal objects of exchange. Dude described one aspect of this new development as it applied to school-age consumers. He said: "A lot of dudes in school who couldn't afford things started buying their stuff from us. We would sell them stuff we couldn't use ourselves, or if we needed the dough." On the other hand, adolescent markets are readily interlocked with adult markets as goods and services demanded by youth are supplemented by commodities demanded by adults. That this interlocking may be initiated by young adults or older adults is illustrated by the following incident, as related to us by an energetic 22-year-old "businessman." Jack said: "I met these three Bean kids [Mexican or Mexican–American boys] in the Safeway [supermarket]. They were trying to steal some groceries. I told them they were going to get caught the way they were doing it. I gave them some advice on how to do it *right*. Outside the store I gave them a line about making money by stealing tires. I told them they would get a percentage on it if they could turn the tires over to me. They'll get practically nothing but I'll string them along until they get wise."

In such cases, however, the adults influence only the subsequent character of theft. They do not usually determine whether the boys will steal systematically in the first place. The adults are unnecessary to the rise of the market, because given the demand crowds, the instrumental ideologies, and the commodification of social life, market relations emerge virtually spontaneously among adolescents themselves. Indeed, interaction with criminal adults, identification with their roles, or interrelation with their markets are not necessary for criminal role making. Criminal relationships can be created solely by enterprising youth.

These enterprising youth, themselves, possess certain characteristics. They create the role of the middlemen and are the most important symbol of illegal market activity. Usually they are at the hubs of social networks and communication chains; consequently, they are in a position to "know everyone," and they are able to deliver the goods by stealing items personally or by contacting someone who can. Their activities catalyze the converging interests of the suppliers, sellers, and consumers of illegal goods and services. This simple everyday equation relating the "go-between" to the other market identities is also described by Dude: "There is your supply and demand. Right there this guy has something to go out for and to get that bread. You see what I mean? You walk into a group and you keep your mouth shut and you hear that this cat wants this. There is your demand. The people around you make your supply. But you don't know what your supply is until the other guys make your demand."

The local context and flow of market events establishes the activities and characteristics of this adolescent middleman. The adolescent who supplies goods to the customers must himself be supplied; hence, as the budding entrepreneur observes, the people around him are a source of supply. These people are thieves who transfer their goods to him, and if he is the only intermediary, the hot merchandise is transferred quickly into the hands of the consumer. Consequently, a dual relationship of trust is involved here: first, the adolescent who connects the customer with the source of supply must be familiar to crowds of customers. Second, he must also be known and trusted by the primary suppliers. Though others can and do fulfill these requirements, one type of youth fills them best of all: the leader (or lieutenant) of streetcorner formations. As indicated, a leader fits these requirements because his own social position provides him with the qualities and connections critical for an entrepreneurial career. Prior to his systematic involvement in irregular market relationships, the leader has already enjoyed greater prestige, an authoritative position, and extensive social connections. Such qualities and relations increase the chances of having the necessary "connections" for successful entrepreneurial activity.

Leaders have other business advantages. They can appeal for help from old fighting friends to eliminate weaker competitors quickly and easily. In such circumstances, rationalizations readily come to mind. In the next illustration, righteous indignation is expressed at the "falling out" of Sam, a dealer in marijuana and other goods. Sam was badly beaten up and forced out by friends of a club leader who was also trying to set himself up in "business." Long John remarks: "That punk Sam was scratched because he is a Punk! He's always been out of the crowd. He was dealing in merchandise and weed, but you know that we didn't trust him. You never know when a guy like that will put the stinger into you. We got Fred to upside his head and he ain't dealing anymore." Sam may have been "scratched," but the competition is never completely suppressed. Hustlers appear spontaneously, every day and everywhere.

Further, there is an extensive chain of entrepreneurial middlemen who become involved before illegal commodities such as suits, jewelry, watches, T.V. sets, portable radios, marijuana, car accessories, and innumerable other items reach their final destination, the adolescent consumer. Once again, our informant, Dude, speaks: "Jack gets the 'hi-fi' set and he goes to a guy and says I give you the hi-fi set for $70. The guy takes it to another guy who gives him a pound of pot for it. That other guy gets the cost of the pot back by selling the set to somebody else. But no matter the way you look at it, the hi-fi set is hot and it will be with the people who know it is hot, or people who will take the chance. But for the most part it will be among kids. They don't know adults. Jack knows them. Or Jose." In this way innumerable social relations are galvanized by the possession of money. The fetishism of ready cash interconnects the widening constellations of illegal behavior.

Among adults such terms as Pimp, Pusher, and Fence denote "professionals" who specialize in types of illegal activities. Adolescent entrepreneurs may also specialize in one type of illegal role, shunning others; yet we frequently found them in multiple roles such as selling narcotics and also handling other merchandise. Whether they deal in narcotics or stolen goods—or even turn a hand to pimping—depends upon many factors: these include the concrete opportunities for illegal gain, the types of behavior being actively repressed by police, the market demand, and the competition within the market itself. Thus, the adolescent entrepreneur emerges in a simple commodity market, where he is initially a middleman, in the most generic sense of the term. Especially during the few years prior to young adult status, the types of illegal goods and services handled may vary at any given time. The entrepreneur's services may also change because of experimentation with various types of entrepreneurial activities. But the important point is that adolescent entrepreneurs will generally do anything to make money, and most distasteful roles are quickly rationalized away if they pay off regularly. Under these circumstances, the fluidity and interchangeability of economic roles is to be expected.

Manny is a young middleman who objectifies these opportunist variations. In his opinion, the word "Connection" does not refer only to the narcotics Pusher. Instead, it also denotes the ability to organize the social connections that bring together opportunities, customers, buying, stealing, and exchanging stolen commodities. He says, "I used to steal with the guys but I dropped this when I started to be a regular Connection. It's less risky being a Connection. For a while I did both things. I would organize a job and be in on it with the guys. Then, I only cased joints or cars and sold them [the observations about illegal opportunities] to the guys for a percentage. They heisted the place. I didn't do anything except case it for them."

Additional differences between the adolescent and "professional" adult entrepreneurs are noticeable. The adult Fence acquires goods from thieves, and if they cannot be disposed of quickly he usually stores them until they can be unloaded safely into the hands of willing customers. The adult Fence, moreover, has ready cash and can purchase stolen goods more easily. By contrast, and with some noteable exceptions, our adolescent entrepreneurs are usually broke. They find it difficult to use their homes for the storage of illegal goods; hence, they prefer to transact business right "in the streets." Jack explains: "This dude came to me with a load of watches. I tried to unload them right away on the streets. Who do I unload to? To the young Dude who likes to jam down the street. He likes to have good clothes and maybe a watch. I sometimes unload to Spooks [blacks] who ain't got much bread but want to look cool anyway. I sometimes sell to guys I know in different places."

On the other hand, the adolescent entrepreneur may unload on an adult Fence. "I couldn't unload, so I unloaded with a Fence," says Jose. "The arrangement is simple. The Heist comes to me with the merchandise and says, 'Sell it on the street.' I go to the Fence if I can't get rid of it on the street and ask him to buy it. The Heist agrees to give me a percentage when I sell the stuff. I burn him for a little more than the percentage by telling him that I sold it for less than I really did. Ninety-nine percent of the time the Fence will buy it if it's good merchandise. If not I take it back to the Heist who burned [stole] it and we're clean."

Also, it is not surprising that as the illegal market emerges, interpersonal relationships are affected by new "impersonal" standards. When there is the possibility of "making money," even one's own best friends become defined as "customers" and "suppliers." As previously mentioned, in time cash values and market necessities contradict older solidary relationships.

This contradiction is illustrated by an incident that occurred while we were visiting Gus. While engaged in conversation, Charlotte knocked on the door of Gus' apartment. As soon as she entered, she produced two new, expensive cameras. She then indicated that her boyfriend (also an old friend of Gus) had been jailed, charged with "grand theft auto," and was desperately in need of bail money. Registered tires, which were finally traced to the boyfriend, had been found by the police in an accomplice's house. The cameras themselves dated from a prior theft. Gus offered Charlotte only fifteen dollars for each camera. She was astonished and complained that he could sell each one for three times that amount. Gus agreed, but he observed that she needed the cash immediately and that she might have great difficulty selling the cameras elsewhere quickly. Charlotte began to cry and plead that she would have to get more money to make bail. Her pleas were unsuccessful. She finally sold the cameras at Gus's price and left the apartment dejectedly. Gus then turned to us and exclaimed, "What the hell did she want? I shouldn't be blamed if that Punk is stupid enough to get caught robbing a car! If I gave her a lot of dough, I would be considered an easy touch by lots of guys. Everybody would put pressure on me if they got in a jam. I've got my reputation to consider!"

Such calculating reflections should not imply that Gus responded to friends coldly in every situation. In some circumstances, Gus certainly was hard as nails; yet, during "social occasions" he spent considerable sums of money on his immediate friends. On the other hand, though he was friendly and a confidante, even on these occasions he often acted like a "politician" whose favors had their price.

Thus, market relations initiate contradictory courses of action among streetcorner youth. While "doing business," the entrepreneur "rises above" everyday concerns with their personal loyalties. Entrepreneurial success calls for amicable yet businesslike relations with an extended circle of associates. But, as associates become potential buyers and sellers, traditional obligations recede. Market exigencies shape the future, fighting is "kid stuff," and wild escapades are condemned if they attract the police. The adolescent entrepreneur's motto for the day becomes: "Act Cool and Take Care of Business."

The entrepreneurial organization of market relationships requires certain abilities and, above all, skillful manipulation of friends, coworkers, sellers, buyers, and victims. Since he operates in a price-making market where prices are bargained, the entrepreneur develops his powers of persuasion. Classified by the word "conning," this power is quickly reified as a "natural instinct." Dude figured it this way: "You get a natural instinct toward this thing. It starts over anything, even over things you never intended to sell in the first place. If a guy was in the room here and suddenly said, 'That's a nice T.V. set!' I automatically fall in with the scene. I'd say, 'How much would you pay for it?' I'd start the bit and try to con the guy into buying it. And the other guy would fall in with it, too."

The entrepreneur eventually employs his ability to con without any apparent effort. After considerable experience, he sometimes even hucksters himself. "I know I need to stay on the [regular] job now that I have a baby. But I don't feel right. Somebody is always hassling me over there [at the factory]. I like it on the street. I've got a good 'con' and I always manage to put out a couple of bucks. Why I sometimes con myself into believing that I'm giving the guy a good deal and try not to sell it at that price."

Also, the entrepreneur applies the "conning" to legal and illegal contexts alike. In either situation, he might enlist the aid of his friends to validate the credibility of a con game. An instance illustrating this process in a legal context involved haggling over the price of an automobile. The purchaser in the sale, Gus, was the entrepreneur mentioned previously. The Seller, Bob, owned a big black 1930s touring car, which looked as if it had been used in a gangster movie for transporting the head of a syndicate round town. Gus wanted the car badly, and as he drove with us over to Bob's house he emphatically pointed out, "Look man, you're a righteous Con in your own way. You get all that information about what's happening among all the Dudes for nothing. Help me out! Rap it down to Joe. Tell him that his car is lousy. It has a lousy motor! Bad tires! Shitty body! Make him want to give the car away to me."

When we arrived, Gus's friend, Larry, was unexpectedly at the scene with Joe. Gus and Larry didn't say a word between them. The bargaining started, and Larry immediately enacted the supporting role that Gus had originally asked us to play. Virtually the identical words were spoken by Larry. Gus did not have to communicate verbally with his friend because their supportive relations in this kind of situation had become highly routinized.

Although leaders of streetcorner groups are in an advantageous position to develop an entrepreneurial status, many of them find it difficult to acquire the ability to con. A good Con must, above all, be flexible and articulate. This contrasts with other delinquent types. To be an outstanding fighter, one does not have to be verbally adroit. In fact, certain qualities associated with the "naturally born Fighter" may restrict his ability to bargain flexibly. For instance, Nate observes, "Conning doesn't seem to work with Chuck or Johnny. They are naturally born fighters. They can't bargain for things. They lay dead behind the scene. They have no 'give'."

Frequently a Fighter's reputation is dependent upon strong emotions and prideful mannerisms that are expressed habitually and unconsciously. As a rule, the Fighter finds it hard to bluff without feeling compelled to fill out the terms of the bluff. Adolescents who react with "blind passion," who see "red" in violent conflicts with others, cannot depersonalize their relationships easily even in nonviolent situations. Hence it is recognized that the Fighter often learns to confront his world with a mask of "no compromise." His forte is violence, and his deportment clearly indicates that "one can only be pushed so far" with impunity.

A Fighter may be affected adversely by irregular markets. While the Fighter (or Bad Stud) may not be as useful in the market, another type, the "Game Stud," has a role to play. In the market, the phrase "Bad Stud" is increasingly replaced by "Game Stud."[2] The Game Stud, like the Bad Stud, has the strength of will and the courage to fight despite the odds. He can "do deeds of daring," but he may not necessarily be the "baddest of them all." Such varied expectations reflect the contexts in which the social identities are embedded. We will draw this comparison a step further.

While the Bad Stud is validated by the Fighters as well as the Punks he has defeated, and since his fierce opponents may be from other territories or groups, the honorific title Bad Stud achieves its most prestigeful connotations during middle adolescence in the ethnocentric milieu. On the other hand, the identity Game Stud is generally granted to all who display the requisite nerve and courage. Moreover, within the market place, it acquires additional connotations that signify nerve in risky economic enterprises. Here, rather than a basic building block in an ethnocentric network, the Game Stud has become an economic type whose role reflects a loosely structured division of labor.

The varied functions of the Game Stud within the irregular market provide new benchmarks for evaluating personal worth. The attributes of the Game Stud are extremely adaptable to the requirements of violent extortion, housebreaking, armed robbery, mugging, and other kinds of theft, where nerve is a major asset. The calculated use of nerve also enters into consideration.

A conversation with an adolescent "businessman" about the importance of nerve illustrates this economically rational view. The conversation took place one evening, after we had attended a club meeting in the company of Dude. The club was composed of younger delinquent boys, and during the meeting they talked heatedly about using four members to "jump an enemy." When the meeting ended, Dude contemptuously remarked, "If they [the younger boys] were in *business* (i.e., in the illegal market] they would be classified as Punks. Because if they are gonna jump this guy they will take four guys to do it. That's crazy! All you need is two guys. As long as they are game, fast, smart. Game is nerve."

Other types, such as the Heist, the Pimp, and the Gambler, begin to emerge in the market. Take gambling, for example. Small games of rummy and poker have already become customary during the early adolescent years, and virtually any place is convenient for a game, so long as there is a spot to lay the cards down. When money increases enormously in importance, the individual delinquent becomes preoccupied with "working his own angle," and gambling is one of these "angles."

Serious gambling for money takes many forms and occurs in a variety of places. It includes small card and dice games at the beach, in the park, on the steps of an apartment house, or in a living room. If a normal pair of dice attracts too much attention, the boys at the corner hangouts liven up "dead time" by shaking a pair of miniature dice that may be enclosed in a transparent cigarette lighter. The small dice may not be as much fun to use, but they are more easily concealed.

These informal events are often completely spontaneous, and they are maintained beyond the end of the adolescent years. Toward the end of adolescence, however, formal occasions for gambling are created by energetic promoters. "Gambling nights" are promoted by entrepreneurs who, for a percentage, line up players, dealers, rooms, small roulette wheels, dice, cards, several card tables, and an assortment of chairs. Some of the younger "clients," who may be only 14 or 15 years old, are invited to such a "set up" because gambling with one's age mates is not as lucrative as a game with the younger dudes. In their admiration for the older delinquents, these dudes scarcely realize that they are being taken for every cent they have.

Thus, organizing a "gambling night" and raking off a percentage for "the house" is a workable scheme for making money. Some of the boys who are very adept at cards become known as good to have around at such events. These boys are hired by an entrepreneur to play for the house at one of the tables, and their take is a percentage of the winnings. Successful experiences of this sort go into the shaping of the adolescent gambler.

Other money-making schemes are constructed by youth always on the lookout for "a way to make a buck." The market, for example, includes buyers of cash. Many boys require credit to pay for automobile loans or to tide themselves over to the next night's successful caper. They may "touch" their friends for a temporary loan; however, old reliable friends may be having their own financial difficulties. They may then turn to the usurious older adolescent loan shark, usually the rare entrepreneur who has successfully accumulated cash from other illegal ventures. These entrepreneurs extend short-term loans, payable in a week or a month, at extremely high rates of interest. Collateral may take the form of an automobile "pink slip" (i.e., certificate of ownership and bill of sale), or a watch, which is held by the adolescent who advances the loan.

As the market begins to stabilize (if only for a temporary period), each member of a streetcorner stradom formation finds his place and makes his way as well as he can. Each person tries his hand at gambling, burglary, entrepreneurial activities, and other ways of making a living. Some streetcorner youth simply remain buyers rather than active workers in the market. Others run through a variety of legal as well as illegal pursuits only to end up routinely with one foot in both legal and illegal markets. Still others turn their hand to illegal activities for maintaining or supplementing their incomes only when times are tough.

For reasons of his own, each person develops his own working relationships with the generally regular and the highly irregular economies. Speaking of his own friends, Whitey, a streetcorner youth, talked about their econcmic activities. He said: "Don won't fuck around with burglary because he is married. Norm doesn't work. His parents give him a little money but he's got a car to keep up. He burglarizes to get money to live it up. He doesn't make deals [he doesn't operate as an entrepreneur]. He rarely makes deals for money but for other stuff like pot and things he can use [personally]."

"Walter can't find a job and he's gotta pay for his car," Whitey added. "So he goes to Gootch and deals with him and tells him, 'I got three guys who need tires and what can I make on it?' Or he burglarizes [a house or store] himself."

So it goes. Each member of the marketplace knows the current status of the other. Like the workers and shop owners in those sections of town where there is a concentration of shops in the same trade, these youth also meet daily and engage in shop talk and small talk. In like manner, the young workers and entrepreneurs of the adolescent market point things out to each other:

Dude says: "Jester ain't stealing now because he's going to junior college and works six hours every night. He wants to keep clean." Nick replies, "Don't kid me! Jester is too lazy to hold a job. He'll be back in business in a few months."

Oscar insists, "Whitey can't fight. You don't hear anybody calling him the Bad Stud, or 'Watch out for Whitey! He can kill you!' It's just that he's got the con." Walter responds: "That's true. But it's the con that makes the bread."

Gus announces, "Hear about Sammy? He got scratched. About time! If the Heat busted him he would cop out on everybody." Bobo agrees and remarks that you can't trust your friends any more.

In the snatches of conversation one can detect short-hand guides to marketplace conduct in the form of aphorisms and proverbs. These pithy comments reveal the instrumental principles that increasingly regulate the lives of the active workers in the illegal market:

> "It's fuck your buddy week, fifty-two weeks of the year."
>
> "Do unto others as they would do unto you . . . only do it first."
>
> "Anybody *that* stupid deserves to be swung [victimized in some way]."
>
> "If you have a buddy kind and true, you fuck him before he fucks you."
>
> "You may be a Con but don't let your mouth overload your ass."
>
> "If I don't cop it . . . somebody else will."
>
> "Just a case of Marty taking care of Marty."

Underneath the shifting identities and high turnover of the "labor force" in the market, stable reciprocities develop and are symbolized in metaphors and phrases such as "Dealer," or "he dealt weed," or "he dealt in hot merchandise." The terms "bargaining," "conning," "dealing," or "heist" and "gameness," usurp the popularity of former words such as Fighter, Bad Stud, and "One for all and all for one," which are charged with ethnocentric meanings. The relationships between these adolescents become atomized, and they hustle alone or combine with one or two partners to take care of "business."

NOTES

1. See Horton (1967) for an outstanding article on the rationality and habit patterns establishing the daily "rhythm" of social activities in an older streetcorner group.
2. The boys rationalize this change in their own words, indicating that actually "everybody knows" only one or two Dudes who are really entitled to be called "Bad Studs" because they are completely ruthless. On the other hand, the Game Studs are a more familiar part of the scene because they are more prevalent.

22

Concluding Years

When the high-school years end, local socialite groups usually disintegrate if their members move on to college. But socialite styles of life make a strong resurgence among informal college groups and in college fraternity and sorority relationships. The deviant aspects of socialite styles of life may also be maintained in college. For instance, Hills (1983:263) writes about "Preppy University," a northeastern upper-middle-class college listed in *The Preppy Handbook*. He notes (1983:257–58) that "alongside of . . . the values of hard work, academic diligence, and deferred gratification is a pervasive set of 'subterranean' values at Preppy U. that emphasize hedonistic pleasures of the moment, thrills, excitement and risk-taking; an equation of masculinity with toughness and aggressive sexual behavior; and a rejection of self-denial and the work ethic." These values tend to prevail during weekends, late evenings, fraternity parties, and special events such as football victory celebrations. Because the grade inflation at Preppy U. enables Preppies to enjoy good grades as well as ample leisure time (the Gentleman's C has become the Gentleperson's B or B+), students study after dinner for a couple of hours, but hundreds gather later in a dozen or more bars several nights a week

> to get plastered, smashed, stoned, party, or indulge in a little pickup "fun sex" for the evening. . . . Unfortunately, sexual assault, property damage, "dine and dash" larceny, car theft, and other untoward behavior are frequently an accompaniment

> of such alcohol and drug consumption (whose mind-altering effects provide convenient social excuses the morning after to absolve students of any moral responsibility for their illicit activity). (Hills, 1983:257–58)

Hills concludes that this behavior is routine and among some student groups has become normalized and

> socially approved, almost semi-institutionalized, often accompanied by a playful, sporting quality—whether it be the graffiti-defaced brand new library addition, the destruction inflicted on the residence halls, causing thousands of dollars annually in damages, or the use of recycled term papers. Many of these injurious acts are so thoroughly rationalized by a socially shared vocabulary of justifications that few participants are likely to experience any strong feelings of guilt or shame. . . . (Hills, 1983:262)

Hills believes that "the increasing prolongation of adolescence in our credential-inflated society" has made residential colleges such as Preppy University a "youth ghetto," where students discover that they have ample time to take risks, test limits, and indulge themselves while they mark time until graduation. However, we would question the causal effects of the segregation of youth or ample leisure time and suggest that the manipulative and deviant behavior observed by Hills may be due to the individualistic attitudes and insensitivities toward other people that are discussed in Part III. Similar standpoints are also mentioned by Clark (1958:250), who bemoans the lack of a theoretical framework for explaining delinquency among privileged youth. Clark writes, "If delinquency is to be defined in terms of its essentials of lack of social sensitivity, lack of empathy, a callow regard for humanity and dignity of others, a punitive and seductive approach to others who are considered weak and defenseless, then these privileged individuals must be considered delinquent in spite of the fact that they are not part of the court records and the presently available statistics." Clark complains about the lack of data regarding these youth. He observes,

> the fact that we do not at present, know the number of such young people who are developing in our schools; that we do not have the theoretical framework and methods for recognizing them . . . does not necessarily diminish the social gravity of this aspect of the delinquency problem. Indeed, the fact that these

> patterns are not generally recognized or discussed as part of the delinquency problem or that they may even be accepted as indications of "normal" and "natural" patterns of a discriminative middle and upper class way of life suggest their insidiousness and gravity. This more obscure aspect of juvenile delinquency will be infinitely more difficult for society to deal with, precisely because it is so inextricably woven into the fabric of the valued and privileged aspect of our society.

While socialite high-school domains usually disappear or are transported elsewhere, the final developments in streetcorner domains are more dependent on local conditions. We have seen, for instance, that the rapid accommodation of cliques to illegal marketplace activity transforms the ethnocentric standards previously sustained within streetcorner groups. Streetcorner life certainly continues after high school, as young adults hang around together or cruise about in cars scanning the social scene. On the other hand, wherever the illegal market is highly developed, it intrudes into the life of the group, and the peers who become heavily engaged in market activities change. The ideology of the market reworks old beliefs. Close friendships that are not adaptable to marketplace goals are loosened, and new partners are adopted for criminal activities. The effect of the market on old friendships can be seen in the use of its calculating terminology.

"I hate Jasper's guts," says Jester. "He's got a big mouth. The other day these guys I know wanted to buy some yellow jackets [pills]. I told them I'd set it up with them and tell them where to get it. Who comes by the house but Jasper with a bunch of guys? I says as long as Jasper is your friend I won't do you guys one favor. You can't trust him."

"Jean is a sneak," snaps Peter. "If she doesn't have anything in it for herself she says 'Fuck you!'"

"Carl is a dip, man. He knows the crowd is around him but he doesn't know what the crowd contains. He knows the world is about to fall but he doesn't know when. I can't depend on him," Dude observes.

"Bob is an easy-going guy. He'll get high with you any time but he'll pay attention to what Jose says. I trust him only up to a point," says Chuck.

"Marlon is the kind of guy that would buy off the president [of the United States]," remarks Whitey painfully. "Marty burns me and cuffs me and fucks me around. He don't come around for weeks and he knows I get pissed off. Then he'll come around and say: 'Whitey, why don't you double [date] with me and my broad next weekend? We're going out to the Pike.' I'll say, 'Hey man, I ain't working.' He'll say, 'Don't worry, the *treat's on me*!' Or something like that . . . that line that just grabs you by the balls and squeezes the hell out of you. It hurts me to see that he is trying to buy me . . . buy my friendship back again. He knows it ain't gonna work, you know."

In some groups, these disintegrating effects in the patterns of trust show up almost immediately. The solidarity maintained by mutual aid, the ethnocentric awareness of common enemies, and the sheer weight of common understandings based on years of association crack under the impact of market standards. These new standards are often applied in unpredictable and arbitrary fashion, depending upon the success of the night's work or pressure from the police.

In the disintegration of trust and group identity, personal security is elevated as the preeminent guide to action. This priority is revealed by the following argument between two brothers, Blackie and Dan, who operated as a burglary team. We were talking with the team a day after the burglary mentioned in the argument. The argument itself was triggered when, in the course of conversation, we asked how well they trusted each other. Blackie suddenly remarked, "We were robbing this house and Dan says that he has to take a crap. Can you believe it? He asked me to come up to the second floor and wait on the landing near the bathroom. He said that he wanted to make sure if the Heat [police] showed up." Dan turned to Blackie and explained, "If the Heat came you might have left me without letting me know." Indignant, Blackie retorted: "Hell, if the Heat came I'd let you know . . . but I ain't gonna wait around to wipe your ass!" At this point we cut into the conversation and asked what would be done if the police pressured one brother to inform on the other. Blackie melodramatically replied: "We have an understanding. We help each other out but when the end comes it's THE END. Even you would look after your own ass if it was THE END."

Thus each young economic criminal begins to assess personal survival by the degree to which everyone around him will "cop out," "stool," or "burn him." Whitey remarks: "Don will accept a Dude simply because he is a friend of a friend and is already accepted by somebody. That's the way the majority of people think. But it's more than that. When I look at a person I want to know whether he's gonna burn me or not. I can tell by his basic personality or even his family life. For instance, this one kid . . . I kept telling everybody about him: 'Don't mess with him, man. He's gonna burn you, man!' You know who he is: Jackson! The reason I knew he would burn you is because he is so afraid of his parents. He had a great fear of them. They were the only existing thing he had. When he did burn . . . he copped out! [He squealed on his friends] Why? One reason . . . because he's afraid of his family and what his impression on society will be when he walks out [of prison]. Whitey continued: "Why did he cop out? Well it's that he's a Punk! But it's more than he's a Punk, man. It's something else. Like Chuck. He copped out on Al and Hank. I knew why. He was scared shit because he would have done a lotta time [in jail]. He only did three months and he was cut loose. That's real wrong. [Implicit here is that a shorter sentence was given to this narcotics user because he informed on friends.] *It's just that you can't trust a person.*"

The belief that most people are concerned with their own selfish advantage is revealed in a discussion with an 18-year-old Heist, Steve, before he was to meet his partner for a night's job. (We were leaving a club meeting and, after indicating that he had some time to spend with us, he said "I have to leave at 11:30 because I've got to meet some guys. . . . We've got a perfect set-up. A store that's easy to get into." During the discussion that followed, this exchange took place:

Researcher: You say that if you haven't got the 'coins' you can burn someone who has the coins and that way you can be equal to him?

Steve: That way you can have what everyone else has.

Researcher: What about the guy you burn? What do you say about that guy?

Steve: Tough shit! If you burn him and get away with it . . . more power to you!

Researcher: You mean getting the coins is enough of a justification?

Steve: Yeh, if a guy is fool enough to let himself get fucked . . . well, then, too bad! Almost anyone who has got the coins to start out with, got them somehow. And, in my opinion, I suspect that maybe he didn't burn somebody for those coins, but in a roundabout way those coins were burnt. Otherwise, he wouldn't have so much coins. No matter how he lived in the business world . . . there is always some chicken-shit stuff going on in it. Somebody's burning somebody and one of them is gonna get the coins.

As they become young adults, streetcorner men and women continue to aid each other and share food, booze, and narcotics to some degree. But the rational calculation of interests and risks that arises in the marketplace undermines sentimentality and elevates its own forms of reciprocity that binds these people economically. A new kind of "trust" emerges under these conditions. Power, nerve, and calculating ability now come to the fore. Power is not just equated with physical superiority. Money and "contacts" make the weak strong. Like the stereotyped television "heavy" who can call upon an "enforcer" at will, the young criminal entrepreneur brags melodramatically that he can "pick up a phone and in ten minutes a pal of mine will be down here to show you just how big I am."

Among young adults heavily engaged in criminal activity, with the destruction of older group identities personal interests converge on their own economic welfare and avoidance of arrest. Yet even with such striving, stable arrangements are still possible. These arrangements are based on accommodation to naked self-interests and power. Who are the friends that can be trusted under these conditions? In the opinion of Dude, they are the boys who are "too active to cop out. They can't wriggle out of it and push it onto someone else. They can't do nothing. They'll burn with other people." These friends can be trusted, at least for the moment.

In this setting, it is agreed that one doesn't have to like a person to predict his behavior, to abide by his ways, or—above all—to respect him. Jose says, "I don't trust Jo-Boy with all my heart. I respect him but I can't trust him because he cares more about himself than he cares about anybody. But if it's a deal, his word is good. He keeps his side of the deal. I respect him because he is power crazy." Thus, when police pressure mounts and economic needs intensify, the integrity of friends is increasingly doubted. Most people are considered opportunistic at heart, and a distinctive moral rhetoric supports this instrumental conception of Everyman.

We have presented an explanation of the forms of delinquency emerging on the level of the group. We have suggested that these forms are linked to the general properties of our society. In addition to this linkage we have proposed that the phasic developments of relatively autonomous, stratified domains of groups are important for understanding the motivated character of delinquent acts.

In our depiction of these phasic developments in earlier chapters we have suggested that ideological conceptions of personal relationships emerge, become elaborated, and provide standards by which social worth is estimated. These conceptions, in turn, affect subsequent patterns of activity. Also, in each phase, the emerging standards are woven into conceptual frameworks that modify older modes of thinking. Toward the end of these collective developments, an instrumental ideology strongly mediates the relations between other human beings and the young criminal who is heavily engaged in marketplace activities.

We have also suggested that instrumental justifications are mediated by collective forms of adolescent conduct. In other words, even though we consider the instrumental mode of organizing moral utterances important, we do not assume that it operates by itself, or that it invariably expresses individual attitudes. The instrumental mode operates in the context of collective relationships. It structures interpersonal communication and facilitates group decisions. Furthermore, the material and ideological sources of interpersonal communication and group decisions are dependent upon macroscopic economic and political relationships beyond the comprehension of the adolescent actors. The members of streetcorner formations, in particular, rarely understand what forces determine their lives even when they are older. Their relationships with one another and with society at large express an individualism and indifference that are usually taken for granted.

In time, however, the more reflective and self-conscious delinquents stop for a moment to look back at their own histories. Often on these occasions they express vague feelings of hopelessness at the present state of their lives. The very justifications uttered by these older youth when continuing the course of their careers—"I'm going to make out. It's them or me!"—reveal their anxiety about loss of control over everyday events. With age, many streetcorner delinquents increasingly see themselves caught in a trap. They have, themselves, been turned into instruments by forces they neither control nor comprehend.

BIBLIOGRAPHY

Adorno, T. W., Elsa Frenkel-Brunswick, Daniel J. Levinson, and R. Nevitt Sanford. 1950. *The Authoritarian Personality*. New York: Harper Bros.

Ash, William. 1964. *Marxism and Moral Concepts*. New York: Monthly Review Press.

Aydellote, Frank. 1913. *Elizabethan Rogues and Vagabonds*. Oxford: Clarendon Press.

Bachrach, Peter, and Morton Baratz. 1970. *Power and Poverty*. New York: Oxford University Press.

Bairoch, Paul. 1975. *The Economic Development of the Third World Since 1900*. Berkeley, Calif.: University of California Press.

Baltzell, Digby. 1958. *Philadelphia Gentleman: The Making of a National Upper Class*. Glencoe, Ill.: Free Press.

Bauman, Richard. 1978. "Teenage drinking and driving," *The California Highway Patrolman* 42.

Berger, Edmund. 1948. "Injustice collectors." In Edmund Berger (ed.), *The Battle of the Conscience, A Psychiatric Study of the Inner Workings of the Conscience*. Washington, D.C.: Washington Institute of Medicine, Monumental Printing Co.

Besant, Sir Walter. 1904. *London in the Time of the Tudors*. Adam and Charles Black.

Biddle, George. 1939. *An American Artist's Story*. Boston: Little, Brown and Co.

Blashfield, R. K., and R. A. Isleib. 1984. "Book review of *Cluster Analysis for Social Scientists*." *Journal of Classification* 1:137–38.

Bluestone, Barry. 1972. "Capitalism and poverty in America: A discussion." *Monthly Review* 2:64–71.

Blumer, Herbert, Alan Sutter, Samir Ahmen, and Roger Smith. 1967. *The World of the Youthful Drug User. ADD Center Final Report.* Berkeley, Calif.: School of Criminology, University of California, Berkeley.

Bonger, William A. 1915. *Criminality and Economic Conditions.* Boston: Little Brown.

Bordua, David. 1961. "Delinquent subcultures: Sociological interpretations of gang delinquency." *The Annals* 338:119–36.

Bowles, Samuel, and Herbert Gintis. 1973. "I.Q. in the U.S. class structure." *Social Policy* 3:65–96.

Braithwaite, John. 1981. "The myth of social class and criminality reconsidered." *American Sociological Review* 46:36–57.

Brake, Mike. 1974. "The skinheads: An English workingclass subculture." *Youth and Society* 6:179–200.

Bremner, Robert H. (ed.). 1970. *Children and Youth in America: A Documentary History, I.* Cambridge, Mass.: Harvard University Press.

Brinton, Crane. 1959. *A History of Western Morals.* New York: Harcourt, Brace.

Buchholz, E., R. Hartmann, J. Leckschas, and G. Stiller. 1974. *Socialist Criminology.* Lexington, Mass.: Saxon House/Lexington Books.

Burgum, Berry. 1967. "The sociology of Oscar Lewis as a critique of imperialism." *Science and Society* 31:323–37.

Chambliss, William. 1973. "The Saints and Roughnecks." *Society* 11:24–31.

Christie, Nils. 1978. "Youth as a crime-generating phenomenon." In Barry Krisberg and James Austin (eds.), *The Children of Ishmael: Critical Perspectives on Juvenile Justice.* Palo Alto, Calif.: Mayfield, pp. 221–30.

Clark, Kenneth. 1958. "Color, class, personality, and juvenile delinquency." *Journal of Negro Education* 28.

Clarke, John, and Tony Jefferson. 1976. "Working class youth cultures." In Geoff Mungham and Geoff Pearson (eds.), *Working Class Youth Culture.* London: Routledge & Kegan Paul, pp. 138–58.

Clelland, Donald, and Timothy Carter. 1980. "The new myth of class and crime." *Criminology* 18:319–36.

Cloward, Richard, and Lloyd Ohlin. 1960. *Delinquency and Opportunity: A Theory of Delinquent Gangs.* Glencoe, Ill.: Free Press.

Cohen, Albert. 1955. *Delinquent Boys: The Culture of the Gang.* Glencoe, Ill.: Free Press.

Coleman, James. 1960. "The adolescent subculture and academic achievement." *American Journal of Sociology* 65:337–47.

——. 1962. *The Adolescent Society: The Social Life of the Teenager and Its Impact on Education.* Glencoe, Ill.: Free Press.

Cooper, Charles. 1863. *Annals of Cambridge, II.* Cambridge: Warwick and Co.

Cressey, Donald. 1953. *Other People's Money.* Glencoe, Ill.: Free Press.

Dagnais, F., and Leonard Marascuilo. 1972. "Student demonstrations in a multiracial high school." *Youth and Society* 3:457–76.

Davis, Alan. 1968. "Sexual assaults in the Philadelphia prison system and sheriff's vans." *Transaction* 8:15–16.

DeFleur, Lois B. 1971. "Ecological variables in the cross-cultural study of delinquency." In Harwin L. Voss and David M. Petersen (eds.), *Ecology, Crime and Delinquency.* New York: Appleton-Century-Crofts, pp. 283–302.

del Olmo, Rosa. 1979. "The Cuban revolution and the struggle against prostitution." *Crime and Social Justice* 12:34–40.

Dollard, John. 1941. *Frustration and Aggression.* New Haven, Conn.: Yale University Press.

Dos Santos, Theotonio. 1970. "The concept of social class." *Science and Society* 34:166–93.

Dunphy, Dexter. 1963. "The social structure of adolescent peer groups." *Sociometry* 26:230–46.

Edel, Abraham. 1955. *Ethical Judgement: The Use of Science in Ethics.* Glencoe, Ill.: Free Press.

____. 1959. "The concept of levels in social theory." In Llewellyn Gross (ed.), *Symposium on Sociological Theory*. Evanston, Ill.: Row, Peterson and Co., pp. 167–95.

Edel, May, and Abraham Edel. 1959. *Anthropology and Ethics*. Springfield, Ill.: Charles C Thomas.

Elliott, Delbert, and David Huizinga. 1983. "Social class and delinquent behavior in a national youth panel." *Criminology* 21:149–77.

Ellis, Herbert, and Stanley Newman. 1971. " 'Gowster,' 'Ivy-Leaguer,' 'Conservative,' 'Mackman,' and 'Continental': A functional analysis of six ghetto roles." In Eleanor B. Leacock (ed.), *The Culture of Poverty: A Critique*. New York: Simon and Schuster, pp. 299–311.

Empey, LaMar T. 1982. *American Delinquency: Its Meaning and Construction*. Homewood, Ill.: Dorsey Press.

Firmin, Thomas. 1681. *Some Proposals for the Employment of the Poor*. 2nd Ed. London. Excerpted in Wiley B. Sanders (ed.), 1970, *Juvenile Offenders for a Thousand Years*. Chapel Hill, N.C.: University of North Carolina Press, pp. 18–20.

Fisher, F. J. 1948. "The development of London as a center of conspicuous consumption in the 16th and 17th centuries." *Transactions of the Royal Historical Society, 4th Series.*

Friedman, Stanley D. 1969. "A typology of adolescent drug users." Unpublished master's thesis, University of California, Berkeley.

Garfinkel, Harold. 1967. *Studies in Ethnomethodology*. Englewood Cliffs, N.J.: Prentice Hall.

George, C. H. 1971. "The making of the English bourgeoisie, 1500–1750." *Science and Society* 35:385–414.

Gibbens, T. C. N. 1958. "Car thieves." *The British Journal of Delinquency* 8:257–65.

Gitchoff, G. Thomas. 1969. *Kids, Cops and Kilos: A Study of Contemporary Suburban Youth*. San Diego, Calif.: Malter-Westerfield.

Glaser, Daniel. 1956. "Criminality theories and behavioral images." *American Journal of Sociology* 61:433–44.

Glueck, Sheldon, and Eleanor Glueck. 1959. "Family life and delinquency." In Sheldon and Eleanor Glueck (eds.), *Problems of Delinquency*. Boston: Houghton-Mifflin, pp. 136–55.

Goldberg, Theodore. 1969. "The automobile: A social institution for adolescents." *Environment and Behavior* 2:157–86.

Gordon, Wayne. 1957. *Social System of the High School: A Study in the Sociology of Adolescence*. Glencoe, Ill.: The Free Press.

Greenberg, David. 1977. "Delinquency and the age structure of society." *Contemporary Crisis* 1:189–223.

Halbwachs, Maurice. 1958. *The Psychology of Social Class*. Glencoe, Ill.: Free Press.

Hannerz, Ulf. 1969. *Soulside*. New York: Columbia University Press.

Harmon, Thomas. 1930. "A caveat or warning for common cursitors, vulgarly called vagabonds." In A. V. Judges (ed.), *Elizabethan Underworld*. New York: E. P. Sutton and Co., pp. 61–118.

Harrison, Bennett. 1975. "Education, training and the urban ghetto." In *Manpower Research Monograph No. 27*. Washington D.C.: U.S. Department of Labor, Manpower Administration, Superintendent of Documents.

Hartjen, Clayton. 1982. "Delinquency, development, and social integration in India." *Social Problems* 29:464–73.

Healy, William, and Augusta Bronner. 1936. *New Light on Delinquency and Its Treatment*. New Haven, Conn.: Yale University Press.

Hibbert, Christopher. 1963. *The Roots of Evil*. Boston: Little, Brown.

Higgins, Paul, and Gary Albrecht. 1982. "Cars and kids: A self-report study of juvenile auto theft and traffic violations." *Sociology and Social Research* 66:29–41.

Hills, Stuart. 1983. "Crime and deviance on a college campus: The privilege of class." *Humanity and Society* 6:257–66.

Hindelang, Michael J. 1971. "Age, sex, and the versatility of delinquent involvements." *Social Problems* 18:524–35.

Hirschi, Travis, 1969. *Causes of Delinquency*. Berkeley, Calif.: University of California Press.

Hirschi, Travis, Michael Hindelang, and Joseph Weis. 1982. "Reply to 'On the use of self-report data to determine the class distribution of criminal and delinquent behavior'." *American Sociological Review* 47:433–35.

Hobsbawm, Eric. 1954. "The crises of the 17th century—II." *Past and Present* 6:63.

Hollingshead, August. 1949. *Elmtown's Youth*. New York: John Wiley.

Horton, John. 1967. "Time and cool people." *Transaction* 4:5–12.

Irwin, John. 1964. "The development of surfing." Unpublished report.

Jusserand, Jean. 1931. *English Wayfaring Life*. New York: G. P. Putnam's Sons.

Kinney, David A. 1983. "Stratification and delinquency: An examination of adolescent sources of prestige and involvement in deviant behavior." Paper presented at American Society of Criminology annual meeting.

Klapp, Orrin. 1962. *Heroes, Villains, and Fools: The Changing American Character*. Englewood Cliffs, N.J.: Prentice Hall.

Kleck, Gary. 1982. "On the use of self-report data to determine the class distribution of criminal and delinquent behavior." *American Sociological Review* 47:427–33.

Kohlberg, Lawrence. 1970. "Education for justice: A modern statement of the platonic view." In *Moral Education: Five Lectures*. Cambridge, Mass.: Harvard University Press.

Kornhauser, Ruth Rosner. 1978. *Social Sources of Delinquency: An Appraisal of Analytic Models*. Chicago: University of Chicago Press.

Krisberg, Barry. 1974. "Gang youth and hustling: The psychology of survival." *Issues in Criminology* 9:115–29.

Labov, William. 1973. "The linguistic consequences of being a 'lame'." *Language in Society* 2:81–119.

Larkin, Ralph W. 1979. *Suburban Youth in Cultural Crisis*. New York: Oxford University Press.

Latrobe, John H. B. 1840. "Address on the subject of a manual labor school" (Baltimore). An excerpt in Robert H. Bremner (ed.), 1970,

Children and Youth in America: A Documentary History, I. Cambridge, Mass.: Harvard University Press, pp. 753–54.

Lemert, Edwin M. 1951. *Social Pathology.* New York: McGraw-Hill.

Lerman, Paul. 1966. "Issues in subcultural delinquency." Unpublished doctoral dissertation, Columbia University.

——. 1967a. "Argot, symbolic deviance and subcultural delinquency." *American Sociological Review* 32:209–24.

——. 1967b. "Gangs, networks, and subcultural delinquency." *American Journal of Sociology* 73:63–72.

——. 1968. "Individual values, peer values, and subcultural delinquency." *American Sociological Review* 33:219–35.

Lewis, Oscar. 1961. *The Children of Sanchez.* New York: Random House, Inc.

——. 1966. *La Vida: A Puerto Rican Family in the Culture of Poverty—San Juan and New York.* New York: Random House.

Liebow, Elliot. 1967. *Tally's Corner.* Boston: Little Brown.

Lin, Tsung-Yi. 1958. "Tai-Pau and Liu-Mang: Two types of delinquent youths in Chinese society." *British Journal of Delinquency* 8:244–56.

Los Angeles Chamber of Commerce. 1967. *The Dynamics of Youth Explosion—A Look Ahead.* Los Angeles: Chamber of Commerce.

Lynd, Helen M., and Robert S. Lynd. 1937. *Middletown.* New York: Harcourt.

Maitland, Sir William. 1739. *The History of London, from its Foundation by the Romans to the Present Time. In Nine Books.* London: Act, Parl. 14 Car. II Brit. Mus. Excerpted in Wiley B. Sanders (ed.), 1970, *Juvenile Offenders for a Thousand Years.* Chapel Hill, N.C.: University of North Carolina Press, pp. 40–41.

Mann, Michael. 1970. "The Social Cohesion of Liberal Democracy." *American Sociological Review* 35:423–39.

Marx, Karl. 1959. *Capital, I.* Moscow: Foreign Languages Publishing House.

____. 1962. *Capital, III*. Moscow: Foreign Languages Publishing House.

Matza, David, 1964. *Delinquency and Drift*. New York: John Wiley.

McFarland, Ross, and Roland Moore. 1961. "Youth and automobiles." In Eli Ginzberg (ed.), *Values and Ideals of American Youth*. New York: Columbia University Press, pp. 169–91.

Meillassoux, Claude. 1980. "From reproduction to production: A Marxist approach to economic anthropology." In Harold Wolpe (ed.), *The Articulation of Modes of Production: Essays from Economy and Society*. London: Routledge and Kegan Paul, pp. 189–201.

Merton, Robert K. 1938. "Social structure and anomie." *American Sociological Review* 3:672–82.

Messerschmidt, Jim. 1979. *School Stratification and Delinquent Behavior: A Macrosocial Interpretation*. Stockholm: GOTAB.

Miller, Walter. 1958. "Lower class culture as a generating milieu of gang delinquency." *Journal of Social Issues* 16:5–19.

Mills, C. Wright. 1940. "Situated actions and vocabularies of Motive." *American Sociological Review* 5:904–13.

Moore, Joan. 1978. *Homeboys: Gangs, Drugs and Prison in the Barrios of Los Angeles*. Philadelphia: Temple University Press.

Morash, Merry Ann. 1981. "Cognitive developmental theory." *Criminology* 19:360–71.

More, Thomas. 1964. *Utopia*. New Haven, Conn.: Yale University Press.

Mungham, Geoff. 1976. "Youth in pursuit of itself." In Geoff Mungham and Geoff Pearson (eds.), *Working Class Youth Culture*. London: Routledge and Kegan Paul, pp. 82–104.

Myerhoff, Howard, and Barbara Myerhoff. 1964. "Field Observations of Middle-class Gangs." *Social Forces* 42:328–36.

Neavles, J. C., and G. Winokur. 1957. "The hot-rod driver." *Bulletin of the Menninger Clinic* 21:20–35.

Niles Weekly Register, December 15, 1821. Excerpted in Robert H. Bremner (ed.), 1970, *Children and Youth in America: A Documentary History, I*. Cambridge, Mass.: Harvard University Press, pp. 773–74.

New York Daily Times, June 28, 1853. "Walks among the New York poor: Emigrants and emigrants' children." In Robert H. Bremner (ed.), 1970, *Children and Youth in America: A Documentary History, I.* Cambridge, Mass.: Harvard University Press, pp. 414–15.

Obregon, Anibal Quijano. 1980. "The marginal pole of the economy and the marginalized labor force." In Harold Wolpe (ed.), *The Articulation of Modes of Production: Essays in Economy and Society.* London: Routledge & Kegan Paul, pp. 254–88.

Ossowski, Stanislaw. 1963. *Class Structure in the Social Consciousness.* New York: Free Press of Glencoe.

Owen, David. 1981. *High School.* New York: Viking Press.

Papagiannis, George, Robert Bickel, and Richard Fuller. 1983. "The social creation of school dropouts: Accomplishing the reproduction of an underclass." *Youth and Society* 14:363–92.

Parker, Howard. 1976. "Boys will be men: The career of a confusion." In Geoff Mungham and Geoff Pearson (eds.), *Working Class Youth Culture.* London: Routledge & Kegan Paul, pp. 27–47.

Pearson, Geoff. 1976. " 'Paki-bashing' in a North East Lancashire cotton town: A case study and its history." In Geoff Mungham and Geoff Pearson (eds.), *Working Class Youth Culture.* London: Routledge & Kegan Paul, pp. 138–58.

Peattie, Lisa R. 1971. "The structural parameters of emerging life styles in Venezuela." In Eleanor Leacock (ed.), *The Culture of Poverty: A Critique.* New York: Simon and Schuster, pp. 285–95.

Perlman, Janice. 1976. *The Myth of Marginality: Urban Poverty and Politics in Rio de Janeiro.* Berkeley, Calif.: University of California.

Petras, James F. 1976. "Class and politics in the periphery and the transition to socialism." *The Review of Radical Political Economics* 8:20–35.

Pfuhl, Edwin. 1980. *The Deviance Process.* New York: D. Van Nostrand.

Pinchbeck, Ivy, and Margaret Hewitt. 1969. *Children in English Society, I.* London: Routledge & Kegan Paul.

Polk, Kenneth. 1972. *Schools and Delinquency.* Englewood Cliffs, N.J.: Prentice-Hall.

___. 1973. "Schools and delinquency experience." *Criminal Justice and Behavior* 2:315–37.

Poveda, Anthony. 1970. "Drug use among the major social types in high school." Unpublished doctoral dissertation, University of California, Berkeley.

Quicker, John C. 1983. *Homegirls: Characterising Chicana Gangs.* San Pedro, Calif.: International Universities Press.

Reynolds, David. 1976. "When pupils and teachers refuse a truce: The secondary school and the creation of delinquency." In Geoff Mungham and Geoff Pearson (eds.), *Working Class Youth Culture.* London: Routledge & Kegan Paul, pp. 124–37.

Richards, Catherine. 1958. "Finding a focus for work with hostile groups." In *Social Work with Groups, Selected Papers from the National Conference on Social Welfare.* New York: National Association of Social Workers, pp. 75–86.

Riggle, William. 1965. "The white, the black, and the gray: A study of student subcultures in a suburban California high school." Unpublished doctoral dissertation, University of California, Berkeley.

Rubin, I. I. 1972. *Essays on Marx's Theory of Value.* Detroit: Black and Red.

Sanders, Wiley B. (ed.). 1970. *Juvenile Offenders for a Thousand Years.* Chapel Hill, N.C.: University of North Carolina Press.

Schelling, Thomas C. 1967. "Economic analysis and organized crime." In *Task Force Report: Organized Crime, Appendix D.* President's Commission on Law Enforcement and Administration of Justice. Washington, D.C.: Superintendent of Documents, pp. 114–26.

Schwartz, Gary, and Don Merten. 1967. "The language of adolescence: An anthropological approach to youth culture." *American Journal of Sociology* 72:453–68.

Schwendinger, Herman. 1963. "The Instrumental Theory of Delinquency: A Tentative Formulation." Unpublished doctoral dissertation, University of California, Los Angeles.

Schwendinger, Herman, and Julia R. Schwendinger. 1963. "Big shots, fatsos and smarty pants: Social types among pre-teen girls." *Pacific Sociological Conference.*

——. 1965. "The swinging set, delinquent stereotypes of probable victims, Part 2." In Malcom Klein and Barbara Myerhoff (eds.), *Juvenile Gangs in Context*. New York: Prentice Hall, pp. 91–105.

——. 1974. *Sociologists of the Chair: A Radical Critique of the Formative Years of American Sociology 1884–1922*. New York: Basic Books.

——. 1976a. "Delinquency and the collective varieties of youth." *Crime and Social Justice* 5:7–25.

——. 1976b. "Marginal youth and social policy." *Social Problems* 24:184–91.

——. 1979. "Delinquency and social reform." In LaMar Empey (ed.), *Juvenile Justice: The Progressive Legacy and Current Reforms*. Charlottesville, Va.: University Press of Virginia, pp. 245–87.

——. 1982. "The paradigm crisis in delinquency theory." *Crime and Social Justice* 18:70–78.

——. 1983a. "Delinquency and the labor market." In James Garofolo (ed.), *Delinquency and Juvenile Justice: Linkages Among Systems*. Albany, N.Y.: The Michael J. Hindelang Criminal Justice Research Center, State University of New York, pp. 1–51.

——. 1985. "Adolescent entrepreneurs and illegal markets." In Brian McLean (ed.), *Political Economy of Crime*. Toronto: McClelland and Stewart.

——. (Unpublished). "Analytic induction and the embrace of commonsense realities."

Schwendinger, Julia, and Herman Schwendinger. 1983b. *Rape and Inequality*. Beverly Hills, Calif.: Sage Publications.

Scott, Peter. 1956. "Gangs and delinquent groups in London." *British Journal of Delinquency* 7:4–26.

Seider, Maynard. 1974. "American big business ideology: A content analysis of executive speeches." *American Sociological Review* 39:802–15.

Severson, John. 1964. *Modern Surfing Around the World*. New York: Doubleday.

Sharff, Jagna Wojcicka. 1981. "Free enterprise and the ghetto family." *Psychology Today* 15:41–48.

Shaw, Clifford R. 1933a. "Juvenile delinquency—A case history." *State University of Iowa Bulletin No. 692–713* (New Series 701). Iowa City, Nebraska: University of Iowa.

____. 1933b. "Juvenile delinquency—A group tradition." *Bulletin of the State University of Iowa No. 23* (New Series No. 700). Iowa City, Iowa: University of Iowa.

Sherif, Muzafer, and Carolyn Sherif. 1953. *Groups in Harmony and Tension.* New York: Harper and Brothers.

____. 1956. *An Outline of Social Psychology.* New York, Harper & Brothers.

Short, James F. Jr., and Ivan Nye. 1958. "Extent of unrecorded delinquency: Tentative conclusions." *Journal of Criminal Law, Criminology and Police Sciences* 49:296–302.

Short, James F. Jr., and Fred Strodbeck. 1962. "The response of gang leaders to status threats: An observation on group processes and gang behavior." *American Journal of Sociology* 68:571–79.

____. 1965. *Group Processes and Gang Delinquency.* Chicago: University of Chicago Press.

Short, James F. Jr., Fred Strodbeck, and Desmond Cartwright. 1962. "A strategy for utilizing research dilemmas: A case study from the study of parenthood in a streetcorner gang." *Sociological Inquiry* 32:185–202.

Shumpeter, Joseph A. 1955. *History of Economic Analysis.* New York: Crown University Press.

Smith, William. 1776. *State of the Gaols in London, Westminster and Borough of Southwark.* London [Brit. Mus.]. Excerpted by Wiley B. Sanders (ed.), 1970, *Juvenile Offenders for a Thousand Years.* Chapel Hill, N.C.: University of North Carolina Press, pp. 62–63.

Stark, Rodney. 1979. "Whose status counts?" *Journal of Criminal Law and Criminology* 72:1055–71.

Sutherland, Edwin H. 1947. *Criminology.* Philadelphia, Pa.: J. B. Lippincott.

Swift, Jonathan. 1901. *The Journal to Stella.* London: Methuen and Co.

Sykes, Gresham, and David Matza. 1957. "Techniques of neutralization: A theory of delinquency." *American Sociological Review* 22:664–70.

Tawney, R. H. 1912. *The Agrarian Problem in the Sixteenth Century*. New York: Burt Franklin.

——. 1947. *Religion and the Rise of Capitalism*. New York: New American Library.

Taylor, Ian, and David Wall. 1976. "Beyond the Skinheads: Comments on the emergence and significance of the Glamrock cult." In Geoff Mungham and Geoff Pearson (eds.), *Working Class Youth Culture*. London: Routledge & Kegan Paul, pp. 105–23.

Thrasher, Frederick. 1927. *The Gang*. Chicago: University of Chicago Press.

Tittle, Charles R., and Wayne J. Villemez. 1977. "Social class and criminality." *Social Forces* 56:474–502.

Tittle, Charles R., Wayne J. Villemez, and Douglas A. Smith. 1978. "The myth of social class and criminality: An empirical assessment of the empirical evidence." *American Sociological Review* 43:643–56.

——. 1982. "One step forward, two steps back: More on the class/criminalty controversy." *American Sociological Review* 47:438.

Turner, Ralph H. 1966. "Acceptance of irregular mobility in Britain and the United States." *Sociometry* 4:334–52.

U.S. Department of Labor Statistics. 1975. "A socio-economic profile of Puerto Rican New Yorkers." *Regional Report 46*, New York: Mid-Atlantic Regional Office.

Veblen, Thorstein. 1953. *Theory of the Leisure Class*. New York: Mentor Books.

Wallerstein, Immanuel. 1974. *The Modern World System*. New York: Academic Press.

Warner, William L., and Paul Lunt. 1942. *The Status System of a Modern Community*. New Haven, Conn.: Yale University Press.

Weber, Max. 1958. *Protestant Ethic and the Spirit of Capitalism*. New York: Charles Scribner's Sons.

Weis, Joseph G. 1969. "A social typology of adolescent drug use." Unpublished master's thesis, University of California, Berkeley.

———. 1973. "Delinquency among the well to do." Unpublished doctoral dissertation, University of California, Berkeley.

Welch, Saunders. 1753. "A letter upon the subject of robberies, wrote in the year 1753." In Wiley B. Sanders (ed.), 1970, *Juvenile Offenders for a Thousand Years*. Chapel Hill, N.C.: University of North Carolina Press, pp. 51–52.

Whyte, William E. 1943. *Street Corner Society*. Chicago: University of Chicago Press.

Wiatrowski, Michael D., David B. Griswold, and Mary K. Roberts. 1981. "Social control and delinquency." *American Sociological Review* 46:525–41.

Wilcox, Kathleen, and Pia Moriarty. 1976. "Schooling and work: Social constraints on equal educational opportunity." *Social Problems* 24:204–13.

Wittig, Monika. 1976. "Client control and organizational dominance: The school, its students, and their parents." *Social Problems* 24:192–203.

Wolpe, Harold. 1980. "Introduction." In Harold Wolpe (ed.), *The Articulation of Modes of Production: Essays from Economy and Society*. London: Routledge & Kegan Paul, pp. 1–43.

Woodress, James. 1955. *Booth Tarkington*. Philadelphia: J. B. Lippincott Co.

Yablonsky, Lewis. 1959. "The delinquent gang as a near-group." *Social Problems* 7:108–17.

Yancey, William L., and Eugene P. Ericksen. 1979. "The antecedents of community." *American Sociological Review* 44:253–62.

INDEX

Name Index

Subject Index

About the Authors

Herman and **Julia Siegel Schwendinger** are 1984 Tappan Award winners for their outstanding contributions to criminology. They pioneered the development of "critical criminology" since the late 1960s. The Schwendingers are founding members of *Crime and Social Justice* and have been on the editorial board since 1974. They are on advisory boards of *International Journal of the Sociology of Law, Insurgent Sociologist,* and *Research Annual on Critical Perspectives in Social Policy.* Other books by this unique team are *The Sociologists of the Chair* (1974) and *Rape and Inequality* (1983). Their commissioned works include "Delinquency and Unemployment" and "Delinquency and Social Reform." Numerous articles have appeared in *Crime and Delinquency, Crime and Social Justice, Issues in Criminology, Social Problems, Journal of Marriage and the Family*, and academic anthologies.

The Schwendingers' prior social work experience with delinquents in New York and California became the springboard for the participant observation of adolescents reported in this volume. This research was followed by a large study designed to test and extend their original delinquency theory, which is presented in this volume.

Professors Herman Schwendinger and Julia Siegel Schwendinger are on the sociology faculty at the State University of New York, College at New Paltz. Herman holds a B.S.S. from the College of the City of New York, an M.S.W. from Columbia University, and a Ph.D. in sociology from the University of California, Los Angeles. Julia holds a B.A. from Queens College, an M.S.W. from Columbia University, and a doctorate in criminology from the University of California, Berkeley.

www.ingramcontent.com/pod-product-compliance
Ingram Content Group UK Ltd.
Pitfield, Milton Keynes, MK11 3LW, UK
UKHW020127290926
15471UKWH00003B/331

9 780275 916565